GEORGE ELIOT, POETESS

For William and Ava

George Eliot, Poetess

WENDY S. WILLIAMS
Texas Christian University, USA

ASHGATE

Published by
Ashgate Publishing Limited
Wey Court East
Union Road
Farnham
Surrey, GU9 7PT
England

Ashgate Publishing Company
110 Cherry Street
Suite 3-1
Burlington, VT 05401-3818
USA

www.ashgate.com

British Library Cataloguing in Publication Data
A catalogue record for this book is available from the British Library

The Library of Congress has cataloged the printed edition as follows:
Williams, Wendy S.
  George Eliot, poetess / by Wendy S. Williams.
    pages cm
  Includes bibliographical references and index.
  ISBN 978-1-4724-3793-8 (hardcover: alk. paper)—ISBN 978-1-4724-3794-5 (ebook)—ISBN 978-1-4724-3795-2 (epub)
  1. Eliot, George, 1819–1880—Criticism and interpretation. I. Title.
  PR4688.W55 2014
  823'.8—dc23

2014005020

ISBN: 9781472437938 (hbk)
ISBN: 9781472437945 (ebk – PDF)
ISBN: 9781472437952 (ebk – ePUB)

Printed in the United Kingdom by Henry Ling Limited, at the Dorset Press, Dorchester, DT1 1HD

Contents

Acknowledgments

I am most grateful to Linda Hughes, whose guidance throughout every stage of writing has made this work possible. Constance Fulmer offered helpful feedback and collegial encouragement, and Anne Frey provided valuable insight into several of Eliot's poems. I am thankful to Linda Kinsey Spetter, Steve Sherwood, James Duke, and Richard Enos for reading early drafts. I am also indebted to Charles LaPorte, whom I have not met but whose seminal work, "George Eliot, the Poetess and Prophet," inspired me to study Eliot's poetry.

Chapter 3 includes material first published in *George Eliot-George Henry Lewes Studies*, 64–5 (2013). Thank you to William Baker for permission to reprint. I appreciate the National Portrait Gallery for allowing me to use the image of Frederic Burton's portrait of George Eliot for the cover of this book. I owe thanks to Bill Hamlett for his meticulous copy editing. I am also grateful to Ann Donahue and her colleagues at Ashgate for editorial assistance.

To the John V. Roach Honors College community at Texas Christian University I offer thanks for providing an industrious and friendly workplace environment. I am grateful, too, for the support of my parents, Robert and Frances Williams, my sisters, Dawn Hoffman and Cynthia Siples, my friend, Isabelle Hocquet, and my husband, Chad Juliano. Finally, I am grateful to my children, William and Ava, to whom this study is dedicated.

Introduction

"Every one of those [poems] I now send you represents an idea which I care for strongly and wish to propagate as far as I can. Else I should forbid myself from adding to the mountainous heap of poetical collections."

—George Eliot

George Eliot's initial work on *The Spanish Gypsy* in 1864 caused her continual headaches, "malaise and feebleness," and a "swamp of miseries" (*Letters* 4:166, 169). In 1865, she quit the lengthy dramatic poem at the behest of her partner, George Henry Lewes, who worried about her mental health, and wrote her fifth novel, *Felix Holt, the Radical.* Upon publication of the novel in 1866, her friend Frederic Harrison wrote her to praise its poetic qualities and her potential as a poet:

> I find myself taking it up as I take up Tennyson or Shelley or Browning and thinking out the sequences of thought suggested by the undertones of the thought and the harmony of the lines. Can it be right to put the subtle finish of a poem into the language of a prose narrative? It is not a waste of toil? And yet whilst so many readers must miss all that, most of them even not consciously observing the fact, that they have a really new species of literature before them (a romance constructed in the artistic spirit and aim of a poem) yet all is not lost. I know whole families where the three volumes have been read chapter by chapter and line by line and reread and recited as are the stanzas of In Memoriam … Are you sure that your destiny is not to produce a poem—not a poem in prose but in measure—a drama? (4:284–6)[1]

Harrison recognized that Eliot's "finest artistic mastery [was] devoted to the solution of the greatest problems and the highest purposes" and urged her to use her "feminine influences" as a "priest teacher adviser or friend" to write a "great work of art" (one that he outlined specifically in the letter) that would show the world the possibility of moral living in society (4:289).[2] His placing Eliot

---

[1]   Robert Browning's praise of *Romola* as "the noblest and most heroic prose poem" that he had ever read (*Letters* 4:96) reflected the common practice of using poetry to comment on the level of achievement in prose (LaPorte, *Victorian Poets* 195–6). A number of critics have commented on the poetic achievement of Eliot's prose; however, Harrison wanted Eliot to produce an actual poem—not "in prose but in measure."

[2]   Harrison appealed to Eliot's poetic ambition to urge her to write an epic poem that would promote the Positivist agenda. She wrote neither the Positivist epic that he outlined in this letter nor the Positivist prayers that he requested (*Letters* 4:284–9, 4:300–302, 9:194–5, 6:387–8). Harrison overestimated Eliot's commitment to Positivism, a philosophy founded by August Comte that superseded theology and metaphysics and sought knowledge based on empiricism. Eliot rejected the philosophy as a whole but was influenced by Comte's secular "religion of humanity." Benjamin Jowett recounted her saying that "she was not

alongside Tennyson, Shelley, and Browning and suggesting that families had read the novel with the same reverence as they read *In Memoriam*, no doubt pleased Eliot, who had not given up on the poetic aspirations that had caused her such illness. His letter made a deep impression on her, and she replied that she read it several times and would "read it many times again" (4:300). She assured him that his letter was "an evidence of a fuller understanding than I have ever had expressed to me before," and that his idea to write a great poem to edify humanity was a "great possibility (or impossibility)" that she would keep perpetually in mind (4:300–301). Finally, she confided in him her secret attempt to resume writing *The Spanish Gypsy* (4:301). Although Eliot would never write the particular epic poem that Harrison proposed, she would follow his advice and attempt great works of poetry as a priest and teacher for higher purposes. Her resumption of *The Spanish Gypsy* in 1866 marked such ambition, and in 1868, at the age of 49, she finally launched her career as a poet with its publication.

Already a wealthy and famous novelist, Eliot turned to poetry knowing that it would not earn her significant financial gain. She wrote to her friend Cara Bray that she expected to be despised for "choosing a work by which I could only get hundreds, where for a novel I could get thousands," and she credited Lewes for her turn to poetry:

> I cannot help asking you to admire what my husband is ... in urging me to produce a poem rather than anything in a worldly sense more profitable. I expect a good deal of disgust to be felt towards me in many quarters for doing what was not looked for from me and becoming unreadable to many who have hitherto found me readable and debateable. (4:438)

Eliot's self-effacing comment about Lewes's urging her to write poetry belied the exhausting effort, spanning four years, with which she produced the poem. She appeared the reluctant poet but understood the potential of poetry to boost one's literary standing. Poetry held cultural prestige, and Eliot's decision to turn to verse in her forties after the success of her first five novels[3] suggests a desire to establish a reputation beyond that of a popular novelist.[4] Encouraging her ambition, her

---

a Comtist at all though she acknowledged a debt to him as to every other great thinker" (Collins, *Interviews* 168). For a discussion of how her poem "O May I Join the Choir Invisible" (1867) was received as a Positivist poem and set to music as a hymn, see Martha Vogeler's "The Choir Invisible: The Poetics of Humanist Piety." Vogeler explains that Eliot occasionally met with Positivists who gathered in London, and Positivists embraced her poetry as an expression of their beliefs, but she did not subscribe to their philosophy (77).

[3]   *Adam Bede* (1859), *The Mill on the Floss* (1860), *Silas Marner* (1861), *Romola* (1863), and *Felix Holt, the Radical* (1866).

[4]   Nancy Henry astutely makes this point in her discussion of *The Spanish Gypsy* in *The Life of George Eliot: A Critical Biography*:

> To a Victorian author—even one whose novels were influential in transforming realist fiction in to high art—the most serious form of writing was poetry. Clarifying her grander themes by treating them in verse, she then took those themes back to her domestic English settings in *Middlemarch*, working the

publisher John Blackwood relayed the comments of John Crombie Brown (press proofreader) on *The Spanish Gypsy*, which he thought would "interest and please Mrs. Lewes" (1868): "if Fedalma [an early name for *The Spanish Gypsy*] does not ... place George Eliot as high among poets as she already stands among novelists, my opinion of the reading intellect of the age will go down to zero" (4:441). Brown's projection that Eliot would be placed "high among the poets" meant that with poetry she should secure a reputation as a national sage like Tennyson or Browning. Blackwood also hoped to "please Mrs. Lewes" with his own comments on her potential for greatness. The day after sending Brown's comments, he wrote to her:

> I have been looking into the Poem very often and I am more and more convinced that you have achieved a great and permanent success. I think I like the opening and the end best, but every other page throughout arrests one and discloses something new each time ... Wishing all success for your debut as a Poet. (4:442)

Eliot's poetry proved deeply meaningful to her, and she tended to it arduously throughout the 1860s and 70s, all the while struggling with self-doubt, debilitating headaches, and depression. She published poems regularly in *Blackwood's Magazine*, *Macmillan's Magazine*, and *The Atlantic Monthly* and oversaw two editions of her collected poems in 1874 (*The Legend of Jubal and Other Poems*) and 1878 (*The Legend of Jubal and Other Poems, Old and New*).[5] When Eliot submitted *The Legend of Jubal and Other Poems* to Blackwood in 1874, she wrote:

> I send you by this post a small collection of my poems which Mr. Lewes wishes me to get published in May. Such of them as have been already printed in a fugitive form have been received with many signs of sympathy, and every one of those I now send you represents an idea which I care for strongly and wish to propagate as far as I can. (6:25–6)

---

high elements of tragedy into her study of provincial life. By freeing herself from the restrictions of realism and conforming to the metrical requirements of poetry, she expressed her beliefs in the need to strive for the high ideals of art in 'The Legend of Jubal' (1870) and 'Armgart' (1871). She stressed altruism in 'Agatha' (1869) and 'Armgart'; love in 'How Lisa Loved the King' (1869); and corporate identity in *The Spanish Gypsy*. Now she was not comparing herself to contemporary realist novelists, but rather to Wordsworth, Scott, Goethe, Milton, Shakespeare, and the Greek dramatists ... The poem did not place her as high among poets as novelists, but it was both more popular and critically praised by contemporary reviewers than its subsequent neglect might suggest. She was striving for literary greatness. Poetry helped her express ideas in universal terms, even as the particular stories of Dorothea and Lydgate were taking shape in her mind (174–5).

[5]   The 1874 edition included "The Legend of Jubal," "Agatha," *Armgart*, "How Lisa Loved the King," "A Minor Prophet," "Brother and Sister," "Stradivarius," "Two Lovers," "Arion," and "O May I Join the Choir Invisible." The 1878 edition included these poems and "A College Breakfast Party," "Self and Life," "Sweet Evenings Come and Go, Love," and "The Death of Moses."

Again, although she distanced herself from her poetic ambition by claiming that Lewes wanted her to publish, her painstaking effort to create, publish, and republish through collections signified a desire to do more than please Lewes. Eliot sacrificed her health, energy, and time (that could have been spent earning more by writing fiction) to secure a lasting literary legacy. Upon reading *The Legend of Jubal and Other Poems* manuscript, Blackwood remarked on the beauty, cadence, and "warning voice" of the poems, stating: "You must have been thinking if not writing Poetry all your life, and if you have any lighter pieces written before the sense of what a great author should do for mankind came so strongly upon you, I should like much to look at them" (6:36–7). Blackwood's request for "lighter pieces" revealed his own mixed feelings about the poems, but he seemed to realize what Eliot hoped to do with her "warning voice"—to write as a "great author" for the benefit of humanity.

Blackwood was not alone in having mixed feelings about Eliot's poetry. During her lifetime, her poetry sold well, though not as well as her novels, and received mixed but mostly positive reviews.[6] Some early critics endorsed her poetry unequivocally. Others claimed the verse lacked originality, inspiration, and rhythm. Critics such as Henry James and Rose Elizabeth Cleveland blamed her agnosticism as an undermining force (*Complete Shorter Poetry* 1:xxxvii–viii). After her death, Eliot's novels overshadowed her poetry, and over the years, critics dismissed her poetry as inferior verse. A complete collection of her poems remained unavailable until the publication of Lucien Jenkins's *George Eliot: Collected Poems* in 1989.[7] Thus, Eliot's readership overlooked a significant portion of her writing for more than a century due to critical dismissal and inaccessibility. Few who read Eliot today know of her poetry, despite its great value to her.[8]

---

[6]   See Antoine Gerard van den Broek's introduction to *The Complete Shorter Poetry of George Eliot* (1:xxvii–lii), his introduction to *The Spanish Gypsy* (1:xl–lv), and William Baker's preface to *The Spanish Gypsy* (xxi–xxv) for a thorough discussion of the publication history and critical reception of Eliot's poetry.

[7]   George Creel (1948) and Cynthia Ann Secor (1969) wrote doctoral dissertations on Eliot's poetry, but they were never published. Jenkins's collection was made possible by Bernard Paris's publication in 1959 that included poems found in an autograph manuscript notebook in the Yale University Library's collection. Paris draws attention to these poems in "George Eliot's Unpublished Poetry": "In a London Drawingroom," "Ex Oriente Lux," "Arms! To Arms!," "In the South," five fragments, four untitled poems, "I Grant you Ample Leave," "Erinna," "The Death of Moses," and "Sweet Evenings Come and Go, Love." Bernard briefly discusses the poems and gives particular attention to "In a London Drawingroom" and "I Grant You Ample Leave." He also notes the fact that "The Death of Moses" and "Sweet Evenings Come and Go, Love" had already been published, though the notebook version of "The Death of Moses" was an early draft.

[8]   The following survey demonstrates the scant treatment of Eliot's poetry—her shorter poems in particular—in the twentieth and early twenty-first century. *The Oxford Reader's Companion to George Eliot* (2000) and "George Eliot" in *Dictionary of Literary Biography, Volume 35: Victorian Poets After 1850* (1985) offer useful reviews of her poetry. Both discuss the exclusion of her poetry in critical discussions, the significance of her work

However, recent studies reveal a quickening interest in Eliot's poetry. For instance, Antonie Gerard van den Broek scrupulously edited scholarly editions of Eliot's poems published by Pickering and Chatto: the two-volume *The Complete Shorter Poetry of George Eliot* (hereafter referred to as *CSP*) in 2005 and *The Spanish Gypsy* in 2008. These invaluable works, which include extensive editorial notes and textual variants, now stand as the authoritative editions of Eliot's poetry.[9]

---

as a poet, and the poems themselves. While helpful introductions to Eliot's poetry, these sources are each only a few pages.

Until recently, Eliot's biographers noted her poetry writing but had little to say about it, treating it as a departure from her novel writing for the most part. Gordon Haight, in *George Eliot: A Biography* (1968), briefly relays information on the production of Eliot's poems but always in relation to her novel writing. He discusses *The Spanish Gypsy* somewhat more extensively, citing in a few pages the poem's background and Eliot's motivation for writing it (376–9, 402–406). Likewise, more recent biographers such as Gillian Beer (*George Eliot*, 1986), Jennifer Uglow (*George Eliot*, 1987), Rosemarie Bodenheimer (*The Real Life of Mary Ann Evans*, 1994), Tim Dolin (*George Eliot*, 2005), and Barbara Hardy (*George Eliot: A Critic's Biography*, 2006) mention Eliot's poetry writing in the context of her novels but do not provide in-depth commentary on the poems or their significance to her writing career. Rosemary Ashton (*George Eliot: A Life*, 1997), Kathryn Hughes (*George Eliot: The Last Victorian*, 1999), and Nancy Henry (*The Life of George Eliot: a Critical Biography*, 2012) offer helpful commentary on *The Spanish Gypsy* in relation to *Felix Holt, the Radical*. Angela Leighton includes biographical information and presents "Brother and Sister" and an excerpt from *Armgart* in her anthology, *Victorian Women Poets* (1992). Leighton rightly points out the fact that Eliot's poetry reveals her attitudes on art and womanhood, which are not seen in her novels, but she dismisses the poetry as "the work of a novelist on leave" (221).

Many critics who discuss Eliot's poetry focus either on *Armgart*—for its treatment of authorial and gender issues—or *The Spanish Gypsy*—for its treatment of race and nationalism. Critics such as Bonnie Lisle and Rosemarie Bodenheimer read *Armgart* as a dramatization of Eliot's own anxiety about artistic ambition, and Louise Hudd views the poem as a feminist treatise. Several scholars, including Rebecca Pope, Susan Brown, and Grace Kehler, comment on the dramatic form and context of the poem. Critics of *The Spanish Gypsy* mostly concentrate on race and nationalism. Herbert Tucker discusses heredity, free choice, and the epic aim of *The Spanish Gypsy*, after lamenting the fact that it is "one of the most conspicuously neglected major works left behind by any Victorian writer of the first rank" (414). Joss West-Burnham, Alicia Carroll, Deborah Epstein Nord, and Victor Neufeldt read *The Spanish Gypsy* in terms of race, gender, and inheritance and draw parallels to Eliot's novels. Isobel Armstrong mentions Eliot in her discussion of the feminine tradition of women poets and briefly argues that *The Spanish Gypsy* was an attempt to write a humanist myth (*Victorian Poetry* 370).

[9]   *CSP* also contains appendices with unattributed epigraphs, poetic fragments, Eliot's essays on poetry ("Notes on Form in Art" and "Versification"), "Leaves from a Note-Book," facsimile title pages, sample pages from the Jubal manuscript, and contemporary reviews. *The Spanish Gypsy* includes Eliot's "Notes on The Spanish Gypsy and Tragedy in General," "Eliot's Notes on Gypsies," "Eliot's Notes on Spain," and "Eliot's Notes on the Inquisition." William Baker served as consulting editor to both *CSP* and *The Spanish Gypsy*.

Charles LaPorte's seminal work, "George Eliot, the Poetess as Prophet" (2003), focuses on Eliot's feminine poetess stance and her coordinate use of religion to sound a prophetic note in her poetry. His article draws attention to Eliot's poetry through its discussion of the moral voice and authority of the prophetess, poetry as salvation, and the use of the Bible in the poetess tradition—a tradition marked by feminine piety. He analyzes Eliot's poems: "O May I Join the Choir Invisible," "The Legend of Jubal," "The Death of Moses," and "A Minor Prophet." LaPorte's treatment of Eliot in *Victorian Poets and the Changing Bible* (2011) is an extension of his article and focuses on the influence of higher critical thinking on her poetry. He shows how Eliot applied recycled domestic and feminine tropes (such as the grieving mother), biblical themes and passages, and a higher critical understanding of prophecy to further her humanistic moral vision. LaPorte's insightful examinations of Eliot's poetic contribution laid the groundwork for further in-depth studies of Eliot's poetry.

The special issue of the *George Eliot-George Henry Lewes Studies*, "The Cultural Place of George Eliot's Poetry" (2011), contains the first collection of essays focused entirely on Eliot's poetry, further demonstrating a renewed interest in her poetic oeuvre. In the preface, Isobel Armstrong promises the collection will "transform our reading of her work" (3). And so it does. The essays reveal an Eliot "who is barely visible in the novels" by showing a poet who contemplates feminist issues, takes unconventional stances, and experiments with form and language (3–5). The collection, edited by Kyriaki Hadjiafxendi, explores a variety of issues and offers new ways of reading Eliot's poems.[10] Additionally, Gregory Tate

---

[10]   The special issue includes the following: Kyriaki Hadjiafxendi discusses Eliot's experimentation with form and the reception of her poetry in "Introduction: George Eliot and the Poetics of Disbelief." In "Quantity and Quality: The Strange Case of George Eliot, Minor Poet," Herbert Tucker argues that Eliot's desire to practice a wide range of forms resulted in her self-fashioned status as a "minor poet." Linda Peterson analyzes Eliot's reliance on the traditions of the poetess and the neo-Greek poet in *The Spanish Gypsy* as a means of achieving the high literary status of Elizabeth Barrett Browning in *"The Spanish Gypsy* as George Eliot's Poetic Debut." In *"The Spanish Gypsy*: Geography, Photography, and Ethnography in Spain," Kathleen McCormack shows how Eliot's use of photography and guidebooks from her travels in Spain aided ethnographic constructions in *The Spanish Gypsy* and also reinforced ethnic stereotypes. Stella Pratt-Smith, in "Inside-Out: Texture and Belief in George Eliot's 'Bubble-World,'" analyzes "A Minor Prophet" and "I Grant You Ample Leave" to show how Eliot's ideas of self were informed by the contemporary science of her day. Valerie Sanders's "'My Father Shook my Soul Awake:' Salvaging Family Relationships in George Eliot's Poetry" examines domestic relationships in *The Spanish Gypsy*, "Brother and Sister," and *The Mill on the Floss*, proposing that her poems, more than her novels, "allow the possibility of a feminine prophetic space not always shriveled by masculine scorn" (90). In "The Poetics of Criticism: Dialogue and Discourse in George Eliot's Poetry," Kimberly Stern discusses Eliot's understanding of the relationship between poetry and philosophy by analyzing "A College Breakfast-Party." She argues that the poem demonstrates Eliot's belief in heterogeneous ideas and uncertainty as a means of achieving sympathetic understanding and intellectual progress. Alexis Easley

considers the representation of psychology in Eliot's poetry in the fourth chapter of his book, *The Poet's Mind: The Psychology of Victorian Poetry 1830–1870* (2012). In "Poetry: The Unappreciated Eliot" (2013), Herbert F. Tucker addresses the performative nature of Eliot's adroit versification and diversification in poetic genre, and rightly argues that "the fact that nobody adores or analyzes [Eliot's poetry] opens a rare opportunity ... to appreciate Eliot's writing as if for the first time" (179). More studies like these will greatly contribute to the understanding of Eliot's work as a whole and its relation to Victorian literature.

This book aims to fulfill such a task by providing further insight into Eliot's poetry and her role as a poetess.[11] I analyze in depth poems that have had little or

---

explains in "Poet as Headliner: George Eliot and *Macmillan's Magazine*" that Eliot's choice to publish "The Legend of Jubal" and *Armgart* in *Macmillan's*, which had a policy of signed publication, showed a desire to capitalize on her growing celebrity to promote and argue for the significance of her poetry. Katherine Newey connects Eliot and Augusta Webster in her discussion of the difficulties of female authorship and Eliot's overshadowing of other Victorian women writers in "The 'British Matron' and the Poetic Drama." Finally, Charles LaPorte challenges the reader to consider the cultural relevance of Eliot's poetry (and poetry in general) in "Postscript: Did Eliot Know Her (Cultural) Place?"

[11] The *OED* states that the term "poetess" first came into usage in 1530 and defines a "poetess" as "a female poet; a woman who composes poetry." This simple definition encompasses a general meaning but does not take into account the complexity with which the term was used in the nineteenth century, at which time the term referred to a feminine tradition of poetry writing. Some take issue with the use of the term "poetess" because of the confusion behind its meaning. Bernard Richards, for example, recognizes its wide usage in the nineteenth century but suggests instead referring to "women poets" rather than "poetesses" (207). Virginia Blain explains the complexity of the term "poetess": "The word 'poetess,' [was] almost ubiquitous in the Victorian period ... We tend nowadays to deride its use, along with all of the feminizing diminutives ... Yet even in Victorian usage 'poetess' is an unstable term, taking on different coloration according to context and being increasingly open to shifting meanings" (31). Blain argues that during the transition from the Romantic to the Victorian periods, the term "poetess" was caught up in the struggle over the feminization of literature. Those threatened by what they perceived to be the female takeover of the male domain of literature used the term in a derogatory manner, "picking up overtones, perhaps, from 'poesy' in the trite or lightweight sense of that word, or from the more trenchantly contemptuous 'poetaster,' an exclusively masculine term commonly applied from the end of the sixteenth century to versifiers who never quite succeeded as poets" (32). The term "poetaster" suggested "a simulacrum of a poet, a rimester who imitates the 'higher' art of a true poet. Like 'poetess,' it can be used for either a professional hack or an amateur dabbler; unlike 'poetess,' it had no meaning that could be construed in any approving way" (32). In her study of the Romantic transatlantic poetess tradition, Laura Mandell points out that critics may disagree as to whether or not a particular woman poet is a poetess. One critic focusing on women poets' domestic poems might classify her as a poetess while another critic looking at her political poems might not. So, argues Mandell, the use of the term "poetess" may refer more to a style of writing than to the poets themselves (12). Although the term "poetess" was at times used to deride and patronize, it could have positive and legitimizing appeal. Eliot and her publisher John Blackwood

no critical attention: "Erinna," "How Lisa Loved the King," "Brother and Sister," "O May I Join the Choir Invisible," "Mid the Rich Store of Nature's Gifts to Man," and "Agatha." I also analyze her better-known poem, *Armgart*, and give briefer attention to a number of her other poems. Through a close analysis of her poetry, I show how Eliot positions herself using the gender-specific and religiously-motivated poetess role to further a non-conventional agenda—that of promoting a doctrine of sympathy rather than orthodox religion—revealing a more complete and accurate view of the author.

Chapter 1 will discuss the poetess tradition by exploring the relationship between religion, poetry, and gender in nineteenth-century Britain. To overcome societal restrictions imposed by a prevalent ideology of separate spheres, women writers turned to religion as a source of power as well as legitimacy. Women capitalized on the notion that they were innately spiritually superior to men and wrote poetry to soothe the nation in a time of religious uncertainty. By employing a feminine voice and poetic conventions, women poets could voice controversial ideas without censure, but as public figures they had to manage their personae and avoid self-display. Like other women poets, Eliot employed poetess conventions that were associated with feeling and spirituality. These associations provided Eliot with an already-established conception that allowed her to promote her unorthodox religious views. Eliot's successful use of the religiously-motivated poetess stance is especially intriguing given her unconventional lifestyle. By the time she began to write poetry, her fame was more influential than her breach of societal decorum, and she was able to adopt a poetess stance without attracting attention for her involvement in the male sphere of society. Eliot used her celebrity to promote her poetry and fashion an image of herself as a living sage. In this chapter, I will examine her poem "Erinna" to show how she employed feminine conventions to situate herself in the tradition of great poetesses while also assuming masculine privileges and agency through use of the epic tradition.

Chapter 2 will explore Eliot's religious background and her transition from orthodox views to an agnostic stance that upheld the sacredness of sympathetic relations. A careful study of her writing reveals the development of Eliot's belief in sympathy as a replacement for orthodox religion. As her views matured, she came to see herself as a prophet-poet whose mission it was to teach others that "fellow-feeling" and sympathetic relations, rather than dogma, led to a moral and just society. Eliot's doctrine of sympathy influenced all her writing—but it especially influenced her writing of poetry. In this chapter, I will analyze "Mid the Rich Store

---

both used the term "poetess" with approbation. Eliot said in a review of *Aurora Leigh* that Elizabeth Barrett Browning "has shown herself all the greater poet because she is intensely a poetess" ("Belles Lettres" 306), and Blackwood referred to Eliot as the "great Novelist and Poetess" (*Letters* 4:452). I employ the term "poetess" in this work, despite its current ability to rankle, not to pigeonhole or diminish women poets but rather to refer to a historically significant tradition of writing that had a legitimizing function in the nineteenth century.

of Nature's Gifts to Man" and "O May I Join the Choir Invisible" to show how Eliot used a poetess stance to forward a secular religion of sympathy.

Chapter 3 will assess Eliot's complex attitudes towards gender. She appeared traditional in many beliefs about women in society, and to the frustration of her friends who were women's rights advocates, she refused to join the cause. She did, however, advocate social progress for women through education. Once liberated by their intellect, she thought, women would gain social power yet retain their femininity. For Eliot, femininity was useful for nurturing sympathy between people and as such was key to the betterment of society. Her stance on women's rights and her attitude towards women writers shed light on her reasons and methods for conveying unorthodox views on women in her poetry. Female characters in her novels often suffer in unconventional settings and thrive in conventional ones, but that is not always the case in her poetry. Some of her poetic heroines speak out against gender inequality and boldly assert themselves in their male-dominant society, and others present a gender normative façade while the narrator subtly conveys unorthodox messages for them. Throughout her works, Eliot promoted sympathy for others, but in some of her poetry she did so by addressing issues of gender. In this chapter, I will examine "Brother and Sister" and "How Lisa Loved the King" to show how Eliot conveyed progressive ideas on gender while appearing feminine and traditional in her beliefs.

Chapter 4 will investigate Eliot's use of two poetess themes, female community and motherhood. Eliot's friendships with women throughout her life provided sympathy during times of loss and offered opportunities to exchange maternal affection. Later in life, Eliot assumed a maternal stance toward younger men and women who became her "spiritual children" in lieu of the biological ones she never had. This chapter will show how Eliot's personal experiences with female community and motherhood shaped her belief in sympathy's consoling power and edified her image as a spiritual mother to the nation. I will analyze *Armgart* and "Agatha" to show how she employed the themes of female community and motherhood to communicate the sacred value of sympathy in society.

Chapter 5 will reassert the case for studying Eliot's poetry through the lens of her poetess stance. By understanding her reliance on the poetess tradition, readers will gain not only a more complete and accurate view of Eliot's overall work but also a fuller appreciation of Victorian poetry as a whole. In this chapter, I will also discuss avenues for future study of Eliot's poetry including examination of poems not covered in this work, overlapping themes in her poetry and novels, Eliot's poetic epigraphs, sympathy in her novels versus poetry, and her technique of including poems within poems. Such studies will bring attention to a neglected area of critical study in the field of George Eliot scholarship.

Chapter 1
The Poetess Tradition

She held the spindle as she sat,
Erinna with the thick-coiled mat
Of raven hair and deepest agate eyes,
Gazing with a sad surprise
At surging visions of her destiny
To spin the byssus drearily
In insect labour, while the throng
Of Gods and men wrought deeds that poets wrought in song
—George Eliot

Eliot's move toward poetry raises key questions: how should critics situate Eliot's poetic work within her canon? Is it a departure from her artistic aim or an extension of it? Is she a major innovator or a novelist gone astray? Ultimately, how should critics understand Eliot, the poet? In answer, one might begin by exploring a tradition of women poets who relied on religion and feminine sympathy to claim authority to write poetry—a traditionally masculine art. Feminist scholars of nineteenth-century British poetry have discussed this tradition at length, and in doing so they frequently refer to the works of Letitia Landon (L.E.L.), Felicia Hemans, Elizabeth Barrett Browning, and Christina Rossetti.[1] They rarely include George Eliot in their investigations.[2] Reasons for this omission might stem from the belief that a renowned woman of intellect with non-traditional religious views and a controversial lifestyle has no place within a tradition marked by feminine piety. However, Eliot's poetry reveals a self-consciously feminine poetics and

---

[1]   See the following works for a discussion of the poetess tradition: Dorothy Mermin, "The Damsel, the Knight, and the Victorian Woman Poet" (1986); Angela Leighton, *Victorian Women Poets: Writing Against the Heart* (1992); Virginia Blain, "Letitia Elizabeth Landon, Eliza Mary Hamilton, and the Genealogy of the Victorian Poetess" (1995); Isobel Armstrong, "The Gush of the Feminine: How Can We Read Women's Poetry of the Romantic Period?" (1995), "Msrepresentation: Codes of Affect and Politics in Nineteenth-Century Women's Poetry" (1999), and *Victorian Poetry: Poetry, Poetics and Politics* (2003); Anne Mellor, "The Female Poet and the Poetess, Two Traditions of British Women's Poetry, 1780–1830" (1999); Jerome McGann, *The Poetics of Sensibility: A Revolution in Literary Style* (1996); Yopie Prins, "Personifying the Poetess: Caroline Norton, 'the Picture of Sappho'" (1999); Susan Brown, "The Victorian Poetess" (2000); Marion Thain, "What Kind of a Critical Category is 'Women's Poetry'" (2003); and Laura Mandell, "Introduction: the Poetess Tradition" (2003).

[2]   Notable exceptions include Charles LaPorte, "George Eliot, the Poetess as Prophet" (2003), Isobel Armstrong, *Victorian Poetry: Poetry, Poetics and Politics* (2003), and Linda Peterson, "*The Spanish Gypsy* as George Eliot's Poetic Debut" (2011).

an assumption of spiritual authority. In order to situate Eliot as a poetess, one must first understand the poetess as a nineteenth-century societal construct rooted in religion. To this end, I will first discuss the religious climate of nineteenth-century Great Britain, poetry as a spiritual province, and the legitimizing function of poetry for women writers. I will then describe the feminine voice and persona of poetesses and consider why Eliot's successful use of the religiously-motivated poetess stance was so unusual.

Religion, Poetry, and a Place for Women Writers

Religion influenced politics and dominated the cultural environment in nineteenth-century Great Britain. At the beginning of the century, the Church of England seemed to hold a stable position as the national religious authority and arbiter of religious thought. However, political and social forces were at work that would lead to radical change in the religious life of the country. The Repeal of the Test and Corporation Acts (1828) removed disabilities imposed on non-Anglican Protestants (Dissenters),[3] and the Catholic Emancipation Act (1829) removed disabilities imposed on Catholics. These acts reshaped the Anglican constitution into a Christian, non-denominational one.[4] This shift resulted in greater acceptance of non-Anglicans, brought about a greater sense of individual choice in regard to religious life, and created a sense of religious uncertainty in the country.

Imperial expansion also contributed to the unsettled religious climate of England. Victorian Christians became increasingly aware of other religions, and this worldwide context forced some to question whether they had sole possession of the truth. Some began to doubt the morality of core Christian doctrines such as eternal damnation and substitutionary atonement (Melnyk, *Victorian Religion* 134). The theory of evolution, along with geological and archaeological discoveries dating the earth into the millions (rather than thousands) of years, unsettled orthodox ideas about God, creation, and humanity's place in the world. Nineteenth-century scientific discoveries challenged the idea of biblical inerrancy and Christian understandings of the world. New ways of interpreting the Bible as a historical or mythological document rather than the Word of God further undermined Christianity's central source of authority. These scientific and societal changes influenced the nature of Christian belief in Britain.

---

[3]   Dissenters gathered in churches that did not identify with the Church of England. Marks of their belief system included personal confession of faith and acceptance of moral discipline. They were viewed as outsiders, and as such were not allowed to hold public office. (Worrall 11–14).

[4]   My discussion of religion will focus on Christianity since it was the dominant religious force in nineteenth-century Britain.

Nineteenth-century writers recorded (and at times contributed to) the national religious turbulence.[5] Authors who engaged with Christianity represented a diversity of perspectives and employed a variety of literary media. Poetry in particular provided a useful space for religious expression. Linda Hughes explains that the connection between Victorian poetry and religious faith "derives from biblical tradition (especially David's authorship of the Psalms), Dantesque and Miltonic epic, English hymnody, and a line of British poets extending from Langland through George Herbert, William Cowper, and the mature Wordsworth among others" (*Cambridge Introduction* 141). The sacred role of poetry was influenced by the Oxford (Tractarian) Movement, which aimed to revive religious faith and traditional practice (141).[6] Leaders of the Tractarian movement, such as John Keble, theologian and professor of poetry at Oxford, and John Henry Newman, priest and Oxford academic, viewed poetry as a form of worship. In his lectures on poetry, Keble expressed the commonplace idea that British religious thought and poetry were inextricably entwined when he explained that poetry was the "handmaid of piety" (2:484):

> [What] more conceivable than that all poetry may have been providentially bestowed on man as the first elements, the prelude, so to speak, of genuine piety? Since, for one thing, ancient records as a rule bear out the conclusion that there has seldom been a revival of religion unless a high and noble order of poets has first led the way: and, for another, both in effect and in character, real Religion is in striking accord with true poetry. (2:473)[7]

The Tractarians believed that poetry resulted from divine inspiration and could communicate virtue and piety through its meter and rhythm. They thought religious poetry could affect the believer emotionally and regarded it as synonymous with religious truth itself (Knight and Mason 100). Those who engaged with poetry, that is, entered into a religious and lyrical experience that allowed for the exploration of three Tractarian issues: "the emotive effect poetry and religion produced on readers; the consolatory quality of such an effect; and the regulation of the

---

[5]   *The Origin of Species* (1859) and *Essays and Reviews* (1860), a collection of articles summarizing a challenge to biblical history by the higher critics and to biblical prehistory by geologists and biologists, shook the religious community.

[6]   Tractarians were members of the Oxford Movement, which was dominated by clerics and educated men (such as Keble) who aimed to restore High Church practice to the Church of England and recover the idea of the Church as a divine institution (Worrall 15–17).

[7]   Kirstie Blair explains that Keble's poetry represented the "fullest and most widely disseminated statement about form and Tractarianism—that poetry and religious feeling are deeply exciting and in some senses disturbing, and that formal elements, in the rituals of the Church and the strictures of poetic form, are necessary to soothe the emotions and offer discipline and control to wayward thoughts and feelings" (50). See the first chapter of Blair's *Form and Faith in Victorian Poetry and Religion* for a thoughtful discussion of Tractarian poetics and form.

consequent feeling in believers (too much feeling, it was feared, could unbalance the believer altogether)" (Tennyson 3). As a sacred manner of expression, poetry was linked with prayer and devotion. Writers seeking solace in uncertain times found that poetry lent itself to spiritual expression. The poetic form freed the believer to feel faith in an age when belief was under threat from enlightenment reason. The form also allowed a space for the non-believing writer and reader to express religious confusion and uncertainty.[8]

Religion was a socially acceptable area of interest and experience for women, and many poured their energies into religious life and literature. Social encouragement of women's religious work and literature generally did not extend to formal theological writing, which society considered a masculine discourse. Women were forbidden from the university and the pulpit and from writing theological genres such as the sermon and treatise.[9] Despite their typical exclusion from nineteenth-century religious and intellectual institutions, women could use poetry as a site to do theology.[10] Poetry offered a sanctioned public forum in which

---

[8]   W.D. Shaw makes the following points to describe how Victorian religion influenced the poetry of the period: first, during the 1830s, recovery of biblical types in the conservative hermeneutics of John Keble and the Tractarians influenced the work of poets such as Alfred Tennyson, Christina Rossetti, and Gerard Manley Hopkins. Second, in the 1850s, the liberal theology of the biblical higher critics, notably David Strauss (and in the 1860s, the "broad church" hermeneutics of Benjamin Jowett), influenced Robert Browning. Also mid-century, the agnostic theology of Thomas Carlyle and the neo-Kantians gave rise to the doubt and cosmic questioning of Tennyson, Arthur Clough, and Matthew Arnold. Throughout the nineteenth century, a theology of human evolution and self-making influenced Browning and Tennyson. Finally, George Eliot created a religion of morality, Matthew Arnold a religion of culture, and Walter Pater a religion of art (457).

[9]   Susan Staves points out that Church of England clergymen helped women writers cultivate their talent and publish. Scholarly bishops and archbishops opened their libraries to learned women with the understanding that they would provide a proper religious education to the nation's children. This access led to women establishing schools to educate poor children and women addressing other women on spiritual matters. By supporting women's spiritual education, the clergy was able to offer to the world models of Anglican feminine belief and piety, thereby enhancing the reputation of the Church of England (85–8).

[10]   Christine Krueger outlines a history of women's literary empowerment that stems from a tradition of informal female preaching. Krueger argues that evangelical hermeneutics allowed women to use the authoritative language of scripture, present female authority in terms of spiritual gifts, condemn the exploitation of women, and urge readers to repent of misogynistic practices (5). Women preachers adopted Old Testament prophetic imagery to disguise their subversive power, and they wielded this power skillfully. Krueger explains: "They exploited the paradoxical foundation of evangelical hermeneutics to appropriate the language of God the Father in order to subvert the authority of their temporal masters. This fruitful but precarious role was the legacy inherited by the female social preachers of the nineteenth century" (10–11). Krueger's analysis shows how eighteenth and nineteenth-century women preachers relied on female predecessors to legitimize themselves and to connect to future generations. Women poets took advantage of the perceived harmony between femininity and Christianity to establish authority to write.

women could give voice to theological ideas. The end of the eighteenth century saw a period of expansion in poetry's popularity, and the genre came to be associated with feminine feeling. Treatises for women discouraged the pernicious influence of novel reading but approved of the reading and memorizing of poetry (Pinch, *Strange Fits* 56). Therefore, women writers could exploit the link between poetry and femininity. Adela Pinch explains that women poets were "conscious of the extent to which they could both take advantage of and be limited by their culture's association of women with sensibility" (57). She argues: "In a period that placed poetic value on 'natural genius,' on the inspired and authentic rather than on the learned and the cultivated, women's natural sensibility gave them an equal, if not greater, qualification for writing poetry" (57). By the nineteenth century, the idea of poet as prophet was commonplace, and poetry, with its inherent relationship to religion, offered women the potential to attain the status of poet-prophet in the public realm.[11] In a society that generally prohibited women's participation in theological discourse, women poets found creative ways to do theology. Women poets often took up religious subjects, rewrote biblical narratives, and focused on prophetic women characters in their poems. They also relied on non-canonical religious texts to claim religious authority. LaPorte states: "the peculiar liminal status of such texts afforded women poets a certain power, for the texts were not sacred in the Protestant churches, yet they were manifestly cousin to much that is, and they showed how sacred-ness in texts is culturally selected" (*Victorian Poets* 217). Eliot's "The Death of Moses," for example, derives from the Devarim Rabbah, a midrashic account of God's descent from heaven to collect Moses' soul at the end of his life. LaPorte explains that the poem does "the cultural work of the Bible without requiring our endorsement of its doubtful historical

---

[11] Scheinberg views the poet-prophet as a man who integrated characteristics associated with men and women in a single prophetic identity. She states: "Because Victorian culture relied so heavily on a system of separate gendered spheres ... this construction of the poet as one who can move between different realms of experience and identity served as a distinct challenge to those explicitly gendered identities" (*Women's Poetry* 39). Male poets, Scheinberg argues, appropriated the female realm of the heart for their own use. The image of the heart symbolized femaleness and femininity, signified sensibility and emotion, and was connected to the body (which stood in opposition to the intellect). Male poets had to reclaim feminine attributes while women only had to excel as poets of the heart. Women could not claim male characteristics the way that men claimed female attributes. The male poet was a universal entity while the woman was more limited. The idea of separate spheres thus relegated women to a certain kind of poetry that did not lead them to transgress gender boundaries as male poets might. So women poets came to be understood as possessing only one side of the poet/prophet sensibility. Women poets therefore had to "transcend" the heart, the domestic realm, and sensibility. According to Scheinberg, women had to challenge patriarchal relegation and claim realms of intellect and philosophy in order to assert poetic authority (38–41). Scheinberg's analysis is revealing; however, I would suggest that women poets did not necessarily have to transcend domestic realms. Some conveyed radical opinions by associating themselves with a feminine tradition that linked femininity and spirituality.

propositions" (214).[12] Eliot took up religious themes throughout her poetry and even rewrote biblical narratives. In "The Legend of Jubal" she elaborated on a passage from Genesis 4 to tell the story of a biblical figure, Jubal, in order to assert the sacred value of art. Eliot's use of a midrashic text and her rewriting of biblical texts indicate her regard for apocryphal texts (including her own) as equally authoritative as canonical ones. Like other women poets, Eliot claimed authority to write religious poetry and soothe the nation in a time of distress, and her ability to benefit from the connection between religion and femininity is all the more intriguing given her own religious skepticism.

The Voice of the Poetess

A feminine language of affect became a dominant mode of poetry in the early and mid-nineteenth-century. Isobel Armstrong explains that women were often given the duty of expressing feeling, pity, and empathy during a period rife with religious uncertainty, fear of revolution, class tension, and racial bitterness ("Msrepresentation" 9). Some women poets drew on the belief that they were emotional, and they used the language of affect to communicate political or social messages.[13] Many found their voice by looking back to precursors such as L.E.L. and Felicia Hemans and worked within an identifiable tradition of feminine writing. Armstrong refers to the woman writers' voice as "a music of [their] own," that might have been pious, simple, and feminine (*Victorian Poetry* 323).[14] Women poets also could escape a societally prescribed feminine identity, protect against self-exposure, and control their objectification by using travel, masks, and role-play, and by setting poems in "other" lands—emotional spaces outside the

---

[12] For an insightful examination of Eliot's engagement with the midrashic text in "The Death of Moses," see LaPorte's *Victorian Poets and the Changing Bible*.

[13] Eliot relied on affect in a number of her poems; salient examples include "Two Lovers," "As Tu Vu la Lune se Lever," "Sweet Evenings," and "Erinna."

[14] Bernard Richards disagrees with Armstrong's case for women poets' creating a language of their own, asserting that women merely coped with an inherited language rather than reinvented a new one (224). However, I think that Armstrong makes a solid case. Women poets used domestic, feminine language and created expressions that other women then used. For example, poetesses often used the adjective "sweet" (as in "sweet enforcement," "sweet home, "sweet antiphony," "sweet instruments," "sweet hay," "sweet repose," and "sweet dreams" in Eliot's "Agatha" and "sweet repose," "sweet nature," "sweet peace," "sweet home," "sweet welcome," "sweet endearments," "sweet guardians," and "sweet communion," in Felicia Hemans's "The Domestic Affections," two poems about home). The reader came to associate such language with the poetess. Richards does, however, agree with Armstrong's idea that women poets shared similar conventions. He says that women poets were alike in that they acted as creators, were recipients of the male gaze, and wrote about love, repression, suffering, sexuality, longing for heaven, and communality (209–26).

rules of the poet's nationality and culture (324–5).[15] Travel and foreign settings allowed women writers to search for the exotic, escape restrictions, or discover a "universal womanhood which transcends cultural differences" (325). Women who followed Hemans and L.E.L. sought to fit their imaginative experiences into an established connection between feminine emotional life and poetry writing.[16] Armstrong argues that women writers negotiated their own sphere of influence and communicated subversive ideas in a feminine, sentimental way easily accepted by society, not to fit into a safe stereotype but rather to negotiate societal conventions and constraints, to create a voice, and to earn a living.

Armstrong's claim that women poets employed similar writing tactics has provoked extensive debate. A number of critics take Armstrong's thesis to mean that women poets were not diverse. This backlash against the idea of the poetess as a united group of women poets is a natural one. Critics wish to honor individual women poets and celebrate their unique qualities. However, acknowledging a poetess tradition does not discount that uniqueness. Rather, it shows how women poets expressed their various views and achieved individual aims by participating in an established tradition that gave them authority to proffer their views. Eliot, for example, wrote within the poetess tradition, but her poetry is far from one-dimensional. She explored a variety of genres: poetic fragments, epigraphs for prose chapters, lyric poems ("In a London Drawingroom," "Two Lovers," "In the South," "Ex Oriente Lux," "I grant you ample leave"), a sonnet sequence ("Brother and Sister"), elegies ("Erinna," "Arion"), hymns and ballads ("O May I Join the Choir Invisible," "Sweet Evenings Come and Go, Love"), narrative verse ("A Minor Prophet," "Agatha," "How Lisa Loved the King," "The Legend of Jubal," "Stradivarius," "The Death of Moses"), philosophical dialogues ("Self and Life," "A College Breakfast Party"), and dramatic poems (*Armgart* and *The Spanish Gypsy*). Eliot's masterful employment of blank verse,

---

[15] For example, George Eliot's *The Spanish Gypsy*, Barrett Browning's *Aurora Leigh*, and Christina Rossetti's *Monna Innominata* all place heroines in distant lands where they escape gendered restrictions of their home culture ("Msrepresentation" 325). Women's poems of displacement allowed for expressive feeling, and their affective expression could serve to reveal or to conceal. Additionally, women poets created new models of poetic agency by displacing themselves in foreign lands. For a discussion of the cultural influence of expatriate women poets, see Alison Chapman's "Poetry, Network, Nation: Elizabeth Barrett Browning and Expatriate Women's Poetry."

[16] Armstrong traces similarities throughout women's writing to show that expressive theory was tied to feminine poetics. For example, she explains how the three Brontës "follow Mrs. Hemans in exploring consciousness under duress" and how Anne Adelaide Procter "follows Letitia Landon in exploring the alien rituals of another culture in her tales" (*Victorian Poetry* 332). Armstrong also discusses Barrett Browning, Dora Greenwell, and Christina Rossetti to establish a women's tradition of expressive poetics in the early and mid-nineteenth century. She turns to the works of Augusta Webster, Amy Levy, Mathilde Blind, and George Eliot to argue that women poets writing in the latter part of the century adopted a poetics of myth and mask.

free verse, heroic couplets, and irregular rhyme schemes further demonstrates her versatility as a poet.

Though Eliot's poetry was diverse, the reader can find poetess conventions throughout.[17] She appealed to feminine modes of expression to elicit the sympathy of her readers by addressing poetess themes such as suffering and alienation ("A London Drawing Room," "Self and Life," and "Erinna"), renunciation and duty ("Brother and Sister," "How Lisa Loved the King," "The Legend of Jubal," *Armgart*, and *The Spanish Gypsy*), and motherhood ("In the South," "Agatha," "The Legend of Jubal," *Armgart*, and *The Spanish Gypsy*). She also set poems in foreign lands ("Erinna," "Agatha," "How Lisa Loved the King," "The Legend of Jubal," "Arion," "Stradivarius," *Armgart*, and *The Spanish Gypsy*) and incorporated religious terminology and concepts such as the afterlife, prophecy, and redemption ("Farewell," "Mid the Rich Store of Nature's Gifts to Man," "Ex Oriente Lux," "The Death of Moses," "A Minor Prophet," "The Legend of Jubal," "O May I Join the Choir Invisible," *The Spanish Gypsy*, "I Grant you Ample Leave," and "A College Breakfast Party"). Eliot did not take overt stands on political and social concerns but discreetly commented on social issues through a stance of sympathy. She sought to express moral truths through the art of poetry, and her use of feminine conventions and her public role as a poetess provided her access to this goal. Understanding the self-conscious tradition of women poets embracing similar literary conventions and modes of expression helps us better discern how Eliot and other women poets were able to thrive.

Self-Display, Separate Spheres, and the Public Image of the Poetess

Women poets found publishing legitimacy by writing seemingly spontaneous, feminine verse and by publishing in popular annuals or literary magazines, with the help of male publishers. In the early part of the nineteenth century, decorated literary annuals—also known as gift books and keepsakes—containing essays, fiction, and poetry of a sentimental or religious nature flourished. Their market appeal equated to high fees for contributors, and though not respected as containing serious work, well-known authors such as Scott, Southey, Moore, Wordsworth, Coleridge, Ruskin, and Tennyson were not above contributing to them (Leighton 49). Women, in particular, found the annuals a safe and appealing place for publication. Angela Leighton explains that "the annuals offered a context for publication which, being largely female, on the one hand presupposed a kind of literary modesty but, on the other, offered a discreetly lucrative living" (49).

---

[17] Margaret Reynolds also notes Eliot's use of "a shared set of formulas and themes which were learned by all the Victorian women poets from their reading, especially, of the many annuals and album books designed for a female readership—an audience which certainly included George Eliot given her close knowledge of *The Keepsake* for 1832" (*Oxford Reader's Companion* 305). Reynolds points out that Eliot complained about the "effeminate feebleness of the 'Keepsake' style" (*Essays* 268) in "The Natural History of German Life" (305).

Women writers, whether or not they wrote out of financial necessity, had to take care not to flout their public role. Publication could appear as self-display or sexual self-exposure. By appearing conventional, women writers could avoid drawing negative attention to their personal lives. Women poets could contribute seemingly simple, pious poems to annuals and literary magazines without threatening traditional notions of womanhood, and readers could happily assume that they wrote spontaneous, emotional lines of verse in the comfort of their homes without shirking household duties.

The necessity for women poets to maintain a domestic image was related to the notion of separate spheres, which associated women with emotion, passivity, and work within the home and men with intellect, power, and work outside the home. Free from the corrupting influences of the outside/male sphere, the domestic/female sphere was safe and pure. Society considered women especially well-suited to govern this realm due to their "natural" ability to care for children and run a household. Christian women had the responsibility to teach virtue in the domestic sphere and were in charge of the religious instruction of children. Leonore Davidoff elaborates on the implications of the separate-spheres ideology for women writers:

> As communicants and parishioners, as upholders of religion in the home, and as the wives, sisters, and daughters of the clergy operating the semi-public life of the vicarage, women played a vital role. As a site of morality, religious belief and practice were ambiguous in their gender imagery. While formal preaching was closed to women, various forms of spontaneous prophecy were not. (19–20)[18]

By mid-century, in association with the separate spheres ideology, women were taking responsibility for moral authority in the home. Consequently, society associated the poetess with qualities that contrasted with the harsh realities of the masculine public sphere: domesticity, sentimentality, and spirituality. Society came to expect the poetess to reflect the elevated British national character, to uphold domestic ideals, and collectively to preserve the noble national identity (Brown, "Victorian Poetess" 187–90).[19]

---

[18] By 1780, the Methodists and the Dissenting Academies supported women preachers, who gained influence and grew in number in the early nineteenth century. Women used the Bible to claim authority to resist those who hindered their pursuit of higher sanctity (Mellor 83). With this authority, they stepped into the public sphere, published, and spoke out on religious, political, and social topics.

[19] Anne Mellor argues that female poets claimed divine authority for their prophetic verse and assumed their role as vessels of the divine (83). Julie Melnyk agrees that women poets claimed divine authority but explains that they did so for a different purpose. She says that women writers revised and subverted the masculine theology they were discouraged from participating in, and they created their own theology (*Women's Theology* xii). They presented arguments (based on Scripture or on the personal experience of "call" or leading) to justify participating in religious discourse and to assert their right to read and interpret Scripture independent of masculine authority. Many stressed equality of men and women before God and focused on Jesus as Bridegroom of a feminized Soul (xv–xvii).

The mark of gender for the poetess was both enabling and constraining. On one hand, the poetess lent herself to sympathetic identification because of the readers' interest in her public life. She offered the reader a personality with which to identify, and readers oftentimes read poetry to find a picture of the poetess in the poem. The figure of the poetess produced an emotional response in the readers who became "sentimental readers, identifying with the personification and effacing [themselves] in order to sympathize with the face of 'the poetess herself in the frontispiece'" (Prins 50–51). On the other hand, the poetess had to manage her reputation carefully, as readers tended to conflate her physical body and her body of work, which was perceived as confessional. Women poets invoked Sappho, the original precedent for the poetess, whose image demonstrated the reader's tendency to pay more attention to the reputation than the work of the poetess. Susan Brown states:

> The fragmented voice of the writer whom the ancients respected as the progenitor of lyric was largely obscured as commentators focused attention on her deeply unhappy biographical legend. In practice this meant that there was little basis for aesthetic judgment of poetesses' work but their lives were scrutinized for conformity to perceived womanly and poetic standards, however conflicting those might be. Sappho's putative biography conveniently enshrined the antagonism between respectable femininity and poetic aspiration. ("Victorian Poetess" 184)

Views of the poetess as an improvisatrice, a statue, or an object of art turned the woman into a form of artistic property created for the man's pleasure (Peterson, "Rewriting *A History*" 116–17). The myth of the poetess as the embodiment of art had the advantage of linking the woman poet to genius and inspiration but the disadvantage of associating her with "infantile poetic effusions," rather than with serious writing (120). Brown explains the problem of women's identification with their art: poetry "is for women a mode, not an occupation. For women writers, the major problem in this formulation is that women are poetry. They live and inspire it but they do not write it, while other people—namely men—have the privilege to do so" ("Victorian Poetess" 181). Eliot understood this concept. In *Middlemarch*, she describes Dorothea Brooke as the representation, not the producer, of art. When Dorothea tells Will Ladislaw that she understands what he means by "knowledge passing into feeling" (for him, the essence of being a poet) but that she could "never produce a poem," he replies: "You *are* a poem—and that is to be the best part of a poet—what makes up the poet's consciousness in his best moods" (223). Though Dorothea understands the poetic sensibility, she cannot write poetry. She can only *be* poetry. Dorothea embodies the problem of the poetess—the difficulty in extricating herself from art. More importantly, she realizes the importance of the poems themselves. She says to Will: "But you leave out the poems … I think they are wanted to complete the poet" (223). Dorothea may not be able to write poetry, but she understands that the true mark of a poet is one who can produce actual work rather than residing in inchoate feeling and imaginative states. Dorothea thus exemplifies the challenge of the poetess, who must call the reader's attention to her art through feminine sensibility and sympathetic identification without encouraging self-display and scandal.

Two strains of poetess demonstrated this difficulty: one in the likeness of Hemans who adhered to domestic ideology, and another in the likeness of L.E.L., who (unlike Hemans) was associated with rumor and sexual scandal. Hemans, though separated from her husband, maintained a feminine ideal by writing poetry that emphasized domestic ideology and nationalism. L.E.L., on the other hand, lived more recklessly. Rumors of affairs invited public scrutiny. Consequently, readers concentrated more and more attention on her actual body than her body of writing, which led to a damaged reputation, a broken engagement, and an early death rumored to be suicide. Leighton points out that both women wrote out of necessity, both risked losing respectability by their appearance in the popular press, and neither had the leisure to develop their talents (51). Linda Hughes explains that both women enjoyed public success and appealed to their readership by upholding domestic and religious ideology in verse while taking risks such as paying homage to Byron (as Hemans did) and identifying with the Sapphic tradition of rendering passion as physical sensation (as L.E.L. did) (170–71). She states: "the poetess pays lip service to contemporary domestic manuals and critical standards even while crafting a less overt rhetorical poetics that enlarges the imagined poetic space within which a middle-class woman could move" (172).

Like L.E.L., Eliot was a public figure associated with scandal. She lived unconventionally and promoted unorthodox views. Her position as assistant editor and contributor of essays and reviews for *The Westminster Review* and her association with a largely male society in London in the 1850s was somewhat unusual for a woman. This activity, along with her blatant choice to live openly with Lewes, placed her in the male sphere and invited ostracism early in her career. She began her fiction-writing career pseudonymously to avoid public disapproval of her lifestyle translating to disapproval of her writing. By the time her identity as the author of *Adam Bede* was discovered, the work was already publicly acclaimed. Her friend Barbara Bodichon wrote to Eliot upon discovering her identity: "1st. That a woman should write a wise and *humourous* book which should take a place by Thackeray. 2nd. That YOU *that you* whom they spit at should do it!" (*Letters* 3:56). Lewes wrote to Bodichon, "It is quite clear that people would have sniffed at [*Adam Bede*] if they had known the writer to be a woman but they can't now unsay their admiration" (3:106). Eliot's reputation was damaged early on, but she established her literary celebrity before she began her poetry-writing career. Having already achieved literary greatness with her novels, Eliot could not be dismissed merely as a woman—or worse, as a scandalous woman—when she came to write poetry.

Eliot as Public Figure

Kathleen McCormack points out biographers' tendency to focus on Eliot's decision to live with Lewes and her early years as a fiction writer. She argues that skimping on Eliot's later years has led to the misconception that she lived outside of respectable society all her life and has given only a limited perspective on who she was (*George Eliot in Society* 4). Eliot enjoyed literary celebrity in the 1860s and 70s and during this time devoted much of her energy to promoting her work and developing a public image. During the years of transformation from social outcast to celebrity, she progressively softened her image. Friends reported a gradual shift in her demeanor. Oscar Browning wrote: "I have been told by those who knew her long that she was awkward in her early womanhood, and had not acquired that repose and dignity which characterized her later years." And Edith Simcox reported that Eliot's childhood friend Maria Congreve observed that "the 'appealingness' of her look ... in later years had turned to graciousness" (Collins, *Interviews* 140).

One way Eliot managed her image was by refusing her readers details of her life—even when information circulating about her was wrong. She also burned her friends' letters to her because, she said, "they were only intended for my eyes and could only fall into the hands of persons who knew little of the writers, if I allowed them to remain till after my death. . . . I hate hard curiosity" (*Letters* 3:376). Furthermore, she refused to allow anyone to write her biography. To John Blackwood she revealed her concern with the public's knowing too much of the author's life, decrying the genre of literary biography (though she had enjoyed reading many herself): "Is it not odious that as soon as a man is dead his desk is raked, and every insignificant memorandum which he never meant for the public, is printed for the gossiping amusement of people too idle to re-read his books" (6:23).[20] In 1870, she flirted with the idea of writing an autobiography—a medium in which she could control the information presented to the public—but ultimately decided not to do it (Bodenheimer, *Real Life* 236–9). She explained to Mrs. Thomas Trollope that though autobiography could offer the reader a portrait of how the mind of an author grew and could be "a precious contribution to knowledge," biographies, she felt, were generally "a disease of English literature" (*Letters* 7:230). Thus, contemporary readers had little insight into her actual life. Collins describes how Eliot fiercely guarded her privacy:

> Apart from the "apocryphal stories" *The Times* would mention in its obituary, only her novels and poetry were available—and these, rumour had it, she never allowed to be mentioned in her presence. So completely did George Eliot distance herself from "newspaper chit-chat," as she called it, so consistently

---

[20]   See Nancy Henry's *The Life of George Eliot: A Critical Biography* for a history of the construction of Eliot's posthumous image through biographies, beginning with the sanitized version of her life in (ed.) John Walter Cross's *George Eliot's Life as Related in Her Letters and Journals* (17–20).

did she withhold information even from standard reference sources, that she managed to ensure distrust of everything printed about her personal life by declining to offer anything in its place. (*Interviews* xvii)

With little biographical information available to the public, Eliot could construct her own image, and she did this in part through the Sunday salons she and Lewes held at their home, famously known as "the Priory." Despite frequent illness, the Leweses kept Sunday salons according to a "rigorous schedule" in the late 1860s to 70s, and in some years the couple held gatherings for five solid months (January through April, November and December, 1871) and received hundreds of guests (McCormack, *George Eliot in Society* 2).[21] These well-attended events brought together prominent and respectable members of society—women as well as men.[22] McCormack describes the environment as lively, fashionable, and intellectually stimulating: "People took light refreshments, advanced their ideas, fell in love, quarreled, confided their troubles, and talked and talked and talked through the Sunday afternoons at the Leweses' Priory" (14). She further explains that "neither scandal nor dullness dominated the parties. Instead, intellectual, artistic, scientific, political, philosophical, wealthy, sometimes titled guests contributed not only to a lively social atmosphere but also to the workings of George Eliot's creative imagination and the marketing of her books" (135). The salons provided a social

---

[21] McCormack explains that Lewes kept meticulous lists of Sunday guests at the Priory. She states: "The host's sense of the importance of the occasions appears in these conscientious records, kept Sunday by Sunday, recording names in their order of arrival. Together with his descriptions of their travels, they occupy the majority of the space in his later diaries and show his eagerness about additional newcomers because each list ends with a comma that suggests he anticipates still another visitor's arrival" (2). These lists are included in Lewes's diaries and journal, which are held in the Beinecke Rare Book and Manuscript Library at Yale University. They are being transcribed and will be published under the editorship of William Baker (2).

[22] Charles Norton wrote critically in 1869: "She is not received in general society, and the women who visit her are either so émancipée as not to mind what the world says about them, or have no social position to maintain. Lewes dines out a good deal, and some of the men with whom he dines go without their wives to his house on Sundays" (*Letters* 5:7). However, Norton was wrong. Women were frequent visitors to the Priory. McCormack explains that Norton's "estimate of an émancipée woman guest" shows "his reluctance to be pleased." She states:

> The first women the Nortons met at the Priory included Eleanor Sellar, Emilia Pattison, and Eliza Lynn Linton, none of whom at the time held or practiced radical ideas about female emancipation. Nor had they abandoned their social status as Norton suggests ... Indeed, the women at the Priory during 1869 made up a mixed bag, the majority of them authors and other intellectuals and/or social activists, but also women primarily occupied with husbands and children, often many children. Norton's determination to represent them as mannish, heedless, or vulgar reveals a standoffishness ... inconsistent with his repeated January visits, made together with women of his own family. (*George Eliot in Society* 7–8)

outlet and served as an arena for networking and self-promotion. Eliot read to her guests from her works in progress, providing a sense of anticipation for the novels and poetry that would soon be out in print. Her eager audience included authors, editors, publishers, reviewers, and fans—people who could write and talk about the famous writer's work in magazines and in society.

Eliot managed to promote her work through readings and socializing at Priory Sundays without self-display. Lewes appeared to instigate readings and business-related discussion at the Priory while Eliot maintained the image of a sweet, feminine, self-effacing woman. Priory visitors frequently described Lewes as circulating the room and telling animated stories while Eliot sat serenely by the fireplace holding intimate, uplifting conversations with first-time guests (see Collins, *Interviews* 87–122). American poet Charles Warren Stoddard described her as "intensely feminine" and "diminutive" with a "gentle persuasive air" and "low, sweet voice" and recalled that while Lewes was the "life of the circle," "Mrs. Lewes was always the same placid, self-poised, kind-hearted, womanly soul, who suffered no one present to feel neglected" (102). Similarly, poet Edward Dowden spoke of her "perfect refined feminine personality," and Eton Chaplain Charles Kegan Paul commented on her "low sweet voice vibrating with emotion," her language "without the faintest tinge of pedantry," her "sympathy which never failed," and her nature which, despite greatness and learning, was "feminine and tender" (111, 109).[23] A number of guests remarked on her low, mellifluous voice, which Henriette Field attested was "an excellent thing in a woman" and "a special charm of the most finely cultured English ladies" (96).

Guests also commonly recalled that she did not say anything great or even noteworthy but rather focused attention on drawing out the best in others. Field explained that in Eliot's conversation there was no "attempt at display," "no wish to 'shine,'" no desire to "attract homage and admiration" (96). Eliot, she wrote, was loth to speak of herself or listen to the praise of others:

> She does not engross the conversation, but is more eager to listen than to talk. She has that delicate tact—which is one of the fine arts among women—to make others talk ... Thus she makes you forget the celebrated author, and think only of the refined and highly-cultivated woman. You do not feel awed by her genius,

---

[23] Public and second-hand accounts corroborated the notion that Eliot was feminine, emotional, and sympathetic. After meeting Eliot in Pau, France in 1867, Nina Lehmann remarked on Eliot's "sweet, mild, womanly presence" which was "so soothing" and "*elevating* above all" (182). Edmund Yates described her voice "of most sympathetic compass and richness" and her manner "full of a grave sweetness, uniformly gentle and intensely womanly" (189). Edward Coley Burne-Jones wrote of her deep knowledge and said that "her heart [was] one of the most sympathetic to me I ever knew" (202). Arthur Compton-Rickett conveyed second-hand knowledge of Eliot (through conversing with Oscar Browning) as "one of the most emotional women I ever met ... emotional, passionate, and dependent ... it wasn't her cleverness that appealed to you—it was her tremendous power of sympathy" (158).

but only quickened by it, as something that calls out all that is better and truer. While there is no attempt to impress you with her intellectual superiority, you feel naturally elevated into a higher sphere. (96)

Dowden wrote: "I cannot report any great sayings of hers—only each thing she said was the most right and best thing (best from an intellectual and spiritual point of view) ... She was very kind ... *sweet*, gracious and beautiful in manner" (111–12). James Sully, psychologist and philosopher, also noted that "If Lewes amused his company by his jocosities, George Eliot enfolded her auditors in an atmosphere of discriminative sympathy. She had a clairvoyant insight into mind and character, which enabled her to get at once into spiritual touch with a stranger, fitting her talk to his special tastes and needs, and drawing out what was best in him" (107–8). Guests often wrote of her ability to draw out their ideas and make them feel more intelligent. Publisher George Smith wrote of her ability to make her listener "pleased with himself" stating:

> I seldom left her presence without having a less modest estimate of my intellectual faculties than I had when I entered it! Perhaps her genius acted as a stimulus to an ordinary brain: or, perhaps, it was her gift of seizing upon a commonplace remark as it fell from your lips, translating it into philosophical terms, clothing it in the choicest words, and giving it back to you with the subtle suggestion that you had uttered some profoundly wise observation! (82)[24]

Eliot embodied the sympathetic ethos she wished to promote in her works. Rosalind Howard wrote of a discussion with Lewes about *The Spanish Gypsy* and its inspiration, Tintoretto's picture of the Annunciation, in which he said that Eliot's "power of entering into another person's point of view is so great that if she is beside a woman praying to a winking virgin—she almost believes in that winking virgin" (67). Eliot's guests often expressed amazement at her ability to make them feel valued, comforted, and spiritually edified.

Her spiritual presence—befitting the quasi-religious function of the poetess—was noted within and beyond the Priory walls. American folklorist and Priory guest Charles Godfrey Leland wrote about a rumor that the greatest men in England, including Carlyle, Froude, and Herbert Spencer sat with their note-books:

> silently taking down from her lips the ideas which they subsequently used in their writings! There seemed, indeed, to be afloat in America among certain folk an idea that something enormous, marvelous, and inspired went on at these receptions, and that George Eliot posed as a Pythia or Sibyl, as the great leading mind of England, and lectured while we listened. (101)

Priory guests and public witnesses referred to her as a "godlike" Oracle (190), a Sybil (118, 124, 126, 154), a "mother-confessor" (158), a "father-confessor"

---

[24] See also the comments of Charles Waltson (90), Annie Sawyer Downs (105), and Justin McCarthy (115).

(184), an Idol (93), to themselves as worshippers (69, 93, 116, 117) and as to her presence as hallowed (145, 155). The public venerated her as a national sage. Thomas Hay Sweet Escott described a time when "the lady" dropped a piece of trash on the street and a Cambridge don "snatched up the precious relic, placed it in his pocket-book, pressed it adoringly to that part of his person where his heart may have been" (124). The same story includes Robert Browning "at a respectful distance" identifying the lady as Eliot to his painter-friend, saying she had the "nose of Dante, the mouth of Savonarola, and the mind of Plato" to which the painter "reprovingly rejoined, 'Hush! She speaks!'" (124). Dubious stories such as these demonstrate to what extent the public mythologized George Eliot. Kathryn Hughes describes the Eliot ethos in London at the height of her fame:

> With Dickens and Thackeray gone and Trollope past his peak, George Eliot was now the country's greatest living novelist. Even in their prime none of this august trio had inspired feelings as intense, personal and reverential as the ones that surged towards the Priory now. Flowers were left anonymously at the door. Adoring fan mail arrived daily. When Marian ventured out strangers pressed forward, wanting to pat, touch and kiss their idol's hand. (303)[25]

Some viewed Eliot's mythic spiritual presence as orchestrated. Escott described Priory Sundays as "more like a religious ceremonial than a social reunion" in which "Mr. Lewes played to perfection the part of Hierophant" and "the gifted lady" sat amidst a "little crowd of worshippers" who "gazed at her reverently and mutely from afar, as if they were looking upon the beatific vision," and if anyone spoke when Eliot was speaking, "he was at once met with a 'hush' of reprehension by Mr. Lewes, and made to feel that he had perpetrated a sort of iniquity" (Collins, *Interviews* 117–18). He described the environment as one of forced worship: Lewes met guests "on the threshold ... yonder was a vase for receiving the votive flowers sacred to the goddess, which visitors often brought. Inside the chamber wherein SHE sat, a space was marked off, behind which the neophytes were not permitted to go" (118). Escott's depiction of Eliot as aloof from her "worshippers" contradicts the many accounts of her attentiveness to guests; however his perception of Eliot's contrived spiritual image was matched by that of Eliza Lynn Linton, who wrote of the:

> goddess on her pedestal—gracious in her condescension—with sweet strains of sympathetic recognition for all who came to her—ever ready to listen to her worshippers—ever ready to reply, to encourage, to clear from confusion minds befogged by unassimilated learning, and generous in imparting her own. But never for one instant did she forget her self-created Self—never did she

---

[25]   Marion Adams-Acton described seeing her at a London exhibition in 1878 where "so great was the crowd pressing round her" that she realized "what a grip she now had on London society" (134). Jane Ellen Harrison wrote of the Eliot "cult" and the ecstasy with which she received a compliment from her, stating that she had met many eminent men, "but there never came again a moment like that" (154).

throw aside the trappings or the airs of the benign Sibyl. Her soft, low voice was pitched in one level and monotonous key, and her deliberation of speech was a trifle irritating to the eager whose flint was already fired. Her gestures were as measured as her words; her attitudes as restrained as her tones. She was so consciously 'George Eliot'—so interpenetrated head and heel, inside and out, with the sense of her importance as the great novelist and profound thinker of her generation, as to make her society a little overwhelming, leaving on baser creatures the impression of having been rolled very flat indeed. (116–17)

It may be tempting to dismiss Linton's observation simply as writer's jealousy; however, one does wonder to what extent Eliot's image was "measured." Eliot often spoke in a self-effacing manner, but her actions sometimes belied her words. Many Priory guests commented on her refusal to hear herself or her works praised in person, but her letters show that she responded to the praise of her friends with deep gratitude for their sympathy and understanding. According to her friend Georgiana Burne-Jones, she claimed to say she was "so tired of being set on a pedestal and expected to vent wisdom" (215). However, she did little to prevent others from putting her on a pedestal. She oversaw Alexander Main's *Wise, Witty, and Tender Sayings in Prose and Verse, Selected from the Works of George Eliot* (1871)—a book of collected passages from her works—and *The George Eliot Birthday Book* (1878)—a diary for recording birthdays of friends and family that was decorated with quotations from Eliot's works. These kitsch publications were not the sort of serious art Eliot liked to associate herself with; nevertheless, she and Lewes encouraged their production. Lewes's response to Main's initial proposal of *Wise, Witty and Tender Sayings* reveals his view of her status as a moral instructor and his wish to encourage others toward such a view. Lewes wrote to Main of a fan's suggestion that excerpts from her works be hung in schoolrooms and railway waiting rooms "in view of the banal and often preposterous bible texts, thus hung up and neglected," but said that Main's book idea was "a far more practical one" and would be "a treasure for readers" (*Letters* 5:192–3). Lewes thus indicated that Eliot's texts were not only more instructive than neglected biblical texts but that the public should regard them with more interest. Eliot likewise embraced Main's idea to disseminate her sayings, and she exchanged numerous letters giving feedback on his choices. Lewes wrote to Main after publication of *Wise, Witty and Tender Sayings* that "Mrs. Cowper Temple told Mrs. Lewes that she had copied passages from 'Romola' into her New Testament. This is strong measure from an English woman, and a devout one, but it shows how deeply the wisdom and beauty of that work has penetrated" (5:276). Both Lewes and Eliot recognized and fostered worship of the great Sybil.

Eliot's mythical status did no harm to her ethos as a poet. The debut of her poetry-writing career coincided with the launch of the Priory Sundays where she gathered about her famous and aspiring poets, theorists, and historians to whom she read aloud poems, which began to appear in periodicals in 1869 (McCormack, *George Eliot in Society* 61). Alexis Easley perceptively argues that Eliot capitalized on her fame in the early 1870s by publishing "The Legend of Jubal" and *Armgart* in *Macmillan's Magazine*—a periodical that had a policy of including authorial signatures. Easley explains: "Eliot's willingness to advertise her poetry and name in a popular literary periodical suggests her recognition of the importance of self-marketing in the ongoing development of her career ... Eliot was able to celebrate her growing fame and cultivate an audience for her poetry" (107).

Eliot promoted herself without self-display at Priory Sundays, in public, and in print, all the while appearing to be the embodiment of spiritual enlightenment and sympathetic understanding. She crafted her poetic persona by masking her feminine identity early in her writing career, by guarding her privacy, and by associating outwardly with femininity later in her career at the Priory, in public, and in her poetry. Through careful self-staging, she embraced the model of the poetess that embodied respectable femininity and avoided the scandalous model that was associated with passion, ambition, and immodest public display. Aside from the autobiographical "Brother and Sister" and possibly *Armgart*, which some critics read as an expression of her artistic anxiety, Eliot's poetry did not readily serve as material for discovery of her life, and she did not offer biographical details to the public. Eliot fashioned her image as that of the wholesome poetess by deflecting attention from her actual life and constructing an image of herself as a sympathetic figure, earning herself the title of the "female Shakespeare" (Collins, *Interviews* 104, 140).

"Erinna" and the Poetess

Eliot's poetry reveals a deliberate engagement with the poetess tradition. Her poem, "Erinna," exemplifies her use of a distinctively feminine voice and conventions to further ideas she would not have stated directly. The poem was inspired by her reading fragments of "The Distaff," a lament written by the ancient Greek poetess Erinna for her childhood friend, Baucis. Eliot introduced her poem with a quote from Karl Ottfried Müller's *History of the Literature of Ancient Greece* (1840):

> Erinna died in early youth when chained by her mother to the spinning-wheel. She had as yet known the charm of existence in imagination alone. Her poem called "The Spindle" – Ἠλἄκάτη – containing only 300 hexameter verses, in which she probably expressed the restless & aspiring thoughts which crowded on her youthful mind as she pursued her monotonous work, has been deemed by many of the ancients of such high poetic merit as to entitle it to a place beside the epics of Homer. (180)

Eliot also included in the poem's preface: "Four lines of the Ἠλἄκάτη are extant. The dialect is a mixture of Doric and Aeolic spoken at Rhodes where Erinna was born; the date about B.C. 612," information she gathered from William Smith's 1846 edition of the *Dictionary of Greek and Roman Biography and Mythology*

(49).[26] Finally, she prefaced her poem with the four extant lines of Erinna's poem in Greek, for which Antoine Gerard van den Broek offers the following translations:

> Thus the sound passes over the waters even into Hades,
> And [it? She?] is silent among the dead; and the darkness covers [her?] eyes[27]
> …
> Thou pompilo, fish that followest folk faring over the fair main,
> follow in pomp at the poop my sweet love. (*Complete Shorter Poetry* 2:281)[28]

Eliot found Erinna's verse fragments, placed after Sappho's poetry, in a book that she and Lewes owned, Theodorus Bergk's *Poetae Lyrici Graeci*; the book contains Eliot's notes on the pages dealing with Sappho's poetry (2:109–10). The placement of Erinna's and Sappho's poetry in Bergk's book points to a trend among scholars connecting Erinna and Sappho throughout the ages. Scholars have called them contemporaries, friends, and lovers, though most today agree that Erinna lived two centuries after Sappho. What we do know of Erinna and Sappho is that they were famous ancient Greek poetesses who were ranked with Homer for their poetic merit, who used a similar verse form, and whose lives invited public scrutiny. Focus on their physical bodies has oftentimes overshadowed attention to their literary bodies. Their literary fragments have been handed down through the ages, used by other poets for inspiration, and mined for biographical details. Their reputations have waxed and waned and been appropriated for various cultural and political purposes. By including Erinna's biographical information and her fragments, Eliot perpetuates the habit of holding up the figure of the poetess for public scrutiny but also asks the reader to pay homage to her literary remains.

Eliot's choice of an elegy—a verse genre associated with a masculine tradition, which could also call attention to the feminine ability to sympathize and mourn—

---

[26] Van den Broek points out that Eliot relied on Smith's work for details on Erinna's dialect and place of birth (*CSP* 2:110). Smith's entry on Erinna also includes the following: "A contemporary and friend of Sappho (about B.C. 612), who died at the age of nineteen, but left behind her poems which were thought worthy to rank with those of Homer" and "She is also called a Lesbian and a Mytilenaean, on account of her residence in Lesbos with Sappho … Three epigrams in the Anthology are ascribed to her … of which the first has the genuine air of antiquity; but the other two, addressed to Baucis, seem to be a later fabrication" (49). Scholars dispute the biographical details of Erinna's life—primarily where and when she lived—and the authenticity of various fragments attributed to her. Most today believe she lived in the fourth century BCE.

[27] As Eliot notes, these fragments were preserved by Stobaeus and Athenaeus. In this fragment, Erinna expresses the hope (or doubt) that her song will reach her friend in Hades, where there is only darkness and silence.

[28] In Greek mythology, Pompilo was a sailor whom Apollo turned into a type of fish named by ancient Greek sailors "pilot fish" because they swam alongside ships, seemingly as guides. According to the *OED*, "poop" refers to church bells. Thus the image in the lines is that of Erinna asking the mythological fish to follow the funeral procession and guide her young friend in death.

allowed her at once to employ and embody the feminine poetic voice that she invites readers to experience through feeling.[29] Her choice of Erinna for the subject of her poem suggests her identification with the ancient poetess tradition. Furthermore, her reproduction of Müller's comment about Erinna's work being entitled to "a place beside the epics of Homer" as an epigraph to her poem might indicate her desire to find a place not only among her female predecessors but, like Erinna, within the great male epic tradition. Eliot, like Erinna and Sappho, alludes to Greek mythological narratives and appropriates them for her own purposes. By making such associations in the preface of her poem, Eliot asserts belief in the potential of the poetess in general, and herself in particular, to achieve the "high poetic merit" of Homer. Eliot's choice of Erinna rather than Sappho (the better-known poetess) for the subject-matter of her poem is curious. She did write a two-line fragment that was inspired by Sappho's fragment 17: "I would not have your beauties in exchange / For the sweet thoughts your beauty breeds in me" and was said to have had the "heart of Sappho" (*CSP* 2:163; Collins, *Interviews* 195). So, why did Eliot write an entire poem about Erinna and craft only a fragment inspired by Sappho? Perhaps the association of Sappho with passion and sexuality deterred Eliot from overtly identifying with her poetic lineage. By writing about the chaste, young Erinna, Eliot associated herself with the pure and respectable poetess who poured out her heart in lament rather than in love and desire.

A papyrus containing 54 lines of "The Distaff" was discovered in 1928, revealing reminiscences of Erinna's shared childhood with Baucis and expressions of grief for the loss of her friend first to marriage and then to death.[30] However, Eliot had access to just four lines of the poem and could only speculate on its content. Her introductory epigraph indicates her interest in Erinna's imaginative life, "the restless and aspiring thoughts" that "crowded on" her "youthful mind" as she pursued her "monotonous work" at the spinning wheel. Eliot's narrator takes on the voice of the mourning poetess, as Erinna did in "The Distaff," weaving into her poem Erinna's sorrowful cries through affective language and meter.[31] Each of

---

[29]   The feminine voice relied on emotion and as such is described as pouring forth from the heart. Linda Hughes explains that Victorian sentimentality and the appeal to the heart can be understood in the context of religion, domestic ideology, and commercialization. "Poetry," she states, "had long been considered the preserve of pathos ... through its link to song, and secular concepts of sympathy reinforced appeals to the responsive heart associated with Victorian piety ... The heart ... was at once an organ of piety, secular morality, intellection, and aesthetic experience" (167).

[30]   To read fragments of "The Distaff" and other epigrams attributed to Erinna, see *Women Writers of Ancient Greece and Rome: An Anthology*. This work also provides useful biographical background on Erinna and a summary of the scholarly debates surrounding her life and her writing.

[31]   For an analysis of "Erinna," see "Aural Sensibility, the Weaver-poet, and George Eliot's 'Erinna'" by Kyriaki Hajdjiafxendi. Hajdjiafxendi is the first to examine the poem and offers an astute reading that compares "Erinna" with Eliot's early essay, "Woman in France: Madame de Sablé" (1854) to show how Eliot uses the image of the imprisoned weaver-poet to propose loneliness as a condition for the creation of women's art.

the five stanzas consists of an irregular combination of tetrameter and pentameter lines and concludes with one hexameter line. The predominantly iambic meter echoes the recurrent turn of the spinning wheel.[32] Stanza one introduces the poem's subject (Art) and setting (Rhodes, Greece), the birthplace of Erinna:

> 'Twas in the isle that Helios saw
> Uprising from the sea a flower-tressed bride
> To meet his kisses—Rhodes, the filial pride
> Of god-taught craftsmen who gave Art its law: (2:113–4)

The image of Helios kissing his bride, Rhodes, rising from the sea, introduces the themes of birth and domesticity. The narrator proudly declares Greece as the place where Ancient Greek poets ("god-taught craftsmen") birthed the poetic form ("gave Art its law") that was sung through the generations and is still revered today.

The narrator then abruptly shifts tone from pride to pity in introducing one of Greece's great artists, Erinna, as she is laboring at the spinning-wheel:

> She held the spindle as she sat,
> Erinna with the thick-coiled mat
> Of raven hair and deepest agate eyes,
> Gazing with a sad surprise
> At surging visions of her destiny
> To spin the byssus drearily
> In insect labour, while the throng
> Of Gods and men wrought deeds that poets wrought in song. (2:114)[33]

The steady iambic rhythm of the spinning wheel intones a sorrowful, monotonous reminder of the young girl's domestic imprisonment. The narrator interrupts the recurrent sound of the wheel with one trochaic line ("gazing with a sad surprise") to alert the reader to Erinna's gaze and visions—of herself in a subhuman state performing "insect labour" and of "Gods and men" who perform epic deeds about which great poems are written. These contrasting visions correspond to the "restless and aspiring thoughts" that Eliot mentioned in her epigraph. To help escape her "insect labor," Erinna relies on her imagination (and the oral tradition of singing poetry) to travel to far off lands where epic heroes perform great deeds. The narrator thus hints of the life-giving potential of poetry

---

[32] Each stanza consists of an irregular combination of tetrameter and pentameter lines and concludes with one hexameter line.

[33] Eliot used these lines as the epigraph to chapter 51 of *Daniel Deronda* in which Deronda meets his mother, who abandoned him to pursue her singing career. The epigraph thus links the themes of motherhood and women's artistic ambition in the novel and the poem. The role of motherhood in "Erinna" is complicated. The mother who allegedly chained Erinna to the spinning-wheel only appears in the poem's epigraph, and of the two mother goddesses that figure in the poem, only one is sympathetic.

amidst suffering. Though Erinna ultimately would die from physical exhaustion, while she was alive, she could live vicariously through imagination and epic song.

Erinna is likened to a spider with her "raven hair and deepest agate eyes" and spins the "byssus," a silk cloth used to wrap mummies in ancient burial customs. As the reader knows, she will die as a result of her own labor. Although she appears to be spinning her own shroud, the "byssus" actually has great worth. She is spinning fine silk rather than ordinary, cheap wool, and her handicraft is valuable art. While she spins silk, she envisions stories of "Gods and men"— stories that will inspire her art. Like Arachne, who weaves stories of gods and men into her tapestry, Erinna will join the great Homeric tradition in weaving stories of epic heroes in song, and in so doing, will weave her own destiny as that of a great poet. In the literal, domestic world, spinning kills the spirit and body of a woman, but in the imaginative realm, spinning creates beauty and life.

The narrator having called attention to her eyes "gazing" at "surging visions of her destiny," transports the reader through her visions to a grand world of epic heroes and daring quests:

> Visions of ocean-wreathed Earth
> Shone through with light of epic rhapsody
> Where Zeus looked with Olympus and the sea
> Smiled back with Aphrodite's birth;
> Where heroes sailed on daring quests
> In ships that knew and loved their guests;
> Where the deep-bosomed matron and sweet maid
> Died for others unafraid ... (2:114)

The narrator emphasizes the location of the heroic action—Erinna's imagination— by repeating the word "where" five times. Each "where" takes the reader to a new vision in Erinna's imagination: Zeus and Olympus smiling on Aphrodite's birth; heroes sailing on quests; matrons and maids dying for others; Pindus echoing songs; Themis seeing fear ennobled into awe. The epic visions in her imagination will ultimately come to life as her own "epic rhapsody," which will echo "to the Ionian shore" to be heard throughout time. The vision of Pindus echoing songs "fed with action and the love / Of primal work" relates to Erinna's song that will be fed with her active imagination and her primal work—that is, the actual and figurative work of spinning. Pindus's echoing songs to the Ionian shore recalls the extant fragment of "The Distaff" ("Thus the sound passes over the waters even into Hades, / And [it? She?] is silent among the dead; and the darkness covers [her?] eyes"). This allusion illustrates that though Erinna may have thought her song echoed out only to fall on the silent dead (or, silent Baucis), it actually found a listening audience that would subsequently remember her, her friend, and her song for generations. The stanza's final vision of Themis, mother of the fates, using her power to ennoble "Brute Fear" into "awe" testifies to the power of Erinna's imagination to weave a fate for herself that will turn her suffering into awe-inspiring art.

In stanza three, the narrator calls the reader's attention back from Erinna's imaginative visions to her physical presence with a direct, emotional, second-person appeal and a shift from steady iambic to forceful, trochaic meter:[34]

> Hark, the passion in her eyes
> Changes to melodic cries
> Lone she pours her lonely pain.
> Song unheard is not in vain. (2:114)[35]

These lines call the reader to enter into Erinna's experience and to witness the process of creating art. Erinna's song ("melodic cries") springs forth from emotion ("passion") roused from imaginative experience and suffering.[36] Erinna "pours" her "lonely pain" into her song. Eliot describes this process of creating poetry in "Notes on Form in Art" (1868): "*Poetry* begins when passion weds thought by finding expression in an image; but *poetic form* begins with a choice of elements, however meager, as the accordant expression of emotional states. The most monotonous burthen chanted by an Arab boatman on the Nile is still a beginning of poetic form" (*CSP* 2:182). The rhythm of the spinning wheel, like the boatman's chant, is the beginning of poetic form, and Erinna's passion, fueled by imagination, finds expression in her song. The poem springs from the artist's passion, and the artist arouses the reader's passion in turn.

The narrator explains why Erinna's "Song unheard is not in vain":

> The god within us plies[37]
> His shaping power and moulds in speech

---

[34] In "Versification" (1869), Eliot explains that in "both verse and music rhythmic and tonic relations are used as a means of moving men's souls by the adjustment of those relations to the bias of passionate experience" (*CSP* 2:185). By varying the meter, she shifts the reader's mood and emotional experience.

[35] "Erinna" shares similar stylistic elements with Barrett Browning's "The Cry of the Children" (1842), a poem that exposes the suffering of child laborers by giving a voice to the children who cry because they are weary from work. Trochaic meter throughout harshly and monotonously pounds like industrial noise in a factory: "Do ye hear the children weeping, O my brothers, / Ere the sorrow comes with years?" (Barrett Browning 2:127). Barrett Browning also uses affective language to create a pitiful mood: "They look up with their pale and sunken faces, / And their looks are sad to see" (2:128). Whereas Barrett Browning employs meter and affective language to elicit the reader's pity for suffering children, Eliot uses these techniques to elicit pity for suffering women.

[36] Kyriaki Hajdjiafxendi aptly observes that Eliot writes poetry (elegy in particular) as a way of reproducing meaning through sound: "Erinna's melodious cries transform not only her pain into singing but also her response to the images she weaves into sound, and hence she herself becomes the elegy—an inter-communicative poetic body whose rhythmic processes the reader shares" ("Aural Sensibility" 110).

[37] "The god within us" reflects Eliot's belief in the Feuerbachian God who is the projection of man's inward nature.

Harmonious a statue of our sorrow,
Till suffering turn beholding and we borrow,
Gazing on Self apart, the wider reach
Of solemn souls that contemplate
And slay with full-beamed thought the darling Dragon Hate. (2:114–15)

Shifting from second to first person, the narrator-poet converges her artistic experience with that of the weaver-poet and all poets to show how creative power ("god within us") uses poetic language ("speech / Harmonious") to give shape to art ("a statue of our sorrow"). Through the creation process, the poet's suffering turns into "beholding"—once created, the poem no longer belongs solely to the poet but also to the public, and the poet can only gaze on her own poem as "Self apart" along with other beholders. The poet offers up her work (her Self) for display while also borrowing from "the wider reach / Of solemn souls that contemplate / And slay with full-beamed thought the darling dragon Hate." In this way, art is a community endeavor of "solemn souls" throughout time who soothe humanity through self-expression inspired by others.[38] In borrowing from Homer, Erinna fulfills her artistic ambition. Likewise, Eliot borrows from Erinna (and Homer) and produces a work for others to behold. The narrator seems to imply that the connective experience of writing applies to all artists; however, she also hints that she is communicating to a more specific community of artists—that of women poets. Nineteenth-century women poets, like Erinna, were restricted by their sex, mythologized by the public, and held up like statues on display for the public to behold. Unlike Homer, who was not restricted by his sex and whose epic poems were sung, memorized, and passed down largely intact throughout the ages, Erinna was forced to create her art while being chained to a spinning wheel— the very symbol of domestic labor—and her art only survived in fragments. For generations, the public regarded her as an artistic genius but focused more on her tragic life and wasted youth.

The quotation marks that enclose stanzas four and five signal a change. In stanzas one and two, the narrator focused on Erinna's experience at the spindle, in her imaginative state, and in the poetic composition process. The second half of stanza three turns to women's experience, and in the final two stanzas, the narrator shifts attention to her own experience. There, she upholds her work as a "statue of [her] sorrow" for others to behold. The quotation marks show that she is "gazing on Self apart," allowing others to "borrow" from, "contemplate," and "slay" the "darling Dragon Hate" with her song that is inspired by Erinna's. As Erinna wove her song from the mythological stories in her imagination, the narrator integrates Erinna's imaginative experience and Homer's epic figures into her poem. In stanza four she addresses Great Cybele (goddess of the earth, mother of the gods) to express the same fear that concerned Erinna—fear that her art would not be heard after her death:

---

[38]   This message echoes that of "Mid the Rich Store of Nature's Gifts to Man": people find spiritual communion through the act of creating and sharing their creative gifts with others. See Chapter 2 for a detailed analysis of this poem.

"Great Cybele, whose ear doth love
The piercing flute, why is my maiden wail
Like hers, the loved twice lost, whose dear hands pale
Yearning, severed seemed to move
Thin phantoms on the night-black air?
But thou art deaf to human care:
Thy breasts impartial cherish with their food
Strength alike of ill and good.
The dragon and the hero, friend and foe,
Who makes the city's weal, and who its woe,
All draw their strength from thee; and what I draw
Is rage divine in limbs fast bound by narrow law. (2:115)

The image of the "piercing flute" connects domestic work, music, and emotion—according to the *OED*, "flute" is both a musical instrument and an instrument used in tapestry weaving.[39] "Piercing" means having an acute effect on the mind or emotions and to pass through with a sharp-pointed object. "Piercing flute" thus alludes to the instrument that pierces to make the tapestry but refers specifically to women's affective song. The narrator wonders why the goddess Cybele, "whose ear doth love" the "piercing flute" would allow women's songs to be lost. The narrator-poet complains that her feminine lament ("my maiden-wail") will be like Erinna's, "the loved twice lost"; she identifies with the double loss of the physical body and potential loss of her art after she is gone.[40] She asks why her "hands" (physical hands), like Erinna's, will become "pale"—indicating her preoccupation with death—and why her "hands" (handiwork, artistic production), like Erinna's, will become "Yearning, severed" and seem to move nothing more than "Thin phantoms on the night-black air." She again expresses Erinna's concern that, once she is dead, her poetry will pass over the waters into Hades and fall silently in darkness. Cybele, who is "deaf to human care," offers no comfort to women writers but instead allows injustice to thrive; her "breasts impartial," rather than nurture and comfort suffering humans, give "Strength alike" to "ill and good." But the narrator does not accept Cybele's impartiality; she explains that while "All draw their strength" from Cybele, what she (the narrator) will "draw / Is rage divine in limbs fast bound by narrow law." The word "draw" means to gather or take, to weave, to take by chance, and to represent in words, and "rage" can refer to

---

[39]   *OED Online*. Oxford University Press, March 2014. Web. Subsequent *OED* citations will use the same edition.

[40]   Use of the word "maiden" with its many definitions allows for multiple readings: "Maiden" refers to an unmarried young woman, a virgin, a spinster of mature years, "the supports in which the spindle of a spinning wheel turns," and a thing which is the first of its kind (*OED*). I take the narrator's "maiden wail" to mean feminine verse composition, as the adjective "maiden" links weaving imagery and womanhood with lament ("wail"), a feminine verse form. However, it would not be unreasonable to read the narrator's "maiden wail" as an expression of sorrow for her (and Erinna's) inability to marry due to being bound by "narrow law."

anger, grief, and "poetic, prophetic, or musical enthusiasm or inspiration" (*OED*). Like Erinna whose limbs are fastened to the spinning-wheel, the narrator's limbs are bound by custom that restricts and devalues women's writing ("narrow law"). Erinna drew poetic inspiration in her domestic imprisonment, and the narrator will "draw" divine, poetic inspiration ("rage divine") in her confinement. She will also write ("draw") inspiration ("rage divine") from her position as a woman writer bound by custom; she will weave feminine experience into her poems.[41]

In stanza five, the narrator turns to a more supportive muse, Athena (goddess of wisdom, knowledge, and art), who promotes justice:

> But Pallas, thou dost choose and bless
> The nobler cause, thy maiden height
> And terrible beauty marshaling the fight
> Inspire weak limbs with stedfastness.
> Thy virgin breast uplifts
> The direful aegis, but thy hand
> Wielded its weapon with benign command
> In Rivalry of highest gifts
> With strong Poseidon whose earth-shaking roll
> Matched not the delicate tremors of thy spear
> Piercing Athenian land and drawing thence
> With conquering beneficence
> Thy subtly chosen dole
> The sacred olive fraught with light and plenteous cheer. (2:115–16)

Unlike impartial Cybele, who favors neither right nor wrong, Athena chooses and blesses the "nobler cause." Athena embodies femininity with her "maiden height" and "terrible beauty," yet she is a warrior. She marshals the "fight" against "narrow law" that binds women and with her "stedfastness" inspires women's hands ("weak limbs," "limbs fast bound") to overcome societal restrictions and to write freely with feminine conviction.[42] She encourages women to write without fear that their work will be devalued and lost over time because of having been written by a woman. Like the pompilo fish that guides ships to shore (and Baucis in death) in "The Distaff" fragment, Athena guides women writers. Her "virgin breast" does not, like Cybele's, cherish "ill and good" alike but instead "uplifts / The direful aegis." The ageless and immortal aegis upon Athena's feminine breast symbolizes the immortal potential of women's writing. Athena's "hand" demonstrates the capacity of the woman writer; it "Wielded its weapon with benign command."

The narrator depicts the power of women's creative ability by recounting the "Rivalry of highest gifts"—the contest between Athena and Poseidon in which they agreed to offer one gift to the city and allow the Athenians to choose which gift they preferred. Poseidon's masculine, "strong," "earth-shaking roll" was

---

[41]   If "rage" is read as anger, then these lines could express the narrator's anger at her confinement and her writing of her indignation.

[42]   Athena also marshals the Homeric fights, and so will the narrator, who weaves Homeric stories into her poem.

no match for the feminine, "delicate tremors" of Athena's spear, which pierced the land and drew forth "with conquering beneficence / Thy subtly chosen dole / The sacred olive." Athenians chose Athena's subtle gift of the olive tree over Poseidon's dramatic display of power, made her their patron deity, and named their city after her. Unlike Poseidon's useless gift, Athena's "sacred" gift of the first domesticated olive tree provided nourishment, warmth, and light from the olives, wood, and oil. The sacred tree met essential domestic needs and allowed the city to thrive. In this way, Athena illustrated the value of women's creative ability and domestic sensibility, and she upheld women as the nation's comforters and life-givers. Athena's "subtly chosen dole" of the tree that was "fraught with light and plenteous cheer" proved that the lot of women should not be confinement within society but to realize "sweetness and light" for the nation.[43] Athena's subtle yet powerful actions demonstrated the ability of women to use the feminine pen ("the delicate tremors of thy spear"), to enlighten the nation ("piercing Athenian land"), and to employ successfully a feminine sensibility ("conquering beneficence") in writing women's experience ("drawing ... / Thy subtly chosen dole").

The narrator credits Athena with inventing the distaff and the loom and explains that her association with domestic work did not diminish her power:

> What, though thou pliest the distaff and the loom?
> Counsel is thine, to sway the doubtful doom
> Of cities with a leaguer at their gate;
> Thine the device that snares the hulk elate
> Of purblind force and saves the hero or the State. (2:116)

The ancients considered Athena to be the inventor of useful and elegant arts as well as all work associated with women. Skilled in women's work herself, she was the "goddess of all wisdom, knowledge, and art, and [was represented] as sitting on the right hand side of her father Zeus, and supporting him with her counsel ... She also maintained the authority of the law, and justice, and order, in the courts and the assembly of the people" (Smith 394). By reminding the reader that Athena invented the spinning wheel, a domestic and creative art that had both the power to kill and to give life, the narrator shows that in Athena what seems limiting and confining is coterminous with greatness and power. She who embodies feminine power has the ability to offer "Counsel" to govern the uncertain fate ("doubtful doom") of besieged cities and devise the plans that capture the powerful warship ("hulk elate / Of purblind force") and save "the hero or the State." The narrator hopes to draw her strength from Athena's feminine example and wise counsel to "sway" the dreadful laws of society ("the doubtful doom / Of cities"), control ("snare") the unwieldy mass of un-insightful discourse ("hulk elate / Of purblind

---

[43]   In writing "fraught with light and plenteous cheer," Eliot may have had in mind the expression that Matthew Arnold made popular in *Culture and Anarchy* (1867–68): "sweetness and light". Arnold urged society to strive for beauty and intelligence, or "sweetness and light," to attain "complete harmonious human perfection" (51, 35).

force"), and write great stories ("[save] the hero or the State").[44] In other words, the narrator as a female poet hopes to overcome societal restrictions and create inspired works that enlighten, elevate, and endure; she hopes to place herself within the lyric and epic traditions and ensure her place "beside the epics of Homer."

Van den Brock dates composition of "Erinna" to a time between 1873–1876, years in which Eliot was struggling with illness and contemplating her own mortality. She also wrote during these years "Mid my Gold-Brown Curls" (1875) a poem that expresses her anxiety about aging:

> 'Mid my gold-brown curls
> There twined a silver hair:
> I plucked it idly out
> And scarcely knew 'twas there.
> Coiled in my velvet sleeve it lay
> And like a serpent hissed:
> "Me thou canst pluck and fling away,
> One hair is lightly missed;
> But how on that near day
> When all the wintry army muster in array?" (*CSP* 2:127)

Eliot's narrator zoomorphizes a single curl of gray hair plucked "idly out" into that of an ominous hissing serpent that portends a full head of gray hair ("the wintry army"). The serpentine hair challenges the narrator to consider that "near day" when she will not be able to "pluck and fling away" a whole army of gray hairs— essentially asking, "what will you do then; how will you overcome inevitable old age?" The narrator answers the question in "Erinna." Like Athena whose "hand / Wielded its weapon with benign command," the narrator will wield her pen to write elevating art that she hopes will echo "to the Ionian shore." The battle imagery in both poems alludes to an internal struggle with mortality. In her mid-fifties, Eliot was feeling the inevitability of her death. She wrote to Mrs. William Smith (1874) that "death seems to me now a close, real experience, like the approach of autumn or winter, and I am glad to find that advancing life brings this power of imagining the nearness of death I never had till of late years" (*Letters* 6:64). Observing Erinna's literary remains—two mere and barely readable fragments written by one who "had as yet known the charm of existence in imagination alone"—caused Eliot to ponder her own failing body. Her anxiety about death and the sustainability of her work prompted her to turn to poetry, which she viewed as superior to all other art forms ("Versification," *CSP* 2:182). She felt strongly called to influence others through her art, especially during the later years of her life, and capitalized on her celebrity to fashion herself as a poetess and living sage and to craft "in speech / Harmonious a statue" for others to behold for years to come.

---

[44]   In addition to fate or judgment, "doom" can refer to a statute, or law; "hulk" means a ship or a bulky, unwieldy mass; "elate" signifies that which is exalted or lofty; "purblind" indicates a lack of understanding or insight; and "force" refers to the strength of discourse, style, or artistic creations (*OED*).

Chapter 2
Prophet of Sympathy

"If Art does not enlarge men's sympathies, it does nothing morally."
—George Eliot

After she left the Christian faith in 1842, Eliot[1] began to consider sympathy, rather than organized religion, as a way of living a moral life. Throughout the 1840s and 1850s, she developed her religious views and eventually settled into a belief in sympathy as a substitute for religion. Much has been said about Eliot's religious views and her concept of sympathy but rarely in relation to her poetry. She wrote religious poems throughout her life. As a young evangelical Christian, she relied on religious terminology and Christian teachings to convey orthodox religious views; and as an apostate, she relied on the same religious language and doctrine to convey unorthodox religious views. It may seem contradictory for an unorthodox believer to rely on religious language and doctrine; however, by the time Eliot began her poetry-writing career, she had successfully fashioned an image of herself as a sage by appropriating such modes of expression. Writing as a venerable poetess, Eliot voiced her belief in the sacred value of sympathetic relationships through religious rhetoric. In this chapter, I address the religious element of Eliot's poetry by discussing the cultural environment in which she lived, her religious upbringing, her conversion from Christianity to a religion of sympathy, and her assimilation of new religious ideas in her poetry with the help of the poetess tradition. I will analyze "Mid the Rich Store of Nature's Gifts to Man" and "O May I Join the Choir Invisible" to reveal Eliot's poetry as the site of her conversion from orthodox religious views to belief in the sacred value of sympathetic human interaction.

George Eliot's Religion and Role as Poet

Eliot's role in England's religious upheaval was significant. She contributed to the increasing sense of religious uncertainty by helping to introduce German ideas of higher criticism to England via her translations of David Strauss's *Life of Jesus* (1846) and Ludwig Feuerbach's *Essence of Christianity* (1854), radical works that demystified and humanized Christianity. Conversely, she participated

---

[1]   Throughout this work, I use the name "George Eliot" to refer to the artist. However, Eliot changed her name a number of times throughout her life. She was Mary Anne Evans, Mary Ann (without the "e") Evans, Marian Evans, Marian Evans Lewes, Marian Lewes, George Eliot, Marian Cross, and Mary Ann Cross. See Rosemarie Bodenheimer's "A Woman of Many Names" to read the reasons for Eliot's many name changes.

in the poetess tradition, one that was associated with the promotion of traditional, spiritual, and feminine ideals. To understand these seemingly paradoxical roles, one must trace her stance toward religion from her youth.

Eliot's religious journey began in the Anglican church that she attended regularly with her family. Her father, a conservative High Church Anglican, had Eliot baptized in their parish church at Chilvers Coton.[2] At the age of nine, she attended school at Nuneaton, where she was strongly influenced by her evangelical (Low Church Anglican) teacher, Maria Lewis, and from age 13 to 16, she went to a Coventry school that was run by Mary and Rebecca Franklin, daughters of a Baptist (Low Church Dissenting) minister.[3] Such evangelical influences during these formative years shaped Eliot into a pious, self-righteous young woman.[4] Her letters from this period reveal a serious girl with a zeal for developing her inner spiritual life through study, prayer, suffering, and austere living. She underwent a

---

[2]   "High Church" and "Low Church" refer to two parties within the Church of England. The High Church party believed in the centrality of sacraments and the importance of the role of the Church in the spiritual lives of its members. The High Church party embraced orthodox theology and rejected enthusiasm. High Church congregants believed the order of bishops, priests, and deacons was essential to its life. The Low Church party de-emphasized sacraments and ritual in worship, emphasized moral behavior, and viewed clergy as models and teachers of manners, not as mediators between God and man. Evangelicals within the Church of England were the most influential of the Low Church party. The Evangelical movement (begun with John Wesley in the prior century) recovered sixteenth-century Reformation doctrines such as justification by faith alone and emphasized conversion, the sinfulness of humanity, future judgment by God, repentance, confession of guilt, awareness of Christ's forgiveness, moral life, and reliance on the Holy Spirit for guidance. Evangelicals downplayed ritual, convention, and rationalism and favored an emotional response to the gospel. They strongly believed in personal salvation and holy living and did not concern themselves much with theology or the Church as an institution. However, they did accept the establishment of the Church of England because they believed that obedience to Christ equated to obedience to the state (Worrall 6–11).

[3]   Rosemary Ashton, who describes the religious climate in the area in which Eliot lived, explains that religious dissent thrived, but the Evans family remained Anglican: "There were chapels of all denominations: Baptist, Wesleyan, Unitarian, Quaker, Congregationalist. Though her own family belonged to the middle-of-the-road Anglican community, Mary Anne herself was strongly evangelical ("Evans"). Haight says that though strongly influenced by her religious experience at the Franklins' school, she did not take an interest in the Baptist doctrines but rather still regarded herself as belonging to the Church of England (20). In short, Eliot identified with the evangelical Anglicans (though not strictly) as opposed to the evangelical Dissenters. She sympathized with her Baptist teachers and her Methodist aunt, but her statements and practices did not show that the dissenters in her life significantly influenced her beliefs.

[4]   Christine Krueger argues that Eliot's evangelical background provided a model in which she and other women expressed spiritual power; this model prepared her for an "extraordinary call, familiar to women preachers" (235). I would add to Krueger's conclusion that Eliot's emerging belief in the sacredness of art in addition to her evangelical background prepared her for a role as spiritual guide to a large audience of readers.

conversion experience at age 15 that led her to study the Bible and religious books with fervor.[5] Eliot began to neglect her appearance in order to show concern for her soul, and she practiced charity and abstained from pleasures such as theatergoing. She later confessed, "I used to go about like an owl ... to the great disgust of my brother" (Cross 1.157). Her letters reveal her commitment to asceticism and self-denial, but there is no evidence that she adhered to the doctrines of atonement and justification by faith. There is also no evidence that she believed in humanity's sinfulness. Avrom Fleishman argues that Christianity for Eliot was not redemptive or salvific. Rather, Christianity provided "an alternative structure to organize a sense of life's inadequacy, the inadequacy both of the world in which she lived and of her own existence" (16). Lacking commitment to key tenets of Evangelical theology, the young Eliot was open to alternate religious views.

In 1841, her family moved to Foleshill where she met and befriended Charles and Cara Bray, freethinking Unitarians who offered Eliot an intellectually challenging environment. They introduced her to liberal thinkers, including the social philosophers Herbert Spencer and Harriet Martineau, the social experimentalist Robert Owen, the radical publisher John Chapman, and Ralph Waldo Emerson on his visits from America (Ashton, "Evans"). During this time, Eliot read historical accounts of the Bible, including Charles Hennell's *Inquiry Concerning the Origin of Christianity* (1838), that explained away the miracles of the New Testament using reason and logic.[6] She may have referred to Hennell's book when she wrote to Maria Lewis: "My whole soul has been engrossed in the most interesting of all enquiries for the last few days, and to what result my thoughts may lead I know not—possibly to one that will startle you, but my only desire is to know the truth, my only fear to cling to error" (*Letters* 1:121).

With the reading of these books, her pious views quickly gave way to skeptical ones.[7] In a letter to her father in February 1842, she explained forthrightly her

---

[5] The formidable knowledge of the Bible and ecclesiastical history she gained during this period of intense religious study would later help her employ religious themes and depict clerical figures in her writing.

[6] Eliot was likely introduced to Hennell's work through his sister, Cara Bray (née Hennell). In his work, Hennell disavowed Christianity as divine revelation but believed it was "the purest form yet existing of natural religion" (vii). Eliot met Hennell frequently at the Bray's home and said of him, "Mr. Hennell seemed to me a model of moral excellence" (Collins, *Interviews* 16).

[7] The Brays' influence on Eliot's conversion from Christianity was undeniable. However, Eliot's change in religious views would have come in any case. Haight cites books she read earlier in life, such as those by Walter Scott and Bulwer Lytton. At age 13 after reading Lytton's *Devereux*, in which there is an "amiable atheist," she was "considerably shaken by the impression that religion was not a requisite to moral excellence" (*Letters* 1:45). Antithetically, she was shocked by the union of religious sentiment and a low sense of morality of the mostly Methodist miners near Foleshill. Haight concludes: "While the Brays certainly crystallized her rejection of orthodoxy, it was long in suspense and inevitable. The surprising thing is that her Evangelicalism persisted until she was twenty-two" (39).

rejection of the Jewish and Christian scriptures: "I regard these writings as histories consisting of mingled truth and fiction ... I consider the system of doctrines built upon the facts of [Jesus's] life and drawn as to its materials from Jewish notions to be most dishonourable to God and most pernicious in its influence on individual and social happiness" (1:128). No longer able to believe in Christianity, she refused to go to church with her father. Strife ensued, but eventually they called an uneasy truce. They agreed that she would go to church and quietly hold her own opinions. Eliot's de-conversion experience was abrupt and confident. She explained to her friend, Mrs. Abijah Pears (Charles Bray's sister), her disbelief:

> For my part, I wish to be among the ranks of that glorious crusade that is seeking to set Truth's Holy Sepulchre free from a usurped domination. We shall then see her resurrection! Meanwhile, although I cannot rank among my principles of action a fear of vengeance eternal, gratitude for predestined salvation, or a revelation of future glories as a reward, I fully participate in the belief that the only heaven here or hereafter is to be found in conformity with the will of the Supreme; a continual aiming at the attainment of that perfect idea, the true Logos that dwells in the bosom of the One Father. I hardly know whether I am ranting after the fashion of one of the Primitive Methodist prophetesses, with a cart for her rostrum, I am writing so fast. (1:125–6)

Interestingly, she used religious terminology ("Truth's Holy Sepulchre," "resurrection," "will of the Supreme," "true Logos," and "One Father") to convey the secular hope that she would be instrumental in revealing the fact that Truth is independent of religious institutions. She saw herself in the same category as "one of the Primitive Methodist prophetesses" and one who would preach "religious" truth to the masses. Eliot would use religious terminology to convey secular meaning throughout her poetry-writing career. From 1842 (her de-conversion) until the end of her career, she employed Christian language to relay unorthodox messages in her poems, including "Mid the Rich Store of Nature's Gifts to Man" (1842), "A Minor Prophet" (1865),[8] "Ex Oriente Lux" (1866), "In the South"

---

[8]   In "Atheist Prophecy," Charles LaPorte shows how Eliot embraced the poetess role by combining sentimental piety and religious skepticism in "A Minor Prophet." LaPorte convincingly argues that the poem, ostensibly about an American zealot, is actually about a skeptical female narrator who doubts the prophecies of her friend and supernatural religious prophecy in general. The "Minor Prophet" refers to the female skeptic, not the male religious zealot. The narrator believes that prophecy is not "the product of supernatural insights, but of sentimental ones: images of the future derive from the prophet's fullness of heart" (429). Her skeptical view of prophecy reveals Eliot's belief in higher criticism; higher critics believed Scripture was inspired poetically. Strauss argued that religious myths came as truths from their authors' sympathies with their subject. This is the idea that Eliot's narrator adopted to describe religious faith in general. Formation of myth derives from a spiritual and affective sympathy that Eliot would come to associate with the poetess tradition, especially as practiced and personified by Barrett Browning. LaPorte states: "Eliot locates prophecy ... in earnest sympathy—the sympathetic soul reflects its desires into its

(1867), "O May I Join the Choir Invisible" (1867), *The Spanish Gypsy* (1868), "Agatha" (1869), "The Legend of Jubal" (1869), "Stradivarius" (1873), "A College Breakfast-Party" (1874), "I Grant You Ample Leave" (1874), "Self and Life" (date unknown), "Mordecai's Hebrew Verses" (1875, from *Daniel Deronda*, Book 5, Chapter 38), and "The Death of Moses" (1875).

Eliot's post-conversion skepticism, knowledge of the Bible, and great intellect made her the ideal candidate for translating Strauss and Feuerbach. Both higher critical analyses set out to demystify scriptures. Strauss in his *The Life of Jesus, Critically Examined* set out to disprove two groups of believers: those who believed the miracles in the Gospels were literally true and supernaturally significant and those who believed the miracles were literally true but explainable by natural causes. Strauss methodically went through the Gospel narratives to distinguish between the historical and unhistorical events related to the life of Jesus and concluded that the New Testament Gospel writers relied on messianic myths and legends to create an account of Jesus' life. They interpreted Jesus' life as fulfilling prophecy and meeting messianic expectation and then perpetuated the myth of Jesus as messiah through their accounts. According to Strauss, these accounts did not intend to deceive; nevertheless, they were historically unreliable. Strauss's method was exhausting, and Cara Bray reported that Eliot was "Strauss-sick— it made her ill dissecting the beautiful story of the crucifixion" (*Letters* 1:206). Eliot's wistfulness for the religion of her youth gave way to exasperation at the monotony of the work, but in the end, she felt satisfied with the time spent with Strauss (1:203, 218). It is difficult to say to what extent his views influenced hers, but his examination of messianic myths may have left a mark. She would later in her own writing rely on the power of myth to influence others. In her poetry, she sometimes elaborated on biblical myths to tell stories with humanist messages. In "The Legend of Jubal," for example, she wrote the story of Jubal, father of the lyre (Genesis 4:21), to relate the value of art to humanity. LaPorte points out that her rewriting of biblical narrative "demonstrates faith in the evolution of biblical hermeneutics away from inspirationism and toward a tradition of sentiment and humanism" (*Victorian Poets* 214). In other words, Eliot proposed a new way to experience religious truth through feminine poetics. Eliot also mythologized the death of a prophet in "The Death of Moses," as if she were a scripture writer, to engender sympathy for Jewish people. As a poetess, she had the spiritual authority to tell biblical stories in her own way, fill in the details, and insert new meaning.

Feuerbach's influence on Eliot is easier to conjecture. In *The Essence of Christianity* Feuerbach took an anthropological approach to analyzing Scripture, offering "more humane ways to interpret religion" and "affirmative understandings of human possibilities" (Ermarth, *Oxford Reader's Companion* 111, 119). In his

---

future, as well as into its past" (429–30). Eliot believed the poetess could best further the ideas of higher criticism and considered imaginative literature as a form of prophecy (428). LaPorte's astute analysis sheds new light on this long-overlooked poem and clearly shows that Eliot embraced religious aspects of the poetess role.

work, Feuerbach explained that God is the projection of man's inward nature. In worshiping God who was incarnated as a human being, humanity worships an ideal form of itself: "The divine being is nothing else than the human being, or, rather the human nature purified, free from the limits of the individual man" (14). Feuerbach's influence on Eliot was pronounced. She proclaimed: "With the ideas of Feuerbach I everywhere agree" (*Letters* 2:153). This overstatement indicates her enthusiasm for his ideas that elevated humanity, and she would continue to uphold a high vision of humanity as her worldview expanded. This appreciation for humanity derived from the German sources was a necessary prerequisite to the practice of sympathy. Her literary writing would soon reveal the view of an author "for whom relations between people have all the sanctity reserved in orthodox religion for the relationship between the individual and God" (Ashton, "Evans"). But that view would come only after she dealt with her frustration with hypocritical and antipathetic models of Christianity.

A Religion of Sympathy

In order to understand Eliot's shift in belief from Christianity to a religion of sympathy, it is essential first to comprehend what sympathy meant to her. The *OED* defines sympathy as: "Conformity of feelings, inclinations, or temperament, which makes persons agreeable to each other; community of feeling; harmony of disposition" (entry 3a); "The quality or state of being affected by the condition of another with a feeling similar or corresponding to that of the other; the fact or capacity of entering into or sharing the feelings of another or others; fellow-feeling" (entry 3b); and "the quality or state of being thus affected by the suffering or sorrow of another; a feeling of compassion or commiseration" (entry 3c). In her letters, Eliot used the word sympathy in all of these significations. For instance, she used the word *sympathy* to refer to a "harmony of disposition" (entry 3a) when she explained her relationship with Lewes to John Chapman: "Affection, respect, and intellectual sympathy deepen" (*Letters* 2:173). To François D'Albert-Durade she also described the "moral and intellectual sympathy" she found with Lewes (3:186). In a letter to Sara Hennell in October 1843, she used the word *sympathy* to mean "community of feeling" (entry 3a). In describing the need for tolerance of others' religious views, she explained that "truth of feeling" is "the only universal bond of union" and urged acceptance: "are we to remain aloof from our fellow-creatures on occasions when we may fully sympathize with the feelings exercised, although our own have been melted into another mould?" (1:162).[9] Her own experience with post-apostasy religious intolerance and subsequent broken relationships taught her that sharing "truth of feeling" with others was

---

[9]   Eliot is explaining her softening attitude toward Christian doctrine. Haight points out in a footnote that Mary Sibree described her shifting views in March 1843: Eliot is "not now so desirous of controversy. She, however, appeared, to me at least, to have rather changed her ground on some points moral in its influence" (*Letters* 1:162).

more valuable than holding dogmatic beliefs. At other times, Eliot used the term *sympathy* to mean feeling compassion (entry 3c). For instance, in response to the death of Sara Hennell's mother, Eliot wrote: "Words are very clumsy things—I like less and less to handle my friends' sacred feelings with them. For even those who call themselves 'intimate' know very little about each other—hardly ever know just *how* a sorrow is felt, and hurt each other by their very attempts at sympathy or consolation … " (2:465). Here, she equates sympathy with consolation while also expressing the difficulty of sympathizing in the sense of understanding another's "sacred feelings." It was this kind of sympathy—sharing the feelings of others, or fellow-feeling—that most interested Eliot.

This sympathy (which we now call "empathy") required understanding the feelings of others. In her letters, Eliot often used sympathy expressly to mean "knowing" or "understanding."[10] For example, when Barbara Bodichon wrote to her "darling Marian" to acknowledge that she recognized her as the pseudonymous author of *Adam Bede*, Eliot responded: "God bless you, dearest Barbara, for your love and sympathy. You are the first friend who has given any symptom of knowing me—the first heart that has recognized me in a book which has come from my heart of hearts" (3:63). Eliot used the term similarly when writing to Charles Bray: "know that wherever I am, there is one among that number of your friends … who enter into your present experience with the light of memories; for kind feeling can never replace fully the sympathy that comes from memory" (3:391). In this statement, she expressed her friendship with the Brays as deeply sympathetic because it was based on years of acquaintance and shared memories.

After leaving the Christian faith, Eliot transformed this idea of sympathy into a philosophy of living. Sympathy for others became the driving force behind her thinking and writing, and the concept of sympathy thoroughly influenced her mature works. Her religious transformation from the High Church Anglicanism of her childhood to the fervent evangelicalism of her adolescence to a strident anti-orthodox position in her 20s finally settled into a sympathetic appreciation for all people and religions that explore truth with honesty and fellow-feeling. She ultimately came to believe that compassion and understanding between humans, whether in a religious or non-religious context, embodied all that is most sacred. This development in Eliot's personal religious journey appears in the religious bent of her works. As a poetess, Eliot relied on religion and sympathy to widen the

---

[10] Suzy Anger explains a similar idea in her discussion of Eliot's "hermeneutics of sympathy." She states: "Eliot's primary concern was understanding others, and, especially, linguistic interpretation" (96). According to Anger, Eliot did not think theological exegesis was helpful, and she tried to make a better secular hermeneutic: a hermeneutic of sympathy (96). Eliot promoted an ethic of sympathy and selflessness and a morality that insisted on people respecting others. She states: "By striving to enter imaginatively into the perspectives of others, one can work against the limitations of subjective perspective, and so more correctly 'divine' (a favorite word of Eliot's) the meanings of their words" (99). Anger views Eliot's concern with sympathy in terms of linguistic interpretation. I relate Eliot's concern with sympathy to religious belief.

English vision, to teach readers how to understand and share in the common lot of humanity, and to lead them toward a fuller consciousness of ethical and moral progress.

Critics track the progression of Eliot's religious belief in various ways. Bernard Paris discusses Eliot's "religion of humanity," citing her reading of Comte, Mill, Spencer, Lewes, and Feuerbach. Paris describes Eliot's "future religion" as a religion of man, not of God, in which sentiment moves man to acts of kindness, unselfishness, and reverence (11–19).[11] Peter Hodgson remarks that Eliot passed through three major religious phases in her life: evangelicalism, a religion of humanity, and a future religion that incorporated the former phases. The "future religion" of George Eliot, he argues, "would be a truthful religion without accusation and consolation, a practical religion oriented to human feelings, needs and deeds, a spiritual religion attuned to the mystery beneath the real, and a religion open to the idea of a sympathetic, suffering, (omni)present God" (13). I agree with Hodgson's view of Eliot's religious progression and her settling into a religious mindset that blended her former beliefs with a new spiritual understanding that included sympathy.[12] However, unlike Hodgson who sees sympathy as one facet of this "future religion," I view sympathy as the core tenet of her mature religion. Hodgson aptly discusses Eliot's concept of a sympathetic and suffering God, who "may be a fiction, but a true and necessary fiction" (22–5). I see Eliot's concept of sympathy extending beyond her belief in a sympathetic God to a consideration of sympathetic humanity.[13]

---

[11]   Paris correctly identifies the place of sentiment, suffering, and humanity in Eliot's religion but perhaps overemphasizes the influence of Positivism on her thinking.

[12]   Rachel Ablow provides a useful summary of eighteenth-century notions of sympathy by which we can situate Eliot's understanding of sympathy. Ablow identifies two aspects of sympathy: as pity or compassion and as a source of identity. Shaftesbury, David Hume, Adam Smith and other eighteenth-century philosophers identified sympathy as the common experience of entering into another's feelings to create a bond and unify communities. Ablow asserts that by the nineteenth century, the meaning of sympathy became more closely associated with the private sphere rather than community. She suggests that sympathy was redefined and became less about feeling than about relating to others and defining self (2–3). Eliot's notion of sympathy is tied to feeling and identification. She emphasizes understanding others and entering into their feelings to create a better and moral community.

[13]   In the introduction to Bernard Paris's *George Eliot's Religion of Humanity*, George Creeger explains Eliot's concept of morality in terms of egoism versus sympathy. He argues that for Eliot, evil was the inclination for self over others. According to Creeger, Eliot was convinced that man's greatest immorality lay in modes of narcissism and the counter to this evil was fellow-feeling, or sympathy. He explains: "No matter how powerful the mind, unless there is a concomitant capacity for compassion, there can be no escape from the prison of the self" (4). Creeger considers Eliot's concept of morality as one of many characteristics of her mindset that finds expression in her writing. His insightful discussion of Eliot's concept of egoism is tangential to this study but merits mention.

Studying how Eliot used the word *sympathy* in the context of her writings sheds light on her concept of the term and its significance.[14] In the numerous reviews of religious books that Eliot wrote for the *Westminster Review*, she often equated sympathy with morality and used the term in the sense of fellow-feeling. In her essay, "Evangelical Teaching: Dr. Cumming" (1855), she railed against religious dogma that bred hatred and expressed the need for fellow-feeling. She decried the evangelical preacher's doctrine pitting his orthodox views—rooted in clannishness (*Essays* 179), immoral doctrines such as that of eternal punishment (182), and "perverted moral judgment" (184)—against moral, sympathetic views. She claimed that his religion "gives a charter to hatred" and "fosters all uncharitableness" (180) and said he "has satisfaction in us only in so far as we exhaust our motives and dispositions of all relation to our fellow-beings, and replace sympathy with men by anxiety for the 'glory of God'" (186). She affirmed the power of humanity instead: "human nature is stronger and wider than religious systems, and though dogmas may hamper, they cannot absolutely repress its growth" (187). Furthermore, she condemned a lack of sympathy for others as perverted and immoral: "But next to that hatred of the enemies of God which is the principle of persecution, there perhaps has been no perversion more obstructive of true moral development than this substitution of a reference to the glory of God for the direct promptings of the sympathetic feeling" (187). For Eliot, Dr. Cumming's perverted concept of God conflicted with human sympathies and hampered moral growth (188). She avowed an alternate view of God as the embodiment of sympathy:

> The idea of God is really moral in its influence—it really cherishes all that is best and loveliest in man—only when God is contemplated as sympathizing with the pure elements of human feeling, as possessing infinitely all those attributes which we recognize to be moral in humanity. In this light, the idea of God and

---

[14] A number of George Eliot critics have written on her concept of sympathy. Most look to her fiction and some to her essays and reviews to discover her understanding of the concept. In *The Marriage of Minds*, Rachel Ablow examines sympathy in relation to marriage plots in the nineteenth-century novel and devotes a chapter to Eliot's *Mill on the Floss*. Forest Pyle, in *A Novel Sympathy: The Imagination of Community in George Eliot*, and Suzanne Graver, in *George Eliot and Community: A Study in Social Theory and Fictional Form*, both discuss the necessity of community for sympathy in Eliot's novels. Audrey Jaffe discusses the link between sympathy and spectacle in *Scenes of Sympathy: Identity and Representation in Victorian Fiction* and shows how this link manifests in *Daniel Deronda*. Elizabeth Deeds Ermarth, in *George Eliot's Conception of Sympathy*, discusses how Eliot's notion of sympathy shifts throughout her career by examining *Romola*, *Silas Marner*, and *Felix Holt, the Radical*. In *Thinking about other People in Nineteenth-Century British Writing*, Adela Pinch discusses how nineteenth-century authors moralized about the practice of thinking about others and how this activity could affect people. She explores this thesis in *Daniel Deronda*. In *Victorian Interpretation*, Suzy Anger devotes a chapter to Eliot's "Hermeneutics of Sympathy" to explain how Eliot's novels reveal an attempt to create a secular hermeneutic (a hermeneutic of sympathy) in exchange for traditional theological exegesis.

the sense of His presence intensify all noble feeling, and encourage all noble effort, on the same principle that human sympathy is found a source of strength: the brave man feels braver when he knows that another stout heart is beating time with his; the devoted woman who is wearing out her years in patient effort to alleviate suffering or save vice from the last stages of degradation, finds aid in the pressure of a friendly hand which tells her that there is one who understands her deeds and in her place would do the like. The idea of a God who not only sympathizes with all we feel and endure for our fellow-men, but who will pour new life into our too languid love, and give firmness to our vacillating purpose, is an extension and multiplication of the effects produced by human sympathy; and it has been intensified for the better spirits who have been under the influence of orthodox Christianity, by the contemplation of Jesus as "God manifest in the flesh." (187–8)

Here, Eliot echoes Feuerbach's notion that sympathy between individuals constitutes an idealized principle of a caring God. For Eliot, the idea of God most conducive to developing human morality was one that embodied sympathy. One who claimed to represent God but could or would not sympathize with others manifested a false idea of God. Only one who sympathized with others could begin to understand the true idea of God and live a moral, purposeful life.

In her signed fiction, as opposed to her anonymous reviews, Eliot ceased to criticize Christianity expressly in favor of promoting sympathetic relations between characters.[15] Her religious scorn was not heard in her first attempt at fiction, *Scenes of Clerical Life* (1857), or in her subsequent novels. Thomas Pinney explains that Eliot outlined in her essays "the morality of sympathy, self-sacrifice, duty, and resignation that later determines the action and values of her novels" (6), and Ashton notes that her novels "all allow for religious belief and endorse it where it is seen to aid or guide sympathetic action … Though she never returned to Christianity in any of its denominations, she remained interested in forms of worship" (*George Eliot: A Life* 276). By 1859, she revealed a softened attitude toward orthodoxy and a firm belief in the sympathetic function of religion. To Beecher Stowe, Eliot described the process of modifying religion to increasingly incorporate a sense of responsibility to fellow humans based on an understanding of their struggles:

I believe that religion too has to be modified—"developed," according to the dominant phrase—and that a religion more perfect than any yet prevalent, must express less care for personal consolation, and a more deeply-awing sense of

---

[15] Kate Field, an American journalist, recalled Eliot saying that she "wrote reviews because [she] knew too little of humanity" (Collins, *Interviews* 178). Eliot's attitude toward Christianity and toward people with whom she disagreed softened over time. Many of her friends and visitors at the Priory wrote of her gentle, feminine manner. Music scholar Sedly Taylor stated in 1877: "She always waits till everybody else has said his say and then sums up in the style of the presiding Judge, though with an ultra feminine softness of voice and manner" (172).

responsibility to man, springing from sympathy with that which of all things is most certainly known to us, the difficulty of the human lot. I do not find my temple in Pantheism, which, whatever might be its value speculatively, could not yield a practical religion since it is an attempt to look at the universe from the outside of our relations to it (that universe) as human beings. (*Letters* 5:31)

In this passage, she described the different vision of religion she was developing for herself, a vision that depended on sympathizing with others. Her belief that religion should be based in sympathy accompanied a strengthening sense that one should extend sympathy to those who hold differing views: "I have no longer any antagonism towards any faith in which human sorrow and human longing for purity have expressed themselves; on the contrary, I have a sympathy with it that predominates over all argumentative tendencies" (2:230). Eliot sympathized with religions whose collective function was the expression of human sorrow and longing because such a function served to unite people and foster mutual understanding. To Bodichon she expressed sympathy for all religious systems that offered "lasting meaning" and inspired "sincere faith":

> Pray don't ever ask me again not to rob a man of his religious beliefs, as if you thought my mind tended to such robbery. I have too profound a conviction of the efficacy that lies in all sincere faith, and the spiritual blight that comes with no faith, to have any negative propagandism in me. In fact, I have very little sympathy with Freethinkers as a class, and have lost all interest in mere antagonism to religious doctrines. I care only to know, if possible, the lasting meaning that lies in all religious doctrines from the beginning until now. (Cross 2:343)

After a period of disdain for dogma, Eliot developed sympathy for religious faiths that manifested a spirit of mutual compassion.[16] She also expressed sympathy toward religious systems to Walter Cross:

---

[16]   In *The Spanish Gypsy*, Eliot sympathetically portrays a pagan religion by equating its faith with its community bond. Zarca, leader of the Zincala gypsy tribe explains:

> it is a faith
> Taught by no priest, but by their beating hearts.
> Faith to each other: the fidelity
> Of fellow-wanderers in a desert place
> Who share the same dire thirst, and therefore share
> The scanty water: the fidelity
> Of men whose pulses leap with kindred fire,
> Who in the flash of eyes, the clasp of hands,
> The speech that even in lying tells the truth
> Of heritage inevitable as past deeds,
> Nay, in the silent bodily presence feel
> The mystic stirring of a common life
> Which makes the many one. (104–5)

All the great religions of the world historically considered, are rightly the objects of deep reverence and sympathy—they are the record of spiritual struggles which are the types of our own ... And in this sense I have no antagonism towards any religious belief, but a strong outflow of sympathy. Every community met to worship the highest Good ... carries me along in its main current, and ... I should go to church or chapel constantly for the sake of the delightful emotions of fellowship which come over me in religious assemblies—the very nature of such assemblies being the recognition of a binding belief or spiritual law. (*Letters* 5:448)

Eliot's appreciation for religions lay in their stories of human struggles, which allowed people to identify and sympathize with the characters, and in their ability to bind together individuals in fellowship.[17] She admired the power of collective belief to unify people and viewed the function of religion as providing an opportunity to gather and worship together "the highest Good." For Eliot, the value of religion lay not in the particulars of a religious belief system (assuming that the belief system promoted mutual compassion and not division) but rather in the community itself. For her, religion served the sacred function of gathering people in a common spirit of mutual understanding. Her appreciation for the unifying role of religion in society thus complemented her personal vision of religion as sympathetic understanding between people. After a visit with her and Lewes in 1877, Benjamin Jowett described her vision as "an Ethical System founded upon Altruism" in which "Her idea of action seemed to be 'doing good to others'" and explained that "She did not seem to object to remaining within an established religion with the view of elevating & purifying it" (Collins, *Interviews* 168–9).

Eliot's deepening conviction that sympathetic interaction led to moral progress in society prompted her to become a teacher of sympathy through her work. To Charles Bray, Eliot stated her belief that societal moral progress depended on individuals showing compassion for one another: "My own experience and development deepen every day my conviction that our moral progress may be measured by the degree in which we sympathize with individual suffering and individual joy" (*Letters* 2:403). She expressed her desire to "touch the hearts of [her] fellow men" (2:416) and to "widen the English vision" (6:304) in the same way that religious stories did. By telling stories, she provided opportunities for the reader to share in the feelings of characters and by extension learn to share in the feelings of fellow humans. She explained to Bray: "If Art does not enlarge men's sympathies, it does nothing morally ... and the only effect I ardently long to produce by my writings, is that those who read them should be better able to imagine and to feel the pains and the joys of those who differ from themselves"

---

[17] Eliot's poem "Ex Oriente Lux" reflects her respect for other religions. She ascribes greater wisdom and spiritual understanding to Eastern religions by explaining that "While the western world was still "cold and sad / Shivering beneath the whisper of the stars," "Asia was the earliest home of light." She concludes that "heavenly Thought" was born in the East, not the West (*CSP* 2:99).

(3:111).[18] For Eliot, art had a moral function; it enabled readers to learn how to sympathize with fellow humans and bound them together in the same way that religious fellowship united members of a community. She wrote in "The Natural History of German Life" (1856) that "Art is the nearest thing to life; it is a mode of amplifying experience and extending our contact with our fellow-men beyond the bounds of our personal lot. All the more sacred is the task of the artist when he undertakes to paint the life of the People" (*Essays* 271). For Eliot, the artist's role was sacred. As a religious leader, the artist's duty was to teach fellow-feeling and compassion and lead society toward a better moral existence. Eliot fulfilled her sacred, artistic role by promoting sympathetic relations in her works of fiction and poetry.

Sympathy in "Mid the Rich Store of Nature's Gifts to Man"

Throughout her poetry-writing career, Eliot used biblical terminology and ideology to further her religion of sympathy. As Barry Qualls states, she "did not write, did not think, without the texts that she abandoned when she lost her faith, without the language of the Bible and the traditions that formed around it, without the histories of its texts that she transformed into contexts and structures for the lives of her characters" (120). During her apostasy in 1842, Eliot wrote a poem— "Mid the Rich Store of Nature's Gifts to Man"—in which she relied on Christian language and principles from which she was distancing herself.[19] This early poem

---

[18] Barry Qualls remarks that throughout her life, Eliot relied on the Bible and its typologies and language. She did this to ensure the "representation, and comprehension, of the sacred in her realistic project" (124). Her famous declaration of art, "If art does not enlarge men's sympathies, it does nothing morally," stems from "this sense of the necessity of faith in a human being's capacity for love and fellowship achieved through suffering; that is: for a human being's capacity to represent, typologically as it were, the incarnation. Her commitment to the 'typical' in her novels was, as she said, her way of securing her readers' lasting sympathies" (124). Qualls is thinking of her novels in this statement; however, we can extend his conclusions to her poetry writing as well. Even though Eliot did not create realistic portrayals in her poetry as she did in her novels, she still believed that the purpose of all art was to tell the truth and to enlarge the sympathies of readers. Whereas she fulfilled this artistic aim in her novels through realism, she appealed to feminine conventions in her poetry.

[19] Eliot's earliest letters include a number of religious poems—some by her own hand and some by other authors who inspired her. She regularly quoted religious poetry to Maria Lewis: *Letters* 1:5 (two lines from Edward Young's *Night Thoughts*), 1:16–17 (a poem by Baptist minister, John Ryland), 1:27–8 (her own poem, "Knowing that Shortly I must put off this Tabernacle"), 1:30 (her "Sonnet"), 1:69 (her "Question and Answer"), 1:75 (Felicia Hemans's "A Spirit's Return"), 1:107 (three lines from Edward Young's *Night Thoughts*), 1:111–12 (an unknown poem followed by George Herbert's "Virtue"). She also included at least one religious poem by Hemans to Martha Jackson in 1841 and two lines of John Milton's *L'Allegro* to Mrs. Abijah Hill Pears in 1842. Of all of these poems, only two ("Sonnet" in

reveals the fact that Eliot was already considering the idea of sympathy in her shifting religious views. In this work, she used the word *sympathy* to mean using one's special ability to create beauty for the purpose of uplifting humanity. She would develop the idea of sympathy (to include the element of fellow-feeling) as a replacement for religion throughout the next two decades.

The context of Eliot's writing "Mid the Rich Store" is crucial to understanding her meaning. Eliot included this poem in a letter to Maria Lewis (February 18, 1842) about a month after her refusal to go to church with her father and ten days before she wrote to her father explaining her rejection of Christianity (*Letters* 1:124, 126–7, 128–30). Her father tried various means to convince her to change her mind: he became angry and then silent, and finally he enlisted the aid of numerous family members, friends, and Christian pastors to persuade her to return to obedience to the faith. Eliot's heartfelt letter to her father explaining her apostasy only served to anger him further and resulted in his sending her to her brother Isaac's home to live. In a state of dejection, she wrote the letter to Lewis. She asked: "How go you for society, for communion of spirit, the drop of nectar in the cup of mortals? But why do I say the drop? The mind that feels its value will get large draughts [doses] from some source if denied it in the most commonly chosen way" (1:127).[20] Here Eliot suggested that she felt deprived of human interaction—the common means of achieving "communion of spirit"—and sought a less usual way to achieve spiritual communion. She turned to the act of writing to achieve spiritual communion since her society was ostracizing her.[21] After this introduction, she included the poem:

> Mid the rich store of nature's gifts to man
> Each has his loves, close wedded to his soul
> By fine associations' golden links.
> As the Great Spirit bids creation teem

1:30 and the unknown poem in 1:111) are not religious. From 1838–1842, she wrote and quoted religious poetry and exchanged heartfelt (orthodox) religious sentiments with her closest friends. She associated poetry and religion throughout these early evangelical years, and when she included "Mid the Rich Store of Nature's Gifts to Man" to Lewis during her transformative phase from orthodoxy toward a religion of sympathy (1842), it was natural for her to convey religious sentiment (albeit changing religious sentiment) via poetry. "Mid the Rich Store" reveals Eliot's shifting views. The poem relies on the Christian language she always used in poetry, and she would continue to employ Christian terminology and imagery in her poetry as her new belief system emerged.

[20]   Eliot was referring to the myth of Psyche, who became immortal after drinking the nectar of the gods. Eliot's equating communion of spirit and society implies that she believed in the life-giving power of the community. Relating to others gives spiritual meaning to humans as nectar in the myth conferred immortality on Psyche.

[21]   After her elopement with Lewes, she would experience even greater societal ostracism. This early lesson in turning to writing as a way to find fulfillment and connectedness would prove useful to the woman who would later be shunned by polite society for her scandalous lifestyle.

With conscious being and intelligence,
So man His miniature resemblance gives
To matter's every form a speaking soul,
An emanation from his spirit's fount,
The impress true of its peculiar seal.
Here finds he thy best image, sympathy! (*Complete Shorter Poetry* 1:25)

This poem represents the first indication of Eliot's turning to her own idea of sympathy as a substitute for religion. Here she describes how sympathy develops by showing that humans project themselves onto objects and people around them. Eliot compares the creation of all life with the development of human sympathy; as the Creator imbues creation with consciousness and intelligence, so humans give meaning to all life by projecting their ideas on to "matter's every form." Such life-giving human activity represents the spring of sympathy.[22]

A more complicated reading of the poem shows how Eliot extended the meaning of sympathy to consider not just the act of projecting ideas onto matter but also the act of sharing gifts with other people. Eliot uses Christian language to communicate the idea that people find spiritual communion through the act of creating.[23] In the first three lines of the poem, Eliot conveys the simple idea that humans have natural abilities. She expresses this simple statement, however, in words laden with complex Christian implications. Thus she establishes her intent to make a religious statement. She explains that among the abundant supply of "nature's gifts to man" (man's abilities and propensities), humans possess some gifts that they especially love and that connect them "By fine associations' golden links" to others who enjoy those same gifts. These lines allude to the New Testament teaching that the Holy Spirit grants spiritual gifts to the body of Christian believers to fulfill the mission of the Church. Spiritual gifts include prophecy, ministry, teaching, exhortation, giving, mercy (Romans 12:6–8, King James Version), wisdom, knowledge, faith, healing, performing miracles, discernment, speaking in tongues, interpreting tongues (1 Corinthians 12:8–10), preaching, helping, administration (1 Corinthians 12:28), evangelism, and pastoring (Ephesians

---

[22] Blank verse allows the reader to experience the poem's rhythm as a heartbeat that signals the continuance of life or as a chant that vocalizes a religious creed or sacred statement about the life-giving capacity of sympathy.

[23] Eliot also expresses this idea in *The Spanish Gypsy*, in Zarca's hope for the "race taught by no prophet" to establish a new land where the tribe will

[Serve] each other's needs, and so be spurred
To skill in all the arts that succor life;
Where we may kindle our first altar-fire
From settled hearths, and call our Holy Place
The hearth that binds us in one family. (106)

Eliot presents a pagan tribe comprising individuals who devote their talents to helping the community. The tribe's religion consists in its devotion to one another.

4:11).[24] The Bible teaches that spiritual gifts are special abilities (and works of service) not earned but granted by the Holy Spirit to each Christian believer for the purpose of unifying and building up the body of Christian believers.[25] Eliot used this Christian concept to articulate a message about the potential of the community. In Eliot's poem, "nature," not the Holy Spirit, distributes gifts to humans, and individual humans cherish these gifts ("Each [man] has his loves") and use them for the good of the community. Spiritual gifts are "close wedded to his [man's] soul / By fine associations' golden links." In other words, gifts or special abilities are individual treasures used to connect and enrich the spiritual community. By using the phrase "fine association," Eliot refers not only to the ways in which people link ideas to one another and to objects, but she also implies that the use of gifts results in a spiritual and virtuous community connection. According to the *OED*, "fine" used as an adjective can mean "consummate in quality," "pure, refined," "Pure, sheer, absolute; perfect," and of persons "consummate in virtue or excellence," while "association" refers to "the action of combining together for a common purpose" and "a body of persons who have combined to execute a common purpose or advance a common cause." For Eliot, the gifts wedded to each human's soul "by fine associations' golden links" serve to create a pure, virtuous body of persons who have a common goal of excellence, and the gifts that these persons exercise also serve to strengthen the community bond. Eliot uses wealth and wedding imagery to impute value to such a bond. The "rich" store of nature's gifts is "wedded" to souls by "fine" associations' "golden links" (symbolic of wedding bands). Eliot expresses the value of a united community through wealth and wedding imagery in the same way the Bible does. Revelation 19:7–8 describes the "marriage" of Jesus (bridegroom) and the Church (bride), dressed in "fine linen": "Let us be glad and rejoice, and give honour to him: for the marriage of the Lamb is come, and his wife hath made herself ready.[26] And to her was granted

---

[24]   *The Holy Bible, King James Version*. New York, NY: American Bible Society, 1999. Print. Subsequent biblical citations will use the same edition.

[25]   Paul wrote the following to explain the communal purpose of spiritual gifts: "For as we have many members in one body, and all members have not the same office: So we, being many, are one body in Christ, and every one members one of another. Having then gifts differing according to the grace that is given to us, whether prophecy, let us prophesy according to the proportion of faith … " (Romans 12:4–6); "But the manifestation of the Spirit is given to every man to profit withal [along with the rest] (1 Corinthians 12:7); "For as the body is one, and hath many members, and all the members of that one body, being many, are one body: so also is Christ. For by one Spirit are we all baptized into one body, whether we be Jews or Gentiles, whether we be bond or free; and have been all made to drink into one Spirit. For the body is not one member, but many" (1 Corinthians 12:12–14); "but God hath tempered the body together, having given more abundant honour to that part which lacked. That there should be no schism in the body; but that the members should have the same care one for another. And whether one member suffer, all the members suffer with it; or one member be honoured, all the members rejoice with it. Now ye are the body of Christ" (1 Corinthians 12:24–7).

[26]   Linen symbolizes status and wealth in the Bible (Ryken 514).

that she should be arrayed in fine linen, clean and white: for the fine linen is the righteousness of saints."[27]

Eliot thus appeals to New Testament theology to establish early in the poem the unifying potential of humanity's natural gifts. She then sets up the poem's controlling analogy, the comparison of the creation of all life with the development of human sympathy. She alludes to the Judeo-Christian creation myth (and perhaps William Paley's design argument) to describe the creation of life: "As the Great Spirit bids creation teem / With conscious being and intelligence" (*CSP* 1:25).[28] She also relies on the prelapsarian principle of humankind's original perfection laid out in Genesis 1:27 ("So God created man in his own image") in stating that "man His miniature resemblance gives" (*CSP* 1:25). She explains that as God fills creation with "conscious being and intelligence," so humanity, who is like God yet part of creation, has consciousness (awareness, feelings, ability to perceive) and intelligence (capacity to understand the needs of others), and gives "To matter's every form a speaking soul."[29] In other words, humans breathe life into everything around them with feelings, perceptions, and intellect by using particular abilities or gifts that nature has bestowed on them.[30] The word "soul" can mean "the principle

---

[27] Typologists connect this passage (and other such New Testament passages) to Hebrew Scriptures that describe the precious relationship between a king (Jesus) and his bride (the Church). For example: "And the daughter of Tyre [the bride] shall be there with a gift; even the rich among the people shall intreat thy favour. The king's daughter is all glorious within: her clothing is of wrought gold. She shall be brought unto the king in raiment of needlework: the virgins her companions that follow her shall be brought unto thee" (Psalm 45:12–14). Leland Ryken's *Dictionary of Biblical Imagery* fully chronicles the wedding imagery in the Bible.

[28] Paley was a Christian apologist and philosopher who posited in the influential *Natural Theology: or, Evidences of the Existence and Attributes of the Deity* (1802) that complex design found in nature necessitated a designer.

[29] According to Feuerbach, humans project their human nature onto God. Eliot may draw on this notion in these lines to depict humans as projecting themselves onto outward objects in a sacred, God-like act of creation.

[30] In her idea of nature's gifts to man serving to impart beauty to all creation, Eliot may have been influenced by Bray's *The Philosophy of Necessity*, which states:

Man possesses feelings and intellectual faculties in common with the brutes, and also several in addition; had he been endowed with more propensities and sentiments than those that now belong to him, more senses and intellectual faculties would probably have been necessary, to enable him to bring them into exercise or use. Even now, we cannot but suppose that we view nature with very different eyes from the brutes, and an additional sense or intellectual faculty might have changed the whole appearance that nature now presents to us. The organ of Ideality [according to phrenology, this refers to the faculty of the brain that perceives beauty] may furnish us with an illustration. Man alone is supposed to possess this faculty. It gives feelings which invest nature with a beauty and splendour foreign to the mere properties of objects, as indicated by the intellectual faculties: it ascribes to it an excellence and charm and perfection which are invisible to those creatures that have it not; and the man in whom it is weak, and he in whom it is strong, truly regard nature with different eyes. (100)

of life" and also "the seat of the emotions, feelings, or sentiments; the emotional part of man's nature" (*OED*). By using the word "soul," Eliot implies that human creation is life-giving in that it provokes an emotional response from whoever experiences the creation and provides the opportunity for that person to connect with the creator and all who partake in the creation. For example, a musician has the special ability to create a piece of music that will provoke an emotional response from the listener, and that listener shares in a spiritual experience with the creator of the music and with all who also feel strong emotion when hearing the same music. Eliot also plays on the multiple meanings of "matter" and "form" in this line to underscore the spiritual element. In addition to physical material, "matter" can mean "the characteristic sensible element or sign used in a sacrament (as water in baptism, the laying on of hands in holy orders, etc.)," and in addition to the shape of matter, "form" can refer to "certain essential formulary words" by which the sacrament is effected such as "I baptize you in the name of the Father, Son, and the Holy Spirit." So Eliot employs sacramental terminology to describe the process of humankind's creation to give human ability divine significance.[31]

Eliot strengthens her claim that human creative ability is sacred by explaining the process as "an emanation from his spirit's fount." The creative act flows forth from the human spiritual center just as creation itself flowed from God in the Judeo-Christian creation myth. The emanation from the human spiritual fount implies a sort of reverse baptism. In New Testament theology, the new believer at baptism receives the gift of the Holy Spirit (Acts 2:38 and 10:45), and the Holy Spirit gives gifts to the believer to enable participation in the building up of the body of believers.[32] In Eliot's version of baptism, the human spirit—not the Holy Spirit—is the source of life in the world; by creating, it gives nature (and itself) meaning, and thus new life. Nature gives humanity gifts, and humanity uses those gifts to give back to nature.

Human creative ability, according to Eliot, is also "the impress true of its peculiar seal."[33] In using special gifts, a person makes a permanent, distinctive mark that represents one's sincere and best self. This mark is a gift to the world and a symbol of a commitment to the community. As "seal" in the Hebrew Scriptures

---

[31]　One further layer of meaning might be drawn from this line. "Matter" also means "The substance of a book, speech, etc." (*OED*). Form can imply "the essential creative quality" of a thing. So, Eliot could also be referring to the creative quality of her own writing.

[32]　Notably, the biblical language associating the Holy Spirit's descent with flowing water in the baptism passage includes: "And they of the circumcision which believed were astonished, as many as came with Peter, because that on the Gentiles also was *poured out* the gift of the Holy Ghost" (Acts 10:45, emphasis added). Eliot's use of the words "emanation" and "fount" acknowledges biblical association of water, baptism, and Holy Spirit.

[33]　Eliot uses the word, "peculiar," to mean special or distinctive. However, she also may have had in mind another meaning of the word. According to the *OED*, "peculiar" in the nineteenth-century meant "A member of the evangelical wing of the Church of England. A disparaging term used by members of the Oxford Movement." "Peculiarism" referred to "exclusivity; adherence to a distinctive doctrine or practice." It is possible that Eliot was gently mocking herself for her former rigid evangelical beliefs.

refers to a symbol of a covenant, "seal" in Eliot's poem refers to a person's distinctive creation as a sign of a covenant with the community. In this seal, "man" finds "thy best image, [which is] sympathy!" Humanity's "best image" is sympathy or the creative ability to bind souls together to make a more unified and virtuous community. Humans manifest the Creator in their special ability to create and impart meaning in the world and so provide opportunities for social and spiritual cohesion. In other words, humans act divinely when they exercise sympathy by offering "communion of spirit" via creation.

After the poem, Eliot wrote in her letter to Lewis:

> Beautiful ego-ism! to quote one's own. But where is not this same ego? The martyr at the stake seeks its gratification as much as the court sycophant, the difference lying in the comparative dignity and beauty of the two egos. People absurdly talk of self-denial—why there is none in Virtue to a being of moral excellence—the greatest torture to such a soul would be to run counter to the dictates of conscience, to wallow in the slough of meanness, deception, revenge or sensuality. This was Paul's idea in the 1st chapter of 2d Ep[istle] to Timothy (I think that is the passage).[34] (*Letters* 1:127)

Eliot's uncertainty of the Bible passage is revealing. She relied on her understanding of the passage but did not need the authority of the passage itself. The exact location in the Bible was no longer relevant for her as she was gaining confidence in her own ideas about morality. In this passage, Eliot seems to be saying that truly moral persons do not consider acting virtuous as self-denial. Moral people enjoy doing or creating for others and detest causing pain (acting unsympathetically) more than anything. It is natural for such persons to feel gratified in performing their beneficial actions. For Eliot, creating for others led to gratification. Her writing the poem was her way to participate in society by producing an edifying work of art for the world to enjoy. She was looking for the meaning of morality and personal fulfillment in a time of isolation from her closest associates, who questioned her morality as a non-Christian.[35] In "Mid the Rich Store," Eliot relied

---

[34] In a footnote, Haight explains that Eliot was referring to 2 Timothy 2:5–12 but suggests that her argument is drawn more from Charles Bray's *Philosophy of Necessity* than the biblical passage (*Letters* 1:127). Haight's statement is probable given the fact that Eliot read Bray's work in December 1841 following Hennell's *Inquiry* (Haight 40). K.K. Collins claims that Bray takes credit for Eliot's "interest in the unforgiving consequences of human actions, and the moral dangers of orienting those actions towards some reward in a future life." Bray's *Philosophy of Necessity*, explains Collins, argued for "a mental determinism which, once accepted, would compel widespread social reform" (*Interviews* 16). Eliot's developing belief in sympathetic action as a means of benefit to others is compatible with Bray's views.

[35] Charles Bray stated in *The Philosophy of Necessity*: "Man has been endowed with certain propensities and sentiments on which his happiness has been made to depend, for their exercise is attended with highly pleasurable sensations, the aggregate of which constitutes happiness" (97–8). Eliot may have had this idea in mind when writing this poem.

on Hebrew Scriptures and New Testament theology, including the sacraments of baptism and marriage, to claim that humanity enjoys spiritual communion within community by creating and sharing creation.[36] Writing for the community was to become her sacramental expression. By employing religious language to address her English readership, despite her personal disbelief, Eliot demonstrates her sympathy with her readers' views and her commitment to the moral edification of and participation within the community.

Sympathy in "O May I Join the Choir Invisible"

Eliot understood sympathy in 1842 to mean something like sharing oneself in service to the community. After "Mid the Rich Store," she did not write poetry again (except the short "As Tu Vu la Lune se Lever" in 1849) until 1865 when her notion of sympathy had matured.[37] Her growing confidence in sympathy as a

---

[36]   In light of Eliot's apostasy, Eliot's father and Maria Lewis did not take communion when they went to church together on January 2, 1842. Perhaps this fact (presumably told to her by Lewis or her father) inspired the inclusion of sacraments in her poem.

[37]   Written from Geneva shortly after her father's death, "As Tu Vu" expresses admiration for the beauty of the noble soul. Van den Broek speculates that Cross omitted the section of the letter that includes the poem because he (as did Haight) considered it bad French verse (*CSP* 1:27). The letter included a note to Sara Hennell explaining that the poem was for an album that the Marquise de St. Germain was compiling: "Thank you for your scrap of L.E.L. I have been invoking the French muse for the Marquise's album—since she would fain have something and it must not be in English which she cannot understand. It will make you smile—so I write it" (*Letters* 1:298). After the poem, she wrote: "I thought it would have done admirably to put in Molière's Misanthrope or Precieuses ridicules. But the thought, dear soul, is a very true one, above all when I apply it to you. Receive it as just what I am feeling and thinking about you" (1:299). Eliot's associating her French verse with Molière's comedies of manners reveals a gentle self-mocking regarding her ability to write poetry in French. She hoped that despite the poem's limitations Sara would feel her sentiment. K.M. van den Broek offers the following translation of the poem:

> Have you seen the moon rise
> In a cloudless azure sky?
> A thousand dewdrops reflect
> Its light like so many stars.
>
> Gather a spring violet
> And hide it in your bosom,
> You and your garments will be heavy
> With its delicious fragrance.
>
> So when a noble spirit appears,
> It invests everything with its grace:—
> Let us remember it that way
> Even though, alas, it moves us to tears. (*CSP* 1:179)

worthy tenet for moral living prepared her for writing poetry. Like many nineteenth-century poets, Eliot used the poetic form to explore religious issues. She took advantage of the prevalent notion of poet as prophet to adopt a prophetic persona and profess sacred and moral truth.[38] She also relied on the poetess tradition—one that associated women poets with sympathy and religion—to promote her belief in living morally by treating others with fellow-feeling. But it was not until after she rejected, decried, and then softened toward Christianity that she began writing poetry in earnest. With a mature mindset towards religion and a strong belief in the ability of humans to make a better society by living sympathetically, Eliot became a poetess.[39]

Eliot's first publication "Knowing that Shortly I must put off this Tabernacle" was a religious poem.[40] The poem was first published in 1840 in the *Christian*

In this poem, Eliot compares the noble soul ("spirit")—such as that of Sara and perhaps also of her father—to the beauty of a thousand dew drops reflecting the moon's light like stars and to the delight of a flower that has been tucked inside one's coat and fills the clothing with an intoxicating aroma. The memory of a loved one has the ability to bring us to tears of sadness (because of the loved one's absence) and of joy (because of the beauty and pleasure-giving ability of the memory).

[38]   Charles LaPorte states: "Eliot embraces stereotypically feminine poetic models as an influence that should change the cultural landscape, and even have a guiding influence akin to that of the Bible" ("Poetess as Prophet" 159). His observation takes into consideration Eliot's association of poet(ess) and prophet(ess). She viewed art as sacred and the role of artist as spiritual guide. Her writing could influence culture as if it was a holy text. LaPorte also notes Harriet Beecher Stowe's observation that the "pure ideal of a sacred woman springing from the bosom of the family, at once wife, mother, poetess, leader, inspirer, prophetess, is peculiar to sacred history" and explains that Eliot capitalized on this connection in her poetry (qtd. in LaPorte 165).

[39]   LaPorte correctly points out that Eliot presented herself as a poetess only after she attained cultural and literary status in the late 1860s and early 1870s, but her belief in the idea that the poetess' work should be intellectually challenging and unapologetically feminine originated in the mid-1850s. He looks to Eliot's review of *Aurora Leigh* to make this claim:

> [In] her criticism, Eliot appropriates for the poetess ... the cultural weight of a supposedly male tradition without jettisoning the figure as one of tenderness, domesticity, and sentimentality. In her opinion, *Aurora Leigh* "superadds" one discourse to another. Eliot believed in a feminine ideal that embraces what Swinburne calls "the whole nature of things" without leaving the "sweet circle of domestic affections" presumed to contain the poetess tradition. And her reconciliation of these ostensibly different perspectives is the more powerful because she herself possessed the "vigor, breadth, and culture" which she praised in *Aurora Leigh*, and the English lack of which she would caricature in her prose. ("Poetess as Prophet" 161)

[40]   Eliot wrote five poems between 1839 and 1849: "Knowing that Shortly I must put off this Tabernacle," "Sonnet," "Question and Answer," "Mid the Rich Store of Nature's Gifts to Man," and "As Tu Vu la Lune se Lever." The poem, "On Being Called a Saint," recorded in Eliot's "School Notebook" in 1834, was first published in Haight's biography

Observer.[41] "Knowing," when contrasted with "O May I Join the Choir Invisible," published in 1867, shows the change in Eliot's religious beliefs from her early evangelical phase to her mature belief in sympathy as a religion. In both poems, Eliot begins with an epigraph to introduce the themes of death and immortality. In "Knowing," the poem's epigraph (and title) is a quote from 2 Peter 1:14. Appropriately, she uses a biblical passage to discuss her longing to bid "farewell!" to earth's gifts, including natural beauties, books, and creatures of the air. She repeats "farewell!" at the end of each stanza to emphasize the finality of her departure and separation from the world after her earthly life. The only things she will not say farewell to are the "Blest volume" and "Dear kindred," whom she will meet in heaven (*CSP* 1:12). In this poem, Eliot expresses the Christian longing for heaven described in 2 Peter. In contrast, Eliot begins "O May I Join" with an epigraph not from the Bible, but from Cicero's *Letters to Atticus* (book 12, letter 18) in which he expresses his longing to carry on the memory of his daughter: "*Longum illud tempus, quum non ero, magis me movet, quam hoc exiguum*" (I am more concerned about the long ages, when I shall not be here, than about my short day).[42] The young Eliot believed so strongly in the sanctity of the Bible that she

---

(Haight 20); Haight and van den Broek note the possibility that this poem was written by Eliot's friend rather than by herself (*CSP* 1:3). From 1849 to 1864 Eliot ceased writing poetry and focused on fiction. Once she began writing poetry again in 1864, she did so consistently until 1879, the year before her death.

[41]   Eliot sent this poem in a letter to Maria Lewis in 1839 with the following note:
I thank you very heartily for your kind note, and I send you in return some doggerel lines, the crude fruit of a lonely walk last evening, when the words of one of our martyrs occurred to me. You must be acquainted with the idiosyncrasy of my authorship, which is that my effusions, once committed to paper, are like the laws of the Medes and Persians that alter not. My attempt at poetry will serve to amuse you, if no more, and you love a laugh so well that it would be ungenerous to withhold the occasion of one. (*Letters* 1:27)

[42]   Cicero's entire sentence reads: "I am more concerned about the long ages, when I shall not be here, than about my short day, which, short though it is, seems all too long to me" (35). Martha Vogeler points out the significance of the role of memory in "O May I Join." Just as Cicero hoped for his daughter, Eliot hoped to carry on George Lewes's memory after his death. She arranged for Unitarian minister Dr. Thomas Sadler to conduct Lewes's funeral at Highgate Cemetery chapel and established a Studentship in Physiology at Cambridge in Lewes's name. Eliot was also concerned with her own mortality. She looked to survive in the memories of her future readers. She placed "O May I Join" at the end of the collected poems in *The Legend of Jubal and Other Poems* to emphasize the poem's significance, as Tennyson would do with "Crossing the Bar" (65). Vogeler also points out the Positivist traits of the poem, explaining that of her poems, "it comes closest to Comte's conception of a new religion in its reliance on memory and meditation as agents of grace and its idealization of the dead as inspiration for the living—termed by Comte 'subjective immortality.' His concomitant assumptions George Eliot also shares: that only the worthy survive in memory and only the good influences the future" (75). However, Vogeler emphasizes that Eliot was not a Positivist and that her poem reflects her own ideas more than Comte's.

wanted to take it with her to heaven. The mature Eliot believed in the sanctity of art, and so for her, Cicero's letter was just as holy as Peter's.[43]

Both poems address the themes of death and immortality. In "Knowing," Eliot emphasizes leaving behind earthly things after death and anticipates heaven, a place where she will "find new joy, / New sounds, new sights" (1:12). By this means, Eliot expresses longing for the New Testament conception of heaven. In "O May I Join," Eliot longs not for the Christian heaven, a place distinct from earth, but for a different kind of heaven, a living in perfect sympathy with others:

> O may I join the choir invisible
> Of those immortal dead who live again
> In minds made better by their presence: live
> In pulses stirred to generosity,
> In deeds of daring rectitude, in scorn
> For miserable aims that end with self,
> In thoughts sublime that pierce the night like stars,
> And with their mild persistence urge man's search
> To vaster issues.
> So to live is heaven (2:85)

Eliot longs to "join the choir invisible," a community of people who lived sympathetically and made other lives better by their presence. This community may include persons past or present who immortalized themselves by showing others how to live more generously and accomplishing "deeds of daring rectitude" (2:85).[44] The choir invisible despises selfish aims and urges humanity to search for "vaster issues" to create a better society (2:85). Eliot's heaven involves living sympathetically and teaching others how to do the same for the betterment of humanity.

---

[43] It is believed that Peter wrote his letter to the Christians of Asia Minor in either 63–65 or 150 CE to warn against false teachers, heretics, corrupt morals, and the end of the world. He wrote to encourage the new converts to practice virtue and turn from false teachers. Some reject the authenticity of Peter's letter. Cicero wrote his letter to his friend, Atticus, in 65 BCE while grieving the loss of his beloved daughter, Tullia.

[44] In "George Eliot: The Poetess as Prophet," Charles LaPorte reads "O May I Join" as a hymn to literature's influence on humanity. The poem is also a hymn to sympathy; it preaches the way to live on in the lives of others through sympathetic acts. Literature is just one way (and it is Eliot's way) to attain that everlasting goal. The choir invisible exerts its influence on, and includes, living humanity. By the end of the poem, Eliot (still alive) declares herself a part of the choir by the creation of the poem. The choir's inclusion of living humanity performing acts of sympathy and compassion is clear by its focus not only on "those immortal dead" and "martyred men," but also the living who perform "deeds of daring rectitude" and have "thoughts sublime" (*CSP* 2:85–6). "So to live [now] is heaven," says Eliot. For her, the choir includes those living and dead who participate in creating the "undying music in the world" (2:85).

Although no longer orthodox in her religious beliefs at the time of writing "O May I Join," Eliot still relies on religious terminology and imagery. She incorporates sin, guilt, forgiveness, justification, sanctification, salvation, sainthood, charity, and fellowship in her portrayal of the process of joining the choir invisible and attaining her idea of heaven. Martha Vogeler states: "The omnipresent Choir constitutes a secular version of the communion of saints; the fellowship of its holy spirits is poured out upon all who believe in them" (67). In Eliot's heaven, humanity makes moral progress by living in perfect harmony and unity: "So to live is heaven: / To make undying music in the world, / Breathing as beauteous order that controls/ With growing sway the growing life of man" (*CSP* 2:85). Little by little humans become better as they are influenced by the "beauteous order" of the choir's "undying music" (2:85). Humans influenced by the choir go through a justification and sanctification process as they join the choir themselves:

> So we inherit that sweet purity
> For which we struggled, failed, and agonized
> With widening retrospect that bred despair.[45]
> Rebellious flesh that would not be subdued,
> A vicious parent shaming still its child
> Poor anxious penitence, is quick dissolved;
> Its discords, quenched by meeting harmonies,
> Die in the large and charitable air. (2:85)

Here Eliot describes the collective purification process of the choir, relying on Christian terminology and putting a twist on Christian doctrine. Members do not earn but rather "inherit" purity; that is, the choir breathes the music of the world into the life of other humans, making them righteous or justified. Then humans go through a sanctification process as they learn to live a life worthy of sainthood. Eliot turns to the example of a vicious parent shaming a child to exemplify the "rebellious flesh that would not be subdued" (2:85). Eliot's portraying an abusive parent as the best illustration of a particularly distasteful sin that results in guilt and forgiveness is a useful reminder to her reader to her role as a poetess who represents domestic and spiritual goodness. (Poetesses often relied on the image of a loving parent and child in their poetry.) Cruelty to a child represents the antithesis of sympathy. However, the guilt that results from unsympathetic behavior can be overcome with the help of the choir that increasingly sways "the growing life of man" through harmonious and charitable actions (2:85). The saints in the choir

---

[45]   Eliot wrote to Charles Ritter in response to his French translation of "O May I Join" in *Fragments et Pensées* (Geneva 1979). She explained the "widening retrospect that bred despair" phrase: "Life is necessarily a widening retrospect as we look back upon it—a journey which we 'lay behind' us as we advance. To many of us—I hope not to you—it is a retrospect of broken resolutions which make each succeeding resolution less hopeful, and in this way breed 'despair.' The words are precise, to one who has had the experience" (*Letters* 7:56).

encourage and uplift the new member(s) by performing acts of charity. Sins are "quenched by meeting harmonies," "die in the large and charitable air" (2:85), and are thus forgiven.

The purification process results in a collective better self, one that is sympathetic and "divinely human" (2:86):

> And all our rarer, better, truer self,
> That sobbed religiously in yearning song,
> That watched to ease the burthen of the world
> Laboriously tracing what must be,[46]
> And what may yet be better—saw within
> A worthier image for the sanctuary,
> And shaped it forth before the multitude
> Divinely human, raising worship so
> To higher reverence more mixed with love—(2:85–6)

Vogeler interprets this passage as a representation of the Eucharist. She states:

> The Eucharist seems to be suggested by the image clusters of a "sanctuary" (the chancel and altar), of a shaping "forth before the multitude" and "raising worship" to "higher reverence" (the public elevation and adoration of the elements), "mixed with love" (the wine and water); while in the midst of these phrases the words "divinely human" characterize the mystery the sacrament celebrates. (70)[47]

Vogeler's insightful interpretation points out the various ways in which Eliot incorporates Christian elements to convey an unorthodox religious notion. In the above passage, Eliot describes the community (that may be taking communion) as one "self." This collective entity is the choir that sobs "religiously in yearning song" and finds ways to ease the burden of the world and make it a better place. The choir is religious because of its moral actions toward others. The "better, truer self" sees within a "worthier image for the sanctuary" and raises worship to "higher reverence" that is "mixed with love" (*CSP* 2:86). Eliot's choir is a past and present community of people who live and have lived sympathetically. They

---

[46] Eliot explains to Ritter: "The 'must be' you have rightly translated ... The great division of our lot is that between what is immodifiable and is the object of resignation and that which is modifiable by hopeful activity—by new conceptions and new deeds" (*Letters* 7:56).

[47] Vogeler also points out the apocalyptic elements in this passage of the poem: "That better self shall live till human Time / Shall fold its eyelids, and the human sky / Be gathered like a scroll within the tomb / Unread forever" (70). She further states: "the Apocalypse seems to lie behind the cosmic imagery with which the strophe concludes. Even the Choir Invisible, it suggests, is not, after all, eternal: it lives only so long as the race and its world— 'human time' and the 'human sky'—prevail. The metaphor of a scroll 'unread forever' must have been particularly painful for a writer!" (70).

worship together in holy fellowship as they act with sympathy and remember others who have done the same. For Eliot, the choir invisible is a community of people living in perfect harmony with one another and with the memory of saints who have died but live on in memory. The choir is divine humanity. The choir is heaven.

Eliot concludes the poem by finding her place in the choir invisible:

> This is life to come,
> Which martyred men have made more glorious
> For us who strive to follow. May I reach
> That purest heaven, be to other souls
> The cup of strength in some great agony,
> Enkindle generous ardor, feed pure love,
> Beget the smiles that have no cruelty,
> Be the sweet presence of a good diffused,[48]
> And in diffusion ever more intense!
> So shall I join the choir invisible
> Whose music is the gladness of the world. (2:86)

At the time of writing, she hoped to live a life worthy of the choir, to reach "purest heaven" by being "the sweet presence of a good diffused." Twelve years after writing the poem, she used the same language to affirm her continued belief in the "good diffused." After talking with Eliot in 1879, Benjamin Jowett wrote notes on their conversation. He recalled that she described two motives that greatly influenced her: "1. She desires to do good to others & to diffuse herself—to pour into the lives of others more than was contained or could be contained in any single one. 2. The dread of falling into dulness & not a calling" (Collins, *Interviews* 204). In the poem she preaches sympathetic living (diffusing oneself) as the way to heaven and guides other souls to a sacred way of life. Whereas she begins the poem "*O may I* join the choir invisible," she declares confidently at the hymn's conclusion "*So shall I* join the choir invisible / Whose music is the gladness of the world" (*CSP* 2:86, emphasis added). Eliot's poem was an immortal hymn to sympathy. Through it and her other poetry, she fulfilled her calling and participated in the choir invisible.

This final stanza includes the phrases "purest heaven," "pure love," "sweet presence," "good diffused," all expressions that are also representative of nineteenth-century femininity. LaPorte aptly remarks on Eliot's use of domestic and sentimental terminology that Victorians associated with femininity. Eliot desires to be "*felt* as a nurse to the sick in spirit, to enkindle generosity, to engender love.

---

[48] This line recalls the final description of Dorothea in *Middlemarch*: "But the effect of her being on those around her was incalculably diffusive: for the growing good of the world is partly dependent on unhistoric acts; and that things are not so ill with you and me as they might have been, is half owing to the number who lived faithfully a hidden life, and rest in unvisited tombs" (838).

This humanistic sentimentality is one of the hallmarks of the poetess tradition" ("Poetess as Prophet" 162).[49] The poetess tradition relied on Christian morality to advance culture. Eliot took Christian terminology and theology and recycled it as feminine piety to preach a religion of sympathy. In so doing, she immortalized herself in the minds of her readers and left a sacred message to guide generations to come.

Conclusion

LaPorte explains that "English poetesses often turned to biblical subjects because the Bible afforded them examples of female prophetic authority, an authority made particularly compelling by the quasi-divine moral perspective credited to many women in nineteenth-century culture" (*Victorian Poets* 213). Eliot was no exception. With her knowledge of the Bible and a firm understanding of her society's expectations for female authorship, she consciously participated in a tradition of women poets who relied on feminine piety and poetry to help refine society through compassion and fellow-feeling. Eliot wrote religious poetry throughout her career, but she wrote earnestly as a poetess only after she rejected and then softened her views on Christianity and developed her own religion of sympathy. Eliot came to appreciate the language, lessons, and stories of the faith she once rejected, and she incorporated them into her poetry to preach a religion of sympathy to her readers. Through her poems, she reached out to the reader in ways she did not attempt in her fiction. She adopted a different persona—that of a poetess—and mingled religious terminology and secular ideas to convey a doctrine of sympathy. Readers then and now experience a fuller understanding of the author's work and message by reading her poetry in addition to her fiction. Nineteenth-century and contemporary minds are made better by the presence of one "immortal dead" who lives again to spur us on to "deeds of daring rectitude" and "thoughts sublime" from the choir invisible.

---

[49] LaPorte also notes that Eliot's invocations of "purest heaven," great agony," and "pure love" are in accord with her desire to share in the "sweet presence of a good diffused." The poetess tradition relied on such recycled tropes of feminine piety ("Poetess as Prophet" 162).

Chapter 3
Sexual Politics in Poetry

"There is no subject on which I am more inclined to hold my peace and learn, than on the 'Woman Question.'"

—George Eliot

George Eliot's relationship with Lewes signaled a rejection of a traditional domestic lifestyle. Yet she *appeared* traditional in many of her beliefs about women in society. She rejected requests to sign petitions promoting women's rights and refused to write for the cause. When activist Clementia Taylor pressured her to take a public stand on women's rights, Eliot wrote that she had "grave reasons for not speaking on certain public topics" and that "no request from the best friend in the world—even from my own husband—ought to induce me to speak when I judge my duty to be silent (*Letters* 7:44). Eliot explained to Mrs. Taylor that she was an artist not an activist: "My function is that of the *aesthetic*, not the doctrinal teacher—the rousing of the nobler emotions, which make mankind desire the social right, not the prescribing of special measures, concerning which the artistic mind, however strongly moved by social sympathy, is often not the best judge" (7:44). Activist Elizabeth Malleson explained that although Eliot "always led the talk ... [to] the position of women, education," she took a conservative public stance for fear of drawing attention to her position: "The impression given me was of her conservatism on many points that we [activists] held could only be treated with courageous reform. She seemed to me timid where we were bold. I always attributed this to her isolated hidden position" (Collins, *Interviews* 68–9). Eliot's stance on the Woman Question frustrated contemporary women's rights activists as well as future feminist critics. Feminist critics today generally complain about her anti-feminist attitude and the weak women's roles in her novels, or they reconcile her position and claim her for feminism because of her liberated lifestyle. Neither of these views is clear-cut, and defining her sexual politics is challenging because her opinions are not distinctly one-sided. For example, she supported women's education and women's right to own property but not their right to vote. Similarly, she supported women's writing but sharply criticized much of it.

Eliot's writing reveals a mind at work processing various beliefs on sexual equality throughout her lifetime. Her novels provide mostly conventional portraits of and perspectives on women, but her poetry, while appearing to promote traditional middle-class values, reveals more progressive ideas. Eliot used poetry to work through and express unconventional ideas about gender in nineteenth-century British society in order to inspire sympathy among the sexes. After exploring Eliot's attitudes toward women writers and women's issues, this chapter will show how her poetry manifested her views on gender matters in ways her fiction did not. I will analyze "How Lisa Loved the King" and "Brother and Sister" to demonstrate how she took greater risks and made bolder statements on gender issues in her poetry by appearing to espouse middle-class values while interrogating the claims of patriarchal gender norms.

George Eliot and Women Writers

As an anonymous essayist, Eliot was largely critical of women's writing.[1] Thomas Pinney cites Eliot's reproach that few women writers "exhibit the subtle penetration into feeling and character, and the truthful delineation of manners which can alone compensate for the want of philosophic breadth in their views of men and things, and for their imperfect knowledge of life outside the drawing-room" (qtd. in *Essays* 301).[2] In her essay "Silly Novels by Lady Novelists," Eliot argued that "Silly novels by Lady Novelists are a genus with many species, determined by the particular quality of silliness that predominates in them—the frothy, the prosy, the pious, or the pedantic" (301). She criticized women writers for creating unrealistic stories that conform to a particular storyline and called such writing empty and lacking in feeling (303). She especially railed against writers of "oracular" novels, ones that relayed the author's religious views (311). She called for higher standards and harsher criticism of women's literature so that silly ladies who write

---

[1]   Women wrote novels, journalism, letters, travel writing, diaries, self-help books, translation, biographies, history, cookbooks, conduct books, and poetry but approached "serious" works (such as sermons, treatises, political works, and literary pieces that required knowledge of the classics) more cautiously since society deemed such writing less feminine. Women who breeched public expectations for femininity risked being considered immoral. Publishing presented another dilemma for women writers. To publish meant entering the public realm. Printed books were part of the public sphere and invited admiration. As part of the private sphere, women were subject to the male gaze but had to appear to be unaware of it. Women who risked entering the public sphere invited sexualized self-exposure, akin to actresses whom, as "public women," society often associated with prostitutes (Mermin xiv). The association of ambition with self-exposure did not hinder writing for women, however. Many avoided self-exposure by publishing anonymously and pseudonymously, and those who published using their names could do so by writing works that society deemed acceptable for women writers. Some women writers advocated (or appeared to advocate) feminine domesticity. The woman writer had scandalous potential since her physical body became conflated with her literary body (Brown 181). However, if she adhered to domestic ideology, society viewed her as respectable (187). Authors like Elizabeth Gaskell and Felicia Hemans who wrote on domestic themes and lived outwardly traditional lives enjoyed public approval. Conversely, society gossiped about and scandalized non-traditional authors such as Leticia Landon and George Eliot.

[2]   Pinney's footnote reads: "*Westminster Review*, LXII, 283. The attribution of this review to George Eliot was made by Gordon S. Haight 'on the basis of style alone' in 'George Eliot's Theory of Fiction', *Victorian Newsletter*, 10 (Autumn, 1956), 1–3."

out of "busy idleness" would give up writing and thereby stop promoting a fatuous impression of women writers (323).[3]

Despite her rigorous critical standards, Eliot did praise women writers whom she thought truly merit-worthy. She greatly respected Harriet Martineau as an author (*Letters* 3:201) and admired the work of Harriet Beecher Stowe with whom she exchanged letters from 1869 until her death.[4] With Elizabeth Gaskell she exchanged a few praiseworthy correspondences but remained less impressed with Gaskell's work than Gaskell with hers. When Gaskell wrote to her upon reading *Adam Bede*, "I never read anything so complete, and beautiful in fiction, in my whole life before" (3:197), Eliot responded with gratitude for fellow sympathy between women artists:

> your letter ... has brought me the only sort of help I care to have—an assurance
> of fellow-feeling, of thorough truthful recognition from one of the minds which
> are capable of judging as well as of being moved ... I shall always love to think
> that one woman wrote to another such sweet encouraging words. (3:198)

Sympathy between women artists for Eliot was rare, and though Gaskell's admiration touched her, she was a critic foremost and as such could not overlook literary limitations. To Clementia Taylor, she said that "Mrs. Gaskell has certainly a charming mind, and one cannot help loving her as one reads her books" but that her novel *Ruth* "with all its merits will not be an enduring or classical fiction" (2:86). Though she admired and engaged a few women writers, she seldom befriended literary women due, most likely, to her critical attitude and high standards. Her devotion to the art of writing and desire to see a better quality of women's writing superseded the need to establish friendships with female authors.

Eliot felt that women writers had a responsibility to their readers to present excellent writing from a feminine point of view.[5] Nevertheless, she wrote her essays anonymously (as was standard practice) and often chose the voice of a male narrator. In "Woman in France: Madame De Sablé" (1854), Eliot's male narrator complained that "With a few remarkable exceptions, our own feminine

---

[3]   Elaine Showalter argues that women writers "thought she had rejected them because she avoided intimacy; they thought she had despised them because she had held them to a rigorous standard" (*A Literature of Their Own* 111).

[4]   She met Martineau in 1845 and again in 1852. The two became friends, but the friendship ended with Martineau's disapproval of Eliot's elopement. Eliot never met Stowe, who lived in America, but the two periodically wrote letters to exchange ideas on religion, philosophy, social justice, and writing.

[5]   The situating of middle-class women in the home made writing opportunities attractive to those who were ambitious, restless, or in need of money. Few respectable options were available to middle-class women who needed to earn a living; they could become governesses, paid companions, school keepers, wives, or writers. Writing offered the added benefit of privacy; they could write at home, secretly, and with little expense (Mermin xv). Many women who turned to writing out of financial necessity wrote for mass appeal and not for artistic value. Eliot criticized writers who forfeited quality for monetary gain.

literature is made up of books which could have been better written by men"
but also acknowledged women's unique contribution: "she will necessarily have
a class of sensations and emotions—the maternal ones—which must remain
unknown to man; and the fact of her comparative physical weakness ... introduces
a distinctively feminine condition into the wondrous chemistry of the affections
and sentiments, which inevitably gives rise to distinctive forms and combinations"
(*Essays* 53).[6] In other words, the female experience gave the woman writer a
sensibility derived from maternal instinct and "sentiments" not available to men.
Women, Eliot argued, ought to draw upon their unique resources to provide fresh
insight through writing. She also espoused the idea that "the difference of sex"
provided a source of "variety and beauty" (53). According to Eliot, women who
imitated or exaggerated the masculine style or whose approach was a "composite
of feminine fatuity" (53, 301) did not properly channel the power of their feminine
distinctiveness.

In addition to successful application of feminine sentiment, Eliot attributed
successful female writing to higher intellect (55). To attain a higher intellect, she
argued in "Woman in France," women should be allowed to interact more freely
with men. French women, for example, were more sympathetic with men than
English women because of a "laxity of opinion and practice with regard to the
marriage-tie" (56). She argued that "unions formed in the maturity of thought
and feeling, and grounded only on inherent fitness and mutual attraction, tended
to bring women into more intelligent sympathy with men" (56). Furthermore,
the practice of salons in France allowed men and women to converse on a broad
array of topics and thus helped bolster feminine culture (57).[7] Eliot believed
women writers could contribute uniquely to literature if they employed feminine
sensibility together with intellect. As an anonymous (presumably male) writer,
she advocated less rigid rules of decorum that would allow men and women to
interact and experience diverse knowledge. Women confined to the home and to
the company of women, by contrast, had no access to masculine perspectives.
A life spent discussing needlework, etiquette, dress, manners, marriage, child-

---

[6]   Ermarth explains that the essay's guiding thoughts are ideas at the heart of Eliot's
work. The first thought "is that society is a homeostatic condition: for better or worse, all
parts affect all other parts. Where women are marginalized, ill-educated, and positively
confined to a corner and to needlework, their whole culture feels the pang; and conversely,
where women have among all citizens an equal opportunity to develop, their culture reaps
the reward" ("Woman in France" 443). The second thought "is that every individual makes
a difference but that individuals alone do not make conditions: it is an aggregate of women,
not just a few exceptionally privileged ones, who make the critical mass that binds society
to one course or another. English society in the mid-19th century supported social practices
that excluded women by law from almost any exercise of social, political, and economic
rights and responsibilities" (443).

[7]   In a comparison of English and French women writers, she deemed French women's
writing as superior to English women's writing because of the French women's greater
intellect.

rearing, and the behavior of neighbors was limited, and for Eliot such a limited mind should not attempt to influence others through writing. Eliot wrote "Woman in France" in 1854, the same year she began living with Lewes. She therefore lived publicly what she promoted anonymously. She broke societal rules of decorum by living outside the bounds of legal matrimony, and though she thrived as an intellectual and a writer partly as a result of such a union, her reputation suffered early on in her career. Not many women risked their position by associating with a fallen woman, and therefore her social world during the 1850s largely consisted of male companionship—Lewes and other guests who read and discussed humanities, social sciences, and natural sciences. She thus gained masculine perspectives by interacting with men and discussing a broad array of topics while retaining the essential characteristics of femininity. By the late 1860s and throughout the 1870s, the duration of her poetic practice, she had successfully transformed her image into that of a poetess with a masculine intellect and a feminine voice.

Eliot wanted the female voice in the public domain to be reflective of a mature mind and a deep understanding of humanity, one that could provide readers with a balanced understanding of human nature and societal needs. One author who represented ideal feminine writing, in Eliot's opinion, was Elizabeth Barrett Browning. In her review of Barrett Browning's poem *Aurora Leigh* (1856), Eliot wrote:

> Mrs. Browning is, perhaps, the first woman who has produced a work which exhibits all the peculiar powers without the negations of her sex; which superadds to masculine vigour, breadth, and culture, feminine subtlety of perception, feminine quickness of sensibility, and feminine tenderness. It is difficult to point to a woman of genius who is not either too little feminine, or too exclusively so … Mrs. Browning has shown herself all the greater poet because she is intensely a poetess. ("Belles Lettres" 306)

Eliot found in Barrett Browning's poetry "genuine thought and feeling" (307). She explained that *Aurora Leigh* exhibited no artifice but rather control, thoughtfulness, and a profound awareness of human emotions: "there is simply a full mind pouring itself out in song as its natural and easiest medium. This mind has its far-stretching thoughts, its abundant treasure of well-digested learning, its acute observation of life, its yearning sympathy with multiform human sorrow" (307). Eliot's praise of Browning showed her insistence upon women writers using their intellect to create sympathetic delineations of the human experience. Charles LaPorte points out that Eliot held different standards for women's poetry and women's prose. He cites Eliot's praise of *Aurora Leigh* to assert:

> Certainly no tradition of writing in the nineteenth century is more self-consciously feminine than the poetess tradition, and Eliot's review instructs that only through this tradition is Barrett Browning able to blossom into great poetry. Here, seemingly, is the distinctive female influence that Eliot wished to see in the English tradition, and Eliot's poetry propagates that influence. ("Poetess as Prophet" 160)

The poetess tradition was more thoroughly feminine than any other writing tradition. But Eliot's comments on women's writing in her early essays imply that she wanted women writers of all genres to compose with intelligence and feminine sensibility.

George Eliot's Sexual Politics

Eliot believed women writers had a particular responsibility to develop intellectually since they were public spokespersons, but she also considered acquired intellect a benefit to women in general. She thought that education would eventually lead to social elevation for women but believed that such change should occur slowly and gradually. Although she strongly advocated equal education for women, she was ambivalent about other issues related to the Woman Question. She expressed this ambivalence to her friend Jane Senior (1869): "There is no subject on which I am more inclined to hold my peace and learn, than on the 'Woman Question.' It seems to me to overhang abysses, of which even prostitution is not the worst. Conclusions seem easy so long as we keep large blinkers on and look in the direction of our own private path" (*Letters* 5:58).[8] She indicated that the issue of women's equality was too complicated for her to take a firm stand, and she could not relate to strident advocates since her own position was unsure.[9] She explained to Mrs. Senior her difficulty in relating to activists: "I feel too deeply the difficult complications that beset every measure likely to affect the position of women and also I feel too imperfect a sympathy with many women who have put themselves forward in connexion with such measures, to give any practical adhesion to them" (5:58). She also expressed her ambivalence to John Morley: "I do not trust very confidently to my own impressions on this subject [female enfranchisement]. The peculiarities of my own lot have caused me to have idiosyncrasies rather than an average judgment" (5:364). By the time she wrote this letter in 1867, Eliot's fame had finally earned her social standing after years of ostracism. She did not

---

[8]   Eliot did not explicitly state what she understood the "Woman Question" to mean. This comment to Mrs. Senior provides the only instance in which she used the expression in her letters. We know that she believed society should enfranchise women only after they were educated, and we also know that she believed women should have the right to own property. Otherwise, we can only speculate on her views based on her lifestyle, actions, and statements to others.

[9]   Though some women were silent, and others like Eliot refused to take a stand, many were active rhetorically, addressing public meetings held for promoting temperance and other women's issues (dress, moral purity, married women's property rights, domestic abuse, suffrage, etc.). Carol Mattingly explains that hundreds of thousands of women participated in the woman's movement. Women outside the suffrage movement were considered "conservative." Scholars often connect women's conservatism to religion, but many of the women's rights activists learned their rhetorical skills through working in the church (103).

want to call attention to her personal life by advocating publicly. As Elizabeth Ermarth aptly states: "She did not participate in rallies because of a personal life so continuously fraught by the courageous choices she made that her health nearly buckled under the strain; she simply had not the luxuries available to women who, as she said, get what they want by indirection so they can still be invited to dinner" (*Oxford Reader's Companion* 442). Deeply sensitive to the opinions and criticisms of others, she had to protect herself from more censure than she could physically handle. She put her energy into writing and left the rallies to others.

Eliot's literary success was a draw to the cause, and her activist friends appealed to her for support on a range of women's issues, but she would not lend her backing to the movement. Activist friends Barbara Bodichon, Clementia Taylor, and Bessie Parkes pursued her for support, as did Julia Smith, founder of Bedford College; Emily Davies, founder of Girton College; Isa Craig, poet and co-worker at the *English Woman's Journal*; Dr. Elizabeth Blackwell, champion for medical education for women; Florence Nightingale, Bodichon's cousin; Octavia Hill, campaigner for women's education; and Caroline Cornwallis, writer and co-contributor to the *Westminster Review*.[10] These women did not succeed in gaining Eliot's full support, but they prompted her to participate in some ways. She signed the Married Women's Property Bill petition, contributed to Girton College and to a fund that enabled Octavia Hill to pursue philanthropic work, and helped Bessie Parkes in her publishing pursuits (Nestor 160–61).[11] She favored justice for married women and hoped to see women better educated, more sympathetic toward others, and more talented as writers, but she was reluctant to engage in women's politics because she felt her talent was that of a writer, not that of an activist.

Eliot often thought about the issues regarding the Woman Question but stood publicly neither on the side of feminism nor on the side of anti-feminism. In 1853, Eliot wrote to Clementia Taylor: "'Enfranchisement of women' only makes creeping progress; and that is best, for woman does not yet deserve a much better lot than man gives her" (*Letters* 2:86). Such statements have led a number of contemporary feminist critics to express disappointment in what they view as Eliot's anti-feminism. Deirdre David, for example, considers Eliot's stance as capitulation to the male-dominated culture (164). Pauline Nestor claims that Eliot's ambivalence was a result of being apolitical and ill-disposed toward activism (162). Karen Chase asserts that Eliot preferred not to engage actively but rather worked out her feelings regarding the Woman Question in her writing (445). A recollection of Eliot written by nineteen-year-old Sofia Kovalevskaya

---

[10]   When Parkes asked her to contribute to the *English Woman's Journal*, Eliot declined, explaining that her "vocation lies in other paths ... I expect to be writing *books* for some time to come ... It is a question whether I shall give up building my own house to go and help in the building of my neighbour's garden wall" (*Letters* 2:431).

[11]   Eliot encouraged Parkes to publish her *Poems* in 1852: "Publish the poems with all my heart, but don't stop there. Work on and on and do better things still" (*Letters* 2:45). She also positively reviewed Parkes's *Gabriel* in *Westminster Review* (Haight 184).

(likely in 1870) demonstrates that though Eliot may have held ambivalent views on the Woman Question she was not anti-feminist. Kovalevskaya described an argument between herself and Herbert Spencer one Sunday at the Priory in which she "argued the 'woman's question' with the enthusiastic fervor of a neophyte … and George Eliot did all in her power to incite me in the discussion" (Collins, *Interviews* 100). The "duel," she explains, "went on for three-quarters of an hour until George Eliot decided to put an end to it. 'You have defended our common concern with such courage,' she said to me, 'and if my friend Herbert Spencer is not yet persuaded, then I am afraid that he must be judged incorrigible'" (100). Eliot commonly ceded the floor to others in her Sunday gatherings, and many Priory guests have noted her keen ability to make them feel all the wiser with her encouragement; however, in this instance, Eliot's inciting Kovalevskaya to speak out on their "common concern" denotes some complicity in thought. She encouraged others to promote women's causes, and she advocated in subtle ways in her writing, but she did not publicly speak out.

Key to understanding Eliot's sexual politics is her belief in a meritocratic society based on education and slow, progressive change.[12] Like other intellectuals of the age, Eliot believed in a shift in societal power from those privileged by gender and class to those who merited power by virtue of intellect. Intellectuals gained power through knowledge and exercised power by writing Truth based on science and reason, untainted by self-interest, and motivated by the good of society, not the good of the individual. Intellectuals such as Eliot thus emphasized literacy and education as means to a better society (see Cottom 4–16). Without equal education, she believed, women lacked the intellect to merit power in society.[13] Eliot thought that education for women (and for all people) would result

---

[12] George Creeger explains that Eliot's "intense conservatism" is a principle characteristic of her mindset. Her conservatism, he suggests, is:

> the value, amounting almost to piety, she gave to the past; the stress she placed upon duty; the insistence that the passions stood in need of a controlling rationality; the acceptance of change and a belief in progress qualified by a fear that any abrupt wrenching would prove harmful to the structure of society; and the yearning, while in London and at the very heart of the world's greatest mercantile and industrial power, for a preindustrial age she had known as a child among the green fields and hedgerows of rural England. (2–3)

Creeger is right. However, I avoid using the term "conservatism" in this discussion as it evokes political connotations and does not account for Eliot's socially liberal views. To be fair to Creeger, he admits that her conservatism was balanced by (or set in a state of tension by) strong liberal-reforming tendencies (3).

[13] In *A Short History of Writing Instruction*, Ferreira-Buckley and Winifred Horner explain in their chapter "Writing Instruction in Great Britain: The Eighteenth And Nineteenth Centuries" that prohibitions against female education were based on cultural and biological grounds. There was a common belief that "rigorous study led to infertility and insanity" (204). Furthermore, medical officials warned that women were "ill-equipped to handle the rigors of study" (204).

in a more universally enlightened society that would naturally produce a fairer distribution of power. But in her view such a change could not take place quickly and should not be forced.

Her belief in steady progress for women is clear in her essay, "Margaret Fuller and Mary Wollstonecraft," written anonymously in 1855, comparing the two women's rights activists. In this essay, she summarized two typical stances on women's roles: "On one side we hear that woman's position can never be improved until women themselves are better; and on the other, that women can never become better until their position is improved—until the laws are made more just, and a wider field opened to feminine activity (*Essays* 205). She argued for gradual change: "There is a perpetual action and reaction between individuals and institutions; we must try and mend both by little and little—the only way in which human things can be mended" (205). Chase explains Eliot's rejection of quick change in favor of slow progress:

> The quick pursuit of a new legal dispensation for women, the insistence on an immediate change in relations of property, the demand for an overturning of the conventions of "separate spheres" for men and women—these hallmarks of a robust new politics struck George Eliot as too hasty and decided ... Her mature thought depends on a conception of social life as a living organism that grows and changes only slowly; transformation cannot be willed in a moment; it must be prepared carefully over time ... Not a hasty, hurried snatching, it is part of a long, organic process leading perhaps to radical change in the relations of the sexes, but not all at once, and not soon. (445–6)

Eliot believed in progressive change that would not disrupt the usual functioning of society. For Eliot, societal progress for women needed to be slow because it required education—an endeavor which took time. To her friends, she boldly asserted her belief in women's right to equal access to education. She wrote to Mrs. Taylor: "I do sympathise with you most emphatically in the desire to see women socially elevated—educated equally with men, and secured as far as possible along with every other breathing creature from suffering the exercise of any unrighteous power" (*Letters* 4:366). Here she pointed to education as a means to social elevation and the avoidance of suffering unjust usage of power. She addressed men's fear of women's education by asserting that education promotes harmonious relationships and healthy families. She explained to Emily Davies that "complete union and sympathy can only come by women having opened to them the same store of acquired truth or beliefs as men have" (4:468). Similarly, to Mrs. Senior she explained that unity among the sexes required education for men and women alike:

> women ought to have the same fund of truth placed within their reach as men have; that their lives (i.e. the lives of men and women) ought to be passed together under the hallowing influence of a common faith as to their duty and its basis. And this unity in their faith can only be produced by their having each the same store of fundamental knowledge. (5:58)

Eliot's defense of women's education indicates a desire for intellectual equality that would lead to social elevation. However, intellectual equality for Eliot would not mean dominance over men. Neither would it mean that women would share masculine gender roles. Rather, she argued, women would continue to have their own functions. She wrote in "Woman in France":

> Let the whole field of reality be laid open to woman as well as to man, and then that which is peculiar in her mental modification, instead of being, as it is now, a source of discord and repulsion between the sexes, will be found to be a necessary complement to the truth and beauty of life. Then we shall have that marriage of minds which alone can blend all the hues of thought and feeling in one lovely rainbow of promise for the harvest of human happiness. (*Essays* 81)[14]

Eliot affirmed to Emily Davies her belief in the "spiritual wealth acquired for mankind by the difference of function," and spoke to the alarm that "women should be 'unsexed'" by explaining: "We can no more afford to part with that exquisite type of gentleness, tenderness, possible maternity suffusing a woman's being with affectionateness, which makes what we mean by the feminine character, than we can afford to part with human love" (*Letters* 4:468).[15] Although she did acknowledge the "special moral influence" that "lies in women's peculiar constitution," she did not believe in the moral or biological superiority of women (4:468).[16] She wrote in "Margaret Fuller and Mary Wollstonecraft":

> Unfortunately, many over-zealous champions of women assert their actual equality with men—nay, even their moral superiority to men—as a ground for their release from oppressive laws and restrictions. They lose strength immensely by this false position. If it were true, then there would be a case in which slavery and ignorance nourished virtue, and so far we should have an argument for the continuance of bondage. But we want freedom and culture for woman, because

---

[14]   Eliot seems to both uphold and subvert gender essentialist ideas in her writings. She extols the maternal, gentle, sympathetic nature of women while championing equal education and vocational success for women. I do not think Eliot was an essentialist. She believed in the unique qualities and functions of the sexes, but she did not assert that these were fixed traits. Rather, she urged men and women to better understand one another and improve society through sympathy and fellow-feeling.

[15]   Jennifer Uglow states that Eliot believed that more opportunities would "both enhance women's capacities *and* maintain their 'precious speciality', the capacity for sympathy" (71). For Eliot, allowing women a greater voice would invite more sympathetic relations between the sexes and thereby lead to a better society.

[16]   Ermarth explains: "To claim that women have special powers, solely because they are biologically women, is an argument from magic of the kind George Eliot has no patience with. Such claims trivialize women's real experience and actively deny them opportunity even to grow up. And this trivialization and this denial is not done only by men, but by women who reinforce the closed circuit of misogynist self-justification" ("Woman in France" 443).

subjection and ignorance have debased her, and with her, Man; for—If she be small, slight-natured, miserable, / How shall men grow?[17] (*Essays* 205)[18]

She likened the argument for moral superiority (based on the oppression of women) to the argument for virtue (based on enslavement). Oppression does not lead to betterment, she claimed, and such an argument would lead to continued oppression. Eliot believed women should neither claim superiority over men nor let society reduce them to servitude or limit them to the domestic sphere. Only in an educated society in which all have free access to knowledge can a culture advance and thrive.

Thus, Eliot believed in women's advancement with qualifications. However, she was reluctant to voice ideas that would appear radical and unfeminine. She strove to present a public image of traditional femininity. John Cross wrote after Eliot's death of her belief in women's advancement and her support of women's higher education. However, he was careful (as was she) to stress the fact that her support of women did not in any way detract from her womanliness:

> She was keenly anxious to redress injustices to women, and to raise their general status in the community. This, she thought, could best be effected by women improving their work—ceasing to be amateurs. But it was one of the most distinctly marked traits in her character, that she particularly disliked everything generally associated with the idea of a "masculine woman." She was, and as a woman she wished to be, above all things feminine—"so delicate with her needle, and an admirable musician." She was proud, too, of being an excellent housekeeper ... Nothing offended her more than the idea that because a woman had exceptional intellectual powers, therefore it was right that she should absolve herself, or be absolved, from her ordinary household duties. (Collins, *Interviews* 222)

To what extent Eliot truly valued her household duties is unclear; what is clear is her desire to be viewed by others as delicate and feminine, and Cross's long digression from the dangerous topic of women's advancement to Eliot's love of household duties served to maintain such an image. Eliot made efforts herself to perpetuate a view of herself as feminine despite her "exceptional intellectual powers," and others readily observed this quality in her. Journalist Bret Harte wrote: "She reminds you continually of a man—a bright, gentle, lovable, philosophical man—without being a bit *masculine*" (210). John Fiske was astounded by her ability to discuss Homer with the intellect of a man and simple language of a woman:

---

[17] This quote is from Tennyson's *The Princess* (175).

[18] Eliot praised activists Fuller and Wollstonecraft for not falling into "sentimental exaggeration," stating: "Their ardent hopes of what women may become do not prevent them from seeing and painting women as they are" (*Essays* 205). A respectful nod to Wollstonecraft was unusual since she was often used as the example of "where feminism leads." Her suicide attempts and extramarital liaisons were publicized in the memoirs of her husband, William Godwin. Eliot typically did not associate with other fallen women, and her praise of Wollstonecraft was a testament to her belief in Wollstonecraft's sensibility, albeit one expressed from behind the safe, genderless veil of anonymity.

> I found her thoroughly acquainted with the whole literature of the Homeric question; and she seems to have read all of Homer in Greek ... She didn't talk like a bluestocking ... but like a plain woman, who talked of Homer as simply as she would of flat irons ... I never before saw such a clear-headed woman. She thinks just like a man, and can put her thoughts into clear and forcible language at a moment's notice. And her knowledge is quite amazing. I have often heard of learned women, whose learning, I have usually found, is a mighty flimsy affair. But to meet a woman who can meet you like a man, on such a question as that of Homer's poems, knowing the ins and outs of the question, and not *putting on any airs*, but talking sincerely of the thing as a subject which has deeply interested her—this is, indeed, quite a new experience ... I think Lewes a happy man in having such a simple-hearted, honest, and keenly sympathetic wife. (*Letters* 5:465)

Fiske's effusive praise of a woman who could meet him "like a man" in intellectual matters and also talk "of Homer as simply as she would of flat irons" reveals Eliot's ability to maintain an "angel in the house" image despite her great learning.

Gender Roles in "Brother and Sister"

Eliot maintained her feminine image by avoiding direct engagement in politics, but she did address women's struggles in her writing. Her fiction presents mostly traditional views and at times engages women's issues—but indirectly and cautiously.[19] Her poetry, however, reveals more fully her complex attitudes toward gender politics.[20] On the surface, Eliot's poems seem to promote traditional views

---

[19]   Chase asserts that Eliot's fiction reveals indirect engagement of the Woman Question: "The engagement occurs in her own terms and within the realm of her fictional project, and if it yields no brisk recommendations for public policy, it makes a persistent challenge to the work of narrative" (443). The debates in the 1850s surrounding the laws of divorce and married women's property were going on at the time when Eliot was beginning her literary career, and the contemporary debates crop up throughout her works. As Parliament discussed a legislative response to domestic brutality, "Janet's Repentance" narrated a story of physical abuse of a woman by her husband. As feminists sought to establish a woman's college, Eliot exposed the neglect of Maggie Tulliver's education in *The Mill on the Floss* (444–5).

[20]   Mathilde Blind describes another unique quality of Eliot's poetry: the reliance on idealistic portraits versus the truthful representations found in her novels. Blind states that having portrayed "the most marvelously truthful delineations of her fellow-men as they are ordinarily to be met with, she now also felt prompted to draw the exceptional types of human character, the rare prophets, and the sublime heroes" in her poetry (165). Blind explains Eliot's departure from realism in *The Spanish Gypsy*: "Here, as in her novels, we find George Eliot's instinctive insight into the primary passions of the human heart, her wide sympathy and piercing keenness of vision; but her thoughts, instead of being naturally winged with melody, seem mechanically welded into song" (168).

with respect to gender;[21] poetic heroines like fictional ones follow a sense of duty and sacrifice their will for others. However, Eliot applied the poetess technique of inserting subversive views while appearing to advance middle-class values. A close reading of her poems reveals the opinions Eliot was reluctant to convey in public and in her novels.

For example, "Brother and Sister," a story told in a sequence of eleven sonnets, appears to be a straightforward poem about the love between siblings, but an in-depth examination presents an unusual challenge to traditional gender roles. Eliot's choice of the sonnet form (and sonnet sequence) was strategic.[22] First, the sonnet form allowed her a place to relay a personal story.[23] Eliot avoided autobiographical expression in general, and she especially avoided self-display in poetry, as readers tended to make autobiographic assumptions about women poets via their poetry. However the sonnet form was associated with autobiographical truth and expression of feeling and therefore provided a natural place to tell one's story.[24] By choosing the sonnet form, which thematized confinement within both social and poetic rules, Eliot could write her personal experience in a formal, controlled

---

[21] *Armgart* is one exception. The heroine speaks out boldly on gender matters; however, by the end of the poem, circumstances force her into a more feminine role.

[22] A brief history of the sonnet will give context for Eliot's use of the form: Petrarch and his followers caused the sonnet form to flourish in fourteenth-century Italy. The English adopted the form in the sixteenth-century, creating new rhyme schemes but keeping its use of amatory sonnet sequences. Milton kept the Italian structure but did not use the amatory context, applying it to political and personal issues. The eighteenth-century produced few sonnets until the end of the century when Della Cruscans and popular poets of sentiment such as Charlotte Smith revived the sonnet form. Wordsworth and Romantic poets used the sonnet form for descriptive and philosophical purposes, and Victorian poets revised and responded to the form in ways largely unnoticed until recently (Houston 247–8).

[23] Eliot wrote two other sonnets. One appears as an epigraph to Chapter 57 of *Middlemarch* and recounts the idyllic lives of two children influenced by the stories of Walter Scott. The similarities in theme (childhood unity and eventual separation), imagery (the "thrill" of flower "buds"), and language ("lines" and the "little world of [their] childhood") with "Brother and Sister" indicate the likelihood that this sonnet was initially written for the sequence. Eliot also wrote "Sonnet" in 1839, a poem in which the narrator reflects on childhood to express a sense of loneliness and disenchantment with life. Margaret Reynolds correctly notes that "Sonnet" expresses a wish for freedom from societal constrictions (*Oxford Reader's Companion* 305). In "Sonnet" and "Brother and Sister" Eliot uses the sonnet form and the adult narrator reflecting on childhood to protest forms of social confinement.

[24] Wordsworth and his contemporaries repositioned the sonnet as a form for autobiographical expression. This effort was connected with the rediscovery of Shakespeare's sonnets, which had been critically neglected but then were transformed into the ideal example of the sonnet sequence as disguised autobiography (Phelan 43). Eliot wrote to John Blackwood (1873) of her poem: "A good while ago I made a poem, in the form of eleven sonnets after the Shakspeare type, on the childhood of a brother and sister— little descriptive bits on the mutual influences in their small lives" (*Letters* 5:403).

setting. She strictly adhered to the formal rules of the sonnet form to express her feelings of confinement in a sibling relationship that assumed traditional gender roles.[25] Eliot's rigid adherence to form provided a structured medium for the story of a young Eliot who faithfully conformed to society's expectations for her but who grew into an independent thinker and writer. Second, the sonnet form allowed Eliot to use her personal experience to make a point of national importance. Critical discussion about the sonnet's rules and qualities shows that the sonnet, above other poetic forms, "connects narratives of literary history with aesthetics at the level of form" (Houston 247). Nineteenth-century readers connected the structure of the sonnet to national history. Those who argued over the definition of the sonnet appealed to England's cultural and literary history, as represented by the differing major rhyme schemes created by Sidney, Surrey, Shakespeare, and Spencer, to make their claims. Natalie Houston explains: "Assertions about the national character of the sonnet and its writers were frequently filtered through discussions of rules for the sonnet's form, presenting it as an engine of cultural transmission (and translation) that best operates by principles of exclusion and codification" (247). Thus Eliot's use of a thoroughly English form of poetry, the Shakespearean sonnet rhyme scheme, rather than the Italian Petrarchan rhyme scheme, for "Brother and Sister" to comment on the unfairness of gendered expectations could be seen as a call to the nation to reconsider its traditions. Eliot conformed to the strict rules of English sonnet form in telling a story of a girl conforming to, yet questioning, the rules of a society that enforced male dominance. By extension, she encouraged English readers also to question such conventions. Finally, the sonnet sequence allowed Eliot to subvert traditional gender expectations by employing a role-reversal technique used by women poets.[26] The love sonnet sequence typically involved a male addressing a female to

---

[25]   Joseph Phelan points out that Tractarian poet John Keble noted the sonnet form as an appropriate vehicle for autobiography because it allowed one to regulate and disguise emotions. This combining of expressiveness and decorum (known by Keble as "modest reserve") allowed women poets to express themselves in the confines of a rule-bound form (46–7). Phelan states:

> The place of the sonnet within the "expressive" poetics underlying the practice of the "poetesses" has not yet been noted. What Isobel Armstrong calls the "aesthetics of the secret," which dominates women's poetry during the early nineteenth century gives rise not only to various forms of masking and displacement (such as the dramatic monologue), but also to the retention of a privileged site of encoded personal utterance in the sonnet. This heavily rule-governed yet apparently spontaneous form allowed women poets to articulate what Dora Greenwell, in revealingly Wordsworthian language, calls the "Open Secret, free to all who could find its key—the secret of a woman's heart, with all its needs, its struggles, and its aspirations." (47)

[26]   John Holmes notes that women writing sonnets and sonnet sequences in the late nineteenth-century did not follow models of poetry written by women early in the century that explored female identity by directly addressing questions of sexuality and gender. He

express his love; however, women poets allowed a female voice to speak to a male either to laud (as with Elizabeth Barrett Browning's *Sonnets from the Portuguese*) or to reject a lover (as with Christina Rossetti's *Monna Innominata*).[27] Eliot adds her own twist to the love sonnet sequence in having a woman describe her devotion not for a lover but for her brother. She includes romantic love imagery to depict a sibling relationship, which brings into question the true nature of this traditional relationship. Eliot's use of the confining poetic form appropriately frames the discussion of a relationship struggling within the confines of societal expectations for gendered behavior. The following analysis of "Brother and Sister" will show how such expectations stifled the relationship between a brother and sister but did not inhibit the sister's artistic development. The sister learns to free herself from society's rules for gendered behavior and to direct her discipline instead to self-discovery and expression through poetry.

Based on her own childhood relationship with her brother in rural Chilvers Coton, Eliot's coming of age sonnet sequence follows the idyllic adventures of siblings who spent their days wandering through a meadow, playing along the banks of a canal, fishing, and counting trees.[28] The adult narrator is the sister, and she

---

argues that Elizabeth Barrett Browning's *Sonnets from the Portuguese*, Eliot's "Brother and Sister," and Christina Rossetti's *Monna Innominata* and *Later Life* all fail to provide a model of female selfhood that is frank in sexuality or free from a sense of inferiority. None of these sequences, he argues, explore the possibility of defining female identity through sexuality or apart from masculinity (101). Amy Billone argues that women initiated the revival of the sonnet form in England in the nineteenth-century at a time when women had difficulty entering the lyric tradition. The sonnet form was associated with silence and designed for reading, not performing. Its structural affinity for silence allowed women poets to "investigate and promote gendered interpretations of silence" (3). Women poets needed to find ways to describe the problem of feeling silenced. They wanted to enjoy the same literary status of their male counterparts but they had to mask what they were saying (5–6). The sonnet form allowed them a structured venue for voicing gender-related concerns.

[27]   Phelan notes that women found the sonnet sequence a useful form because of "its apparent modesty and humility, its ability to offer them a level playing field, and perhaps most importantly its association with an interior and often secret life of longing and desire." He explains:

> Because it necessarily implies some view of the nature of the relationship between men and women, the amatory sonnet becomes particularly contentious in this respect. Both its chivalrous elevation of women to the status of unattainable near-divinities (Dante's Beatrice) and its tendency to objectify the recipient of the poet's attentions (Petrarch's Laura) render it complicit with patriarchy in certain obvious ways, and produce on the part of many women poets a desire to subvert or reverse its habitual gender roles and characteristics. (6)

[28]   The unusually autobiographical poem depicts meadowlands, rookery oaks, and a canal with barges (all descriptions of Eliot's childhood surroundings), a young girl's love for her brother whom she followed around (Eliot idolized Isaac), her frightening encounter with a gypsy (such as when Eliot as a young girl was frightened by a gypsy near her home), and their separation by school (school parted Eliot and Isaac at ages five and eight). Eliot's

looks back on her early days with the brother she idolized with fond reminiscence, describing their life in romantic terms while at the same time suggesting the confining nature of a relationship characterized by gender normative behavior and learning. The first sonnet begins:

> I cannot choose but think upon the time
> When our two lives grew like two buds that kiss
> At lightest thrill from the bee's swinging chime,
> Because the one so near the other is. (*Complete Shorter Poetry* 2:5)

At this early point in the poem, the sister appears to describe a young lover with whom she was inseparable. Not until the eighth line does she reveal the fact that the object of her affection is her brother. Eliot not only departs from the traditional sonnet sequence in shifting the focus of the girl's affection to a brother rather than a lover; she also changes the recipient of the address. Rather than speaking to a lover, Eliot's narrator speaks in third person. The sister is speaking to a wider audience. She and her brother, though they shared a happy childhood together, no longer speak; the sister-narrator speaks as an adult to her audience (English readers) to explain why the relationship ended. So, while the traditional address-to-lover sonnet sequence views the sequence as mediating a relationship, Eliot's address-to-brother sequence narrates a finished relationship. At the outset of the first sonnet the narrator also makes clear the confining nature of the sibling relationship. The sister is forced by her memory ("I cannot choose but think upon the time") to tell of the elder brother who defined boundaries and set limits for their life together (2:5). She describes him in terms of measurements—he was exactly "forty inches"—and explains how his path determined hers: "I the girl that puppy-like now ran, / Now lagged behind my brother's larger tread" (2:5). In her youthful perception, her brother not only designated their daily path, but he also defined the boundaries of all knowledge:

> I held him wise, and when he talked to me
> Of snakes and birds, and which God loved the best,
> I thought his knowledge marked the boundary
> Where men grew blind, though angels knew the rest. (2:5)

---

novel *The Mill on the Floss* also details the lives of two siblings, Maggie and Tom Tulliver, who grow up in a rural setting. The novel, like the poem, depicts the tension between the siblings due to the sister's non-conformity to gender rules and the brother's disapproval. The novel concludes with the death of the reunited siblings, and the poem concludes with a divorce and a liberated sister-poet. Eliot spoke out on gender matters more freely in her poetry because her poetry presented the material in a less overt manner. Aware of the fact that novels were more thoroughly scrutinized for controversial content, Eliot felt safer to develop these themes more discreetly, through verse. See van den Broek's editorial notes for detailed parallels between "Brother and Sister" and *The Mill on the Floss* (*CSP* 2:269–70).

She unquestioningly obeyed the commands of her God-like brother: "If he said 'Hush!' I tried to hold my breath / Wherever he said 'Come!' I stepped in faith" (2:5). In the first sonnet and throughout the sonnet sequence, the narrator measures the events by time: "Long years" (2:5), "Blest hours" (2:6), "my sunny day" (2:7), "Those hours" (2:7), "the still hours" (2:8), "Those long days" (2:8), "one whole minute" (2:9), "those brief days" (2:10), "that early time" (2:11), "the dire years" (2:11), etc. Eliot's repetition of measurements of time and her use of meter and rhyme (iambic pentameter and the Shakespearean sonnet rhyme scheme) reinforce the idea that though the sister was happy, she was trapped in a relationship marked by gender boundaries. Controlled by her brother who was taught to rule over her, she was content in her youthful ignorance.

Sonnet two further develops the theme of confinement and also introduces a writing motif. The sister-narrator, now old, writes that "Long years have left their writing on my brow," reminding the reader that a wiser woman is writing the poem (2:5). She describes how the young siblings "wandered toward the far-off stream / With rod and line" (2:5-6). The wandering, also referred to as "rambling" (2:7), suggests a freedom the sister enjoys in nature that was different from the pathway laid out by the "brother's larger tread" (2:5), the "trodden ways" their mother bade them keep, and the "firm stepping-stones" where the brother guided the sister with a "measuring glance" (2:10). The "rambling" and "stream" also represent the flow of words of the narrator as she learns the balance between rambling thought and ordered discourse in telling her story. The sister, aware of her brother's greater power because of his sex, states with happy resignation that they set off on their journey with a basket "Baked for us only, and I thought with joy / That I should have my share, though he had more, / Because he was the elder and a boy" (2:6). Conscious of the "loving difference of girl and boy," she acceded to her older brother's power. They each acted according to their own sexual function. Sister learned to obey, and brother learned to master. Even though their relationship was not equitable, she was happy in "those blest hours of infantine content" (2:6) because in her youthful innocence she did not know any other way. The rod and line that the siblings take to fish with have a symbolic as well as practical function. The rod (a biblical term for offspring) and line (meaning lineage) remind the reader of the blood connection that binds the siblings, while also hinting at an impending separation between the two, as the sister associates the rod (also a unit of measurement and an instrument of punishment) with her brother and the line (also words in a poem) with herself.[29] Her brother will learn to measure out punishment when the sister does not follow his path, and the sister will learn to write lines as she pursues her independent course.

The sister reveals her inclination to wander beyond the confinements of the "meadow-path" in sonnets three and four (2:7). She takes an interest in the "dark

---

[29]   The rod also represents a walking stick or shepherd's staff, as in "Thy rod and thy staff, they comfort me" (Psalm 23:4). Thus the rod has the potential to comfort as well as punish.

rooks [that] cawing flew, / And made a happy strange solemnity, / A deep-toned chant from life unknown to me" (2:6). The birds fly freely above the fixed meadow-path and sing of an unknown world. Similarly, flowers "with upturned faces gazing drew / My wonder downward, seeming all to speak / With eyes of souls that dumbly heard and knew" (2:7). With its strange music and mysterious knowledge, nature draws her attention from the pathway laid out by her brother. She begins to see that her brother is not the sole source of knowledge and that she can find truth in the wild. However, the sister learns that sometimes venturing beyond the safe pathways of life can be dangerous. Passing a thicket of trees, "where wild things rushed unseen," she notices "black-scathed grass [that] betrayed the past abode / Of mystic gypsies, who still lurked between / Me and each hidden distance of the road" (2:7). The "dark smile" of a gypsy and the "dark rooks" that fly above her elicit curiosity about and fear of the unknown. Treading from the pathway, she fears, may lead to dangerous consequences, yet the allure is powerful.

Sonnet five relates the tension that develops in the sibling relationship as a result of pursuing different courses. Along their meadow-path, brother and sister are "schooled in deepest lore" and "learned the meanings that give words a soul / The fear, the love, the primal passionate store, / Whose shaping impulses make manhood whole" (2:7). For the brother, the shaping impulses are societally determined, and they make "manhood" (humanity) "whole" (united).[30] He learns to fear the unknown, that which lies outside societal boundaries, and to love conformity. He loves by leading and commanding, and the little sister loves by following and obeying. However, the sister reveals a tendency to seek knowledge and love from outside sources. She begins to discover that there is life beyond the brother's societally-constructed boundaries. Her shaping impulses come not only from society but also from the natural world, and she in turn gives shape to the "meanings" (truths) she learns by writing the poem about her thoughts on society's pressure to conform to gender roles. The impulses that shape her into an independent thinker and writer make her whole in a way that is different from her brother's experience of wholeness. Her adult decisions to deviate from society's gender-bound rules disqualify her from the wholeness and unity that society offers. However, she will experience a completeness that comes with living life in a way that is true to oneself. The sister-narrator uses the words "love," "loving," and "primal passionate store" to remind the reader that the relationship between the brother and sister was once so close that she compared it to a romantic relationship. In their youth, they loved one another by following societal expectations for their genders. But the adult sister interjects a disapproving comment to discredit such a love that depends on societal conformity:

---

[30] Eliot tended to used masculine pronouns to describe humanity (mankind) and humans (he/him). In this case, however, her use of "manhood" instead of "humanity" or even "mankind" may imply that the "wholeness" experienced benefits men more than women.

For who in age shall roam the earth and find
Reasons for loving that will strike out love
With sudden rod from the hard year-pressed mind?
Were reasons sown as thick as stars above,
'Tis love must see them, as the eye sees light:
Day is but Number to the darkened sight. (2:8)

The sister questions the validity of a love that depends on her conforming to a set of rules. Her "reasons for loving" (seeking truth outside rules made by others) cause her brother to "strike out love" for her with "sudden rod from [his] hard year-pressed mind." The "rod," once a symbol of childhood fishing fun, harmony, and oneness through birth and blood, now represents an instrument of punishment. The brother's adult "mind" (way of thinking) has been "year-pressed" over time by tradition and now is hard and unable to perceive reasons for loving that do not conform to its rigid set of rules.[31] As a youth, she viewed her brother's knowledge as marking the boundary "Where men grew blind, though angels knew the rest," but as an adult, she learns that he is not enlightened but rather lives in the dark in matters of truth and love (2:5, 8). For the adult sister, true love naturally understands reasons for loving "as the eye sees light" (2:8). By contrast, because of his "darkened sight," the brother sees that "Day is but Number" (2:8). In other words, life ("Day") based on a collection of rules ("Number") for loving is meaningless. The statement has literary implications for the sister-poet as well. According to the *OED*, "but" can be used to mean "void of." And "number" can signify "metrical periods or feet; lines, verses" or "harmony; conformity, in verse or music, to a certain regular beat or measure; rhythm." The sister is saying that for the unenlightened person, life is devoid of poetry and true harmony. The brother's decision to love according to societal rules means that his life will have only the appearance of order. He will attain societal acceptance but will not understand how to love truly. The sister's decision to love outside of traditional boundaries means that she will live poetically and in harmony with her choices but will suffer for her lack of social conformity. This sonnet may be a comment on Eliot's choice to love Lewes and the consequence of society's and her brother's rejection of her based on that decision. Eliot blames the lack of harmony in her sibling relationship to Isaac's stubborn way of thinking and his inability to understand her reasons for loving Lewes. This sonnet gives a taste of the poem's divisive conclusion.

In sonnet six, the narrator explores the unknown world of nature beyond the familiar spots of the brother's path. She "sat in dreamy peace" on the banks of the "brown canal [that] was endless to my thought" and escaped into a world of imagination where barges rounded a "grassy hill to me sublime / With some Unknown beyond it, wither flew / The parting cuckoo toward a fresh spring time" (2:8). Intrigued by the unknown destinations of the rooks and cuckoos and the mysterious lives of the gypsies and the flowers with "eyes of souls," she seeks

---

[31]   Another reading of this sonnet involves contrasting the ease of loving spontaneously in childhood with the difficulty of loving in the harsh, indifferent world of adulthood.

out unfamiliar territory, takes ownership of hidden, private places that are hers only. Moments in nature alone with her imagination shape her. These hours, she explains, "Were but my growing self, are part of me, / My present Past, My root of piety" (2:8). The repetition of "my" and "me" indicates an awareness of an independent development apart from her brother with whom she once felt her life was inextricably entwined, and her use of the word "piety" implies an obedience to another source of devotion: her writing. She will turn from obedience to her brother and to society's rules for decorum and will instead rely on her own knowledge of the world, love, and art to live her life. She will learn to apply rules not merely to outward behavior but to art. The narrator will use the discipline she learned from her brother and her self-guiding imagination to craft powerful lines of poetry that have the ability not only to conform to rules and not only to express her fancy but that also have the power to make statements of national importance. By learning to write poetry and developing her art, Eliot creates a poem that transcends time, records personal history, and makes a condemnatory comment on a social injustice in nineteenth-century British life.

Sonnets seven and eight return to the theme of writing as they tell of an incident in which the sister learns a lesson in judgment and irony:

> Those long days measured by my little feet
> Had chronicles which yield me many a text;
> Where irony still finds an image meet
> Of full-grown judgments in this world perplext. (2:8)

The narrator again reminds the reader that she is writing a poem and confining herself to the rules of poetry writing. The chronicles of her life provide material for "many a text" that she measures by "little feet," and she will tell of an ironic incident that will show the confusing way in which people in society judge one another (2:8).[32] "Full-grown judgments" also refer to her own judgments that she will render now that she is no longer "little" but "Full-grown." One day, her brother puts her in charge of fishing while he looks for bait, and she obeys his command to "mind the rod" (2:9) for as long as she can; then her own desire to escape into the unknown world overpowers her will to please her brother:

> Proud of the task, I watched with all my might,
> For one whole minute, till my eyes grew wide,
> Till sky and earth took on a strange new light
> And seemed a dream-world floating on some tide—
> A fair pavilioned boat for me alone
> Bearing me onward through the vast unknown. (2:9)

---

[32]   Laura Mandell asserts: "Poetry written in the tradition of ironic simplicity contrasts directly with the overwrought transparency of poetry written by the poetess. In my view, at least, it is difficult to find irony in poetess poetry, and to do so leads to strained readings" (24). However, as my discussions of "Brother and Sister" and "Lisa" will show, Eliot clearly employs irony. Perhaps Mandell is correct and Eliot is an exception. A fuller study of irony in the works of poetesses is needed to refute or substantiate Mandell's claim.

Her will to obey only lasts "one whole minute," and then her powerful imagination takes her on a solo journey to a free and unknown world. However, by happy accident, she catches a fish and receives rich social reward as a result:

> My guilt that won the prey,
> Now turned to merit, had a guerdon rich
> Of hugs and praises, and made merry play,
> Until my triumph reached its highest pitch
> When all at home were told the wondrous feat,
> And how the little sister had fished well.
> In secret, though my fortune tasted sweet,
> I wondered why this happiness befell. (2:9)

Ironically, her disobedience earns her praise. As a child, this is confusing. As an adult, she understands that her imagination was stronger than her will to obey and that she could only gain social favor by luck.[33] She uses her "lines" to describe this incident to show that judgments are not always sound or necessarily based on truth. The adult Eliot can thus say that situations are complicated and not always easy to judge. To those who negatively judge her writing and her non-conforming lifestyle, she uses this ironic situation to point out their short-sighted impressions.

Whereas in sonnet one the narrator emphasizes oneness and unity in the sibling relationship, in sonnets nine and ten, she emphasizes differences. They grew up in the very same world in which they learned to behave according to gender differences:

> We had the self-same world enlarged for each
> By loving difference of girl and boy:
> The fruit that hung on high beyond my reach
> He plucked for me, and oft he must employ

---

[33] The gardener points out that the sister had "luck" in catching the fish (2:9). He whose job it is to make order of disorder in the natural world understands the disparity between wildness and conformity. He knows it can only be by luck that the imaginative child could win praise for obedience. Eliot uses the garden motif throughout to accent the theme of boundaries. Margaret Reynolds equates the garden of their childhood landscape to the Garden of Eden and the brother (who named the animals, held the knowledge, and plucked the fruit from the high tree for the little sister) to God or Adam. The conventional mother and brother in the poem ruled the little sister who "disturbs the untroubled surface of her poem by reading beyond this idyllic landscape" (*Oxford Reader's Companion* 306). Reynolds does not comment on why she perceives the mother as conventional, but the passage about the mother does depict a traditional mother at home caring for and watching after her children:

> Our mother bade us keep the trodden ways,
> Stroked down my tippet, set my brother's frill,
> Then with the benediction of her gaze
> Clung to us lessening, and pursued us still
> Across the homestead to the rookery elms. (2:6)

> A measuring glance to guide my tiny shoe
> Where lay firm stepping-stones. (2:10)

The brother understands that his role is to help, guide, and rule over his sister. He considers it his responsibility to guide his sister along the correct path in life, and by fulfilling his masculine function, he shows her kindness: "This thing I like my sister may not do, / For she is little, and I must be kind" (2:10). The word, "kind," also can mean "of the same sex" and "innate, inherent," which implies that the brother is simply acting as a boy when he tells his sister what to do. The brother learns to master the sister and tries to control her impulses: "Thus boyish Will the nobler mastery learned / Where inward vision over impulse reigns, / Widening its life with separate life discerned" (2:10). The boy's "Will" and "inward vision" reflect a supposedly natural, male tendency to reign over the sister's impulses. However, his "shaping impulse" is not innate but societal (2:7). His "Will" (desire) to rule his sister is reinforced by society's teaching boys to master girls and the enjoyment of the power in doing so. By reining her into safe, societal standards, he exercises the "nobler mastery" ("noble" by society's standards) (2:10). The will to master becomes greater with the exercise of domination. Thus, as the brother performs his sexual function, he becomes aware of the "separate," smaller life of his sister and begins to define his life as greater by its distinctiveness from hers. The sister-narrator implies that society teaches boys that their ability or desire to dominate girls is innate and separates them as a superior class, thus creating a false dichotomy: "A Like unlike, a Self that self restrains" (2:10). Eliot probably borrowed the expression "Like unlike"[34] from Thomas Carlyle whose narrator in *Sartor Resartus* uses the phrasing to compare the romantic union between

---

[34]   This expression appears in book two, chapter five ("Romance") of *Sartor Resartus*. The narrator-editor recounts the story of Teufelsdröckh, a German professor, who at this point in the narrative is a lost and heart-broken wanderer, looking to discover the meaning of love and life:

> "If in youth," writes he once, "the Universe is majestically unveiling, and everywhere Heaven revealing itself on Earth, nowhere to the Young Man does this Heaven on Earth so immediately reveal itself as in the Young Maiden. Strangely enough, in this strange life of ours, it has been so appointed. On the whole, as I have often said, a Person (Person-lichkeit) is ever holy to us; a certain orthodox Anthropomorphism connects my Me with all Thees in bonds of Love: but it is in this approximation of the *Like and Unlike*, that such heavenly attraction, as between Negative and Positive, first burns-out into a flame. Is the pitifullest mortal Person, think you, indifferent to us? Is it not rather our heartfelt wish to be made one with him; to unite him to us, by gratitude, by admiration, even by fear; or failing all these, unite ourselves to him? But how much more, in this case of the *Like-Unlike*! Here is conceded us the higher mystic possibility of such a union, the highest in our Earth; thus, in the conducting medium of Fantasy, flames-forth that fire-development of the universal Spiritual Electricity, which, as unfolded between man and woman, we first emphatically de-nominate LOVE." (93, emphasis added)

woman and man with the God-human connection. Such a disparate connection, the narrator argues, attests to the holiness of human love and makes humanity complete (93). Eliot may have adopted Carlyle's phrase, "Like-Unlike," to state the case that the brother and sister, though of different sexes, share a blood connection and an innate capacity to love one another. The "Self that self restrains" refers to the brother's behaving according to society's rules of decorum and also to his attempts to restrain his sister, whom he should consider a part of himself but does not because of his superior attitude. The brother's separating himself from the sister, because of a false belief in his own superior nature, results in a catastrophic and unnecessary chasm. In the lines that follow, the sister-narrator remarks ironically that her brother's "years with others must the sweeter be / For those brief days he spent in loving me" to point out that the brother must depend on the childhood love he shared with her to love a woman as an erotic partner later in life (*CSP* 2:10). This love, based on subjection, will not really be sweeter for others or for himself since he has learned a false notion of love. The siblings' once close relationship (that was earlier described in romantic terms) will divide unnaturally due to society's destructive indoctrination. Just as Carlyle's narrator promises to tell a story that will benefit his British readers (7–8), Eliot's narrator also repeatedly provides moral commentary for her British audience.

In sonnet ten, the sister-narrator confirms her decision to pursue truth in love and art by showing that she made every effort to conform to societal expectations but that such efforts were impossible. She explains that as a child, she identified with, worshipped, and lovingly followed her brother. She "knelt with her brother at marbles" and "marked his fling" and "watched him winding close the spiral string / That looped the orbits of the humming top" (*CSP* 2:10). These moments of submissive interaction in which she watched her brother and assisted his play were happy, though she was the subordinate and passive player. For love of her brother, she tried to suppress her day-dreaming escapist tendencies, which she knew would not always end luckily as in the fish-catching incident, and submit to the more realistic and fixed set of traditional gender roles:

> Grasped by such fellowship my vagrant thought
> Ceased with dream-fruit dream-wishes to fulfil;
> My aëry-picturing fantasy was taught
> Subjection to the harder, truer skill
> That seeks with deeds to grave a thought-tracked line,
> And by "What is," "What will be" to define. (2:11)

Her use of the word "grasped" indicates the forced nature of the sibling relationship. She had to do what was expected of her in order to receive love, and doing so meant forcing herself to subdue her natural tendency to imagine other worlds. But clues in the passage indicate the impossibility of subduing her will and thus winning her brother's love. The final three lines of this sonnet present two alternate yet agreeable readings. First, the "harder, truer skill" (2:11) that her "vagrant thought" (imagination) was subjected to can refer to the brother's skill of mastering. In this case, "harder" means rigid, as in the "hard" and "year-pressed" mind of the brother (2:8), and "truer" is used to mean legitimate and correct. The sister uses "truer" in this sense ironically to state that though society accepts the brother's skill of mastering as rightful and in accordance with the rules, the narrator does not. This skill for the brother "seeks with deeds to grave a thought-tracked line, / And by 'What is,' 'What will be' to define (2:11). According to the *OED*, "line" can refer to "course of action, procedure, life, thought, or conduct." Thus, the brother creates a "thought-tracked" (calculated, measured) line (course of life, way of thinking) with his "deeds" (actions, conduct), and he defines "What will be" (the future) by "What is" (the present). In other words, the brother measures life by one's actions and believes that one's present actions determine their future worth (and reputation). Or, he sees the future way of the world as conforming to the present way of the world as he understands it. He will, therefore, judge his sister's non-compliance to gender-normative behavior and pursuit of truth outside the bounds of propriety as incorrect and unforgivable in the short and long term. The second way to understand these final lines is to read the "harder, truer skill" as the sister's skill of obedience (in which case the word "harder" means difficult and the word "truer" is again used ironically) to the brother's domination and the suppression of her imagination. This skill aims to do the impossible; it "seeks with deeds to grave a thought-tracked line, / And by 'What is,' 'What will be' to define" (2:11). In this case, "line" refers to poetry, and the sister is saying that it is impossible to "grave" (engrave or write) a "thought-tracked" (imaginative yet measured) line of poetry with "deeds" instead of words. And it is equally impossible for her to define "What will be" (the future) by "What is" (the present) through her conduct. The sister realizes the incompatibility of exploring truth through imagination and falling into line with a set of gendered expectations. She also sees that seeking love based on a code of conduct is futile. In order to develop into the artist she will become, the sister must set her own limits for her life and writing and understand that following a false path is not only destructive but also impossible. The only way the sister-poet can define "What will be" by "What is" is through words, not deeds. The sister can write poetry that foresees the future by describing a "childhood-world" in which she discovers her poetic capacity by freeing herself from the stressful restrictions set by others. Eliot's comment in this passage is likely autobiographical. Isaac's rejection of her throughout the years she lived with Lewes, and his reuniting with her briefly only after her lawful marriage to Walter Cross two years after Lewes's death and near the end of her life, demonstrates his recalcitrant mindset and willingness to forgo a lifetime of loving relations with his sister over an issue of conduct. Eliot's pursuing a life path that did not align with Isaac's caused her pain but afforded her the opportunity to thrive as a writer. Lewes affirmed Eliot's personhood by loving her without condition, and he encouraged her art. For her, the loss was worth the gain.

Sonnet eleven concludes predictably with the siblings' separation. The sister states that school (or, learning the lessons described in the earlier sonnets) parted them and thereafter they

never found again
That childish world where our two spirits mingled
Like scents from varying roses that remain
One sweetness, nor can evermore be singled. (2:11)

Again, the narrator describes the former relationship in romantic terms, likening their inseparability to one combined scent from two roses. She explains that the "twin habit of that early time / Lingered for long about the heart and tongue" (2:11). The "twin habit" that allowed them to be close as youths—his dominance and her submission—provided her many moments on which to ponder, discuss, and write. These lessons learned in youth now provide material for her poetry writing: the "dear accent" of the "one happy clime" to "our utterance clung" (2:11). The reader can only imagine what the brother has to say about the early lessons he learned. The sister, on the other hand, has a voice. In writing the poem, she calls the reader to listen to her story and to sympathize with her view that one must create one's own boundaries in life and not reject or judge based on differences. The experiences of her youth impressed the sister-poet with "its dear accents" (marks), and she recreates those "accents" with the rhythm of her poetry. She draws attention to her ability to stress meaning with meter by altering the poem's predominantly iambic pentameter to trochaic pentameter:

Yet the twin habit of that early time
Lingered for long about the heart and tongue:
We had been natives of one happy clime
And its dear accent to our utterance clung. (2:11)

By altering the meter at the moment of discussing "accent" and "utterance," she shows the control she has over her poetry. Her careful self-confinement, demonstrated by the skillful use of and deviation from iambic pentameter, reveals an ability to express feelings and move others to feel with her in a controlled setting. After self-confidently asserting control over her own world, she concludes, inevitably, with a divorce: "Till the dire years whose awful name is Change / Had grasped our souls still yearning in divorce" (2:11).[35]

The narrator once again uses the word "grasped" to indicate the wrenching nature of the "divorce." No longer "grasped" by the fellowship of her brother, the sister was freer to explore new worlds, truth, love, and art independently of the brother's boundaries. Her use of passive voice emphasizes the inevitability of the severance of the relationship. Dreadful years "shaped them [their souls]

---

[35] Awful "Change" also makes an appearance in "The Legend of Jubal" when Jubal returns to his land of origin after a long journey. Hoping to find familiarity and reconnect with his community and impart the wisdom gained from his journey, Jubal instead meets "dread Change" (1:59). For Eliot, change is often painful, but she realizes that with it can come greater knowledge and clarity of vision. She favors gradual change rather than abrupt, jarring change for society, and her many references to the past and memory in her poetry reveal her wistfulness for lost innocence and simplicity.

in two forms that range / Two elements which sever their life's course" (2:11). Simply read, this passage refers to two people who are shaped differently and go their separate ways. This reading implies that "forms" (behavior according to the rules of decorum) played a role in their separation. An alternate reading involves a literary image. According to the *OED*, "form," "range," and "element" all have meanings that relate to printing. "Form" refers to "a body of type, secured in a chase, for printing at one impression;" and "range" means "to make straight or level; to make (type) lie flush at the ends of successive lines, to align;" and "element" signifies "the letters of the alphabet. Hence, the rudiments of learning, the 'A, B, C'; also, the first principles of an art or science." The image is that of two texts embodying contrasting sets of learning that are side-by-side and completely separate. The author originally prepared the texts for a singular function, but their incompatible principles "sever their life's course" (2:11). The siblings no longer share a "course" in life, and as a result they do not share discourse. Both find their own paths in life based on their own understanding of truth. Such separation is bitter-sweet for the narrator, who concludes, "But were another childhood-world my share, / I would be born a little sister there." Margaret Reynolds explains that these lines reveal a "subversive side" of the sequence. She quotes the final two lines of the poem and asks: "Does it mean that she would actively like to play the role of the little sister? Or does it mean that, unfortunately, she will inevitably be treated as the little sister because that is indeed 'the woman's lot'?" (306). Reynolds is right in suggesting that Eliot is questioning the lot of the little sister because she is a girl. Eliot is also saying, however, that she does not regret her "childhood-world" because it taught her how to define her own life by seeking truth independently. Eliot chose a life that others, including Isaac, considered unnatural when she united with Lewes. As a result, she and her brother divorced. In the poem, she depicts a sibling relationship in which codes of conduct determine love as unnatural and lacking in sympathy. She learns to translate past female obedience to present poetic obedience, and she learns the value of boundaries and discipline, but not of those set by others. As an adult poet, she "engraves" the past with clarity, authority, and control, within the confines of the metered sonnet form and within the confines of a marriage that she recognizes as more legitimate than many legal marriages, and she produces a "thought-tracked line" that will guide future readers who are open to its direction toward sympathetic relations.

Marriage in "How Lisa Loved the King"

Whereas "Brother and Sister" deals with a sibling relationship, "How Lisa Loved the King" (1869) concerns a marriage relationship. The topic of marriage especially interested Eliot due to her personal circumstances. She lived with Lewes from 1854 until his death in 1878 and considered their partnership as a marriage. Lewes, however, was still legally married to Agnes Jervis and could or would not divorce.[36] Divorce was expensive and difficult to obtain prior to the Matrimonial Causes Act of 1857, and though Eliot suffered societal scorn during the early years of their union, she did not overtly express her views on marriage and divorce.[37] However, she did communicate her opinions indirectly—early in her career through anonymous reviews and later in her career through poetry.

Dayton Haskin explains that Eliot anonymously conveyed progressive views on divorce in her two reviews of Thomas Keightley's book, *An Account of the Life, Opinions, and Writings of John Milton: With an Introduction to "Paradise Lost."* The first review, published in *The Leader*, showed support for Milton's stance on divorce, drawing connections to England's parliamentary debates on marriage in the mid-1850s (209). In the review, Eliot also praised Caroline Norton's public account of her husband's abuse and her stance against the injustice of married women's lack of legal status (211–12).[38] Thus, Eliot affirmed the progressive views of others without revealing her own self-interest in the legal matter of divorce. Haskin states: "Urging a parallel between the action taken by Milton and that taken by a contemporary who wrote as one woman speaking for others, she endorsed a kind of courage that the conventions of anonymous reviewing did not permit her to

---

[36] Most critics believe that Lewes could not divorce Agnes due to his having legitimized the first of four children she had by Thornton Hunt. Haight explains: "Today a divorce would have set him free; but then divorce was out of the question. Even if he had had the hundreds of pounds it required for the cumbersome legal process, Lewes, having once condoned her adultery, was forever precluded from appealing for divorce" (132). Nancy Henry refutes what she calls the "condonation theory" that many critics have embraced. She asserts there is no legal or biographical evidence to prove that Lewes's condoning Agnes's adultery resulted in forfeiture of his right to divorce (*The Life* 99). Henry offers a convincing explanation for Lewes's not seeking a divorce:

> [Lewes] did not condone adultery that occurred after he left their home, and he had the legal right to pursue a divorce suit or legal separation, but the fact that he was living with another woman would have put him at an insurmountable disadvantage in a trial. In short, to say that condonation precluded him from appealing for divorce is to judge a trial that never occurred. We can be certain that no one (Lewes, Agnes, Hunt, Eliot) wished to be dragged through the courts and into the public limelight, exposing sensitive and ambiguous questions of sexual conduct and paternity that would be embarrassing to all parties and harmful to the many children now involved, not to mention the new author George Eliot, who came into being the same year as the Matrimonial Causes Act of 1857 (101).

[37] Andrew Dowling explains that the Matrimonial Causes Act of 1857 and the Divorce Court resulted not only in an increased number of divorces but also in public interest in marital conflict: "The Divorce Court worked to transform marital behavior into a public issue ... [The] general literary trend toward the subject of matrimonial misery can be best understood ... as a response to this wider social desire to know in greater detail the intricacies of a previously invisible topic" (329).

[38] Norton detailed her experience in *English Laws for Women of the Nineteenth-Century* (1854) and *Letter to the Queen on Lord Cranworth's Marriage and Divorce Bill* (1855).

exercise herself" (213). The second review, published in *The Westminster Review*, showed support for Milton's role as a father, implicitly likening Milton to Lewes, and suggesting that men and women alike suffered from the unjust marriage laws. Haskin states: "The climactic work of the review was to present Milton not as the author of *Paradise Lost*, but as a stand-in for Lewes, whose personal situation the reviewer was not about the publicize" (214).

As an anonymous reviewer early in her career, Eliot condoned divorce without drawing public attention to her own situation. Later, she expressed progressive views without censure through poetry. By the time Eliot turned to poetry, she was an established author approaching the age of 50. Her fame had overshadowed the scandal of her lifestyle, and she was able to embrace a new image. As a poetess with vatic authority, Eliot did not have to protect her reputation by writing anonymously, but she was subtle in her expression of unconventional beliefs. She voiced subversive messages while seeming to promote traditional values.[39]

Her poem, "How Lisa Loved the King," provides a vivid illustration of this.[40] Yet the poem has received almost no critical attention despite its unusual treatment of topics of interest in the nineteenth century and today: marriage and gender inequality.[41] Written in the same year that she began *Middlemarch* (1869), "How Lisa Loved the King" addresses the theme of marriage in a much different way than the novel does.[42] In *Middlemarch*, Eliot portrays marriage realistically,

---

[39]   Meg Tasker explains that sexual matters were more easily addressed in poetry than in novels, both for men and women authors: "Not only may sexual desire or activity be described indirectly, through metaphor and allusion (this, after all, is possible in prose), but they could be more freely employed *as* metaphor in poetry" (36).

[40]   Eliot finished writing "How Lisa Loved the King" on Valentine's Day in 1869, a day on which she and Lewes held a salon attended by Robert Browning and others interested in poetry. McCormack explains that everyone involved regarded the day as a "triumphant afternoon in the service of poetry and a supreme experience in London literary salonizing" (*George Eliot in Society* 62).

[41]   I have not found an analysis of the poem. Margaret Reynolds briefly mentions the poem in her entry on Eliot's poetry in the *Oxford Reader's Companion* (305), Andrew Thompson contextualizes the poem in *George Eliot and Italy: Literary, Cultural, and Political Influences from Dante to the Risorgimento* (120–23), and van den Broek provides useful background including Eliot's interest in Boccaccio and publication information (*CSP* 1:137–41).

[42]   Eliot wrote to John Blackwood upon completion of the poem: "I am glad that you liked Lisa's story which fascinated me. When I began to write it, it was simply with the longing to fulfill an old intention, and with no distinct thought of printing" (*Letters* 5:16). Andrew Thompson argues that Eliot wrote "How Lisa Loved the King" during the Italian unification and that the poem hints at Eliot's political views on Italy at the time: "The parallels between Eliot's poem and the Italian situation in the late 1860s would not have been lost on her readers. Support for the cause of Italian unification was never stronger than in the 1860s" (123). He also notes that though she typically wrote anonymously, Eliot requested her name appear on the publication. He states: "At a time when Swinburne was writing openly 'political' poetry in support of Italian unity and against Napoleon III, Eliot

but she does not overtly criticize the institution. The novel concludes with the happy union of Dorothea who forfeits her fortune and status to marry Will. "How Lisa Loved the King," on the other hand, appears to tell the story of a girl who loves, obeys, and marries. However, the tale of simple, feminine piety actually challenges nineteenth-century marriage practices and exposes the problem of women's limited choices in society.

Adapted from the seventh tale of the tenth day of Giovanni Boccaccio's *The Decameron* (1353),[43] the poem relates the story of a common girl who falls in love with a king, secretly pines for him until she nearly dies, expresses her love, and then earns his attention in the form of his arranging her marriage to another man, Perdicone.[44] Eliot's choice of a tale that reverses the gender expectations of the medieval convention of courtly love is significant.[45] In Boccaccio's poem

---

preferred to allow her own anti-Napoleonic sentiments to emerge in more muted tones from within the original story by Boccaccio" (123). Eliot's including political issues in "muted tones" demonstrates her strategy of subtly inserting controversial opinions in her poetry. Her subtle approach was suitable for a poetess eager to comment without inviting negative attention.

[43] Boccaccio's *The Decameron* includes 100 stories (novellas) told over ten days by ten young people. Eliot may have gotten the idea to rewrite medieval source material from William Morris, whose best-selling poem *The Earthly Paradise* (1868–1870) included stories ("The Lovers of Gudrun") that retold thirteenth-century Icelandic literature (the *Laxdaela saga*). Eliot and Lewes were reading *The Earthly Paradise* when she wrote "How Lisa Loved the King" (*Letters* 4:450). She admired the work and corresponded with Morris, thanking him for sending a presentation copy with a personal inscription in 1870 (8:472). She also met him on at least one occasion (9:219). Statesman John Bright claims to have discussed poetry, "especially of Wm Morris of *The Earthly Paradise*," with Eliot in 1877 (Collins, *Interviews* 135). Modeled on *The Decameron* and Chaucer's *Canterbury Tales*, the epic-length *The Earthly Paradise* includes 24 framed stories and features a group of medieval pilgrims. These devotees seek an earthly paradise where they can attain immortal life, but experience a sense of displacement and disillusionment as they tell stories of love. In retelling Boccaccio's story, Eliot, like Morris, repurposes her tale to make her own comments on love and disillusionment. For a discussion of Morris's revision of the Laxdeala saga in "The Lovers of Gudrun," see Florence Boos's "Morris' Radical Revisions of the 'Laxdaela Saga'" and Linda Julian's "Laxdaela Saga and 'The Lovers of Gudrun': Morris' Poetic Vision."

[44] The name Perdicone relies on the Italian word "perdita" which means lost (*OED*). This might imply that Lisa's marriage to Perdicone will result in a loss of identity for Lisa.

[45] The concept of courtly love began in the twelfth century among the troubadours of southern France and then spread into surrounding countries. According to Barbara Tuchman, the stages of courtly love included: "worship through declaration of passionate devotion, virtuous rejection by the lady, renewed wooing with oaths of eternal fealty, moans of approaching death from unsatisfied desire, heroic deeds of valor which won the lady's heart by prowess, consummation of the secret love, followed by endless adventures and subterfuges to a tragic denouement" (67). The story of Lisa includes extramarital love, hardship of the lover, worship from afar, declaration of devotion, virtuous rejection, moans of approaching death, and the lovers' sublimation of love.

(and in Eliot's version), a *man* (King Pietro / Pedro) attracts the admiration of a *woman* (Liza / Lisa) at a holiday tournament in thirteenth-century Italy.[46] It is Lisa, not the man, who worships from afar, languishes, and declares her love. Lisa is the hero, and her virginity and obedience are her "heroic virtues" (*CSP* 1:146). Eliot magnifies the role-reversed courtly love context of Boccaccio's poem to emphasize the feminine themes of love and marriage. Furthermore, she adds epic elements not found in *The Decameron* to increase the ironic effect of a woman's ability to love greatly and marry obediently. Upon first reading, the poem appears to ennoble marriage, but a closer examination of Eliot's epic additions reveals a view of marriage as little more than a financial contract between men.

Eliot keeps Boccaccio's storyline intact, but she makes extensive changes to give her version an epic quality that repurposes the story. Eliot, like other nineteenth-century women poets, employed the ancient epic form to explore contemporary gender issues.[47] "How Lisa Loved the King" is not an epic poem, but it undeniably employs epic conventions.[48] The effect of these epic conventions is an ironic tone. Eliot's narrator mentions early in the tale that the festival tournament feels like an "epic song" that "greatly tells the pains that to great life belong" to hint that the tale will be epic-*like* (1:144). The description of the "mock terror" (1:144) and "warlike feigning" (1:160) of the tournament, moreover, reminds the reader of an

---

[46] Sicily "welcomed" Spanish King Pedro who freed Palermo from the "yoke / Of hated Frenchmen" (1:143). Lisa was one Italian subject "of no noble line" (1:144).

[47] Elisa Beshero-Bondar, Herbert Tucker, and Simon Dentith all discuss the significance of the epic form to women writers in the nineteenth century. In *Women, Epic, and Transition in British Romanticism*, Beshero-Bondar discusses women poets and the emphasis on femininity in epics of the early nineteenth century. Women writers of epics, she asserts, dealt with women's agency, cultural conflicts, and identity and used the epic form to criticize traditionally masculine patriotic virtues and promote women's interests as central to the well-being of the nation (5–6). Tucker in *Epic: Britain's Heroic Muse 1790-1910* and Dentith in *Epic and Empire in Nineteenth-Century Britain* discuss epic and gender negotiations in their broader studies of nineteenth-century epic, and both include Eliot in their studies. Tucker analyzes Eliot's *The Spanish Gypsy* as an epic work that explores the themes of identity and heredity (415–25), and Dentith discusses Eliot's reclaiming of the historic prestige of epic in *Middlemarch* and *Daniel Deronda* to translate an ancient masculine form for a contemporary, feminine purpose (99–104). These scholars all recognize the fact that women writers used the epic form, both successfully and unsuccessfully, to negotiate gender in contemporary life.

[48] More often discussed by critics, *The Spanish Gypsy* is recognized as an epic work. Both poems are set in medieval times—"How Lisa Loved the King" in thirteenth-century Italy and *The Spanish Gypsy* in fifteenth-century Spain—and both concern marriage, love, and sacrifice. However, *The Spanish Gypsy* carries a serious tone and ends tragically with death while "Lisa" maintains a playful tone and ends with a marriage. "Lisa" lacks the epic qualities of seriousness and length but contains formal epic conventions, such as an invocation of the muse, epithets, and epic similes. *The Spanish Gypsy*, on the other hand, does not have these formal epic conventions but deals with the epic themes of nationalism, heredity, and renunciation.

element of play in the story. The poem, like the tournament, is a great show that offsets a real message about marriage. As characters play courtly love roles and hold mock tournaments, they draw attention to the values of chivalry. Thus, Eliot playfully draws attention to old-fashioned habits and values related to love and marriage.

Unlike Boccaccio's story, Eliot's version incorporates epic language, including epithets such as "Young Lisa" (1:146), "gentle Lisa" (1:144), "Sweet Lisa" (1:147), "fair Lisa" (1:162); formulaic Homeric phrases such as "wingèd passion" and "wingèd speech" (1:147); and frequent use of the word "hero" (and variant forms "heroes," "heroic") to describe Lisa's lofty aspirations for love (1:146). Eliot thus takes advantage of the courtly love role reversal scenario presented by Boccaccio to call into question the identity of the hero. Lisa describes the king as a hero when she expresses her hope to love "some hero noble, beauteous, great, / Who would live stories worthy to narrate," but it is Lisa who is described in heroic language and whose story is narrated (1:146).[49] Eliot also alters Boccaccio's prose tale by masterfully writing heroic couplets with alexandrines to conclude (and sometimes interrupt) verse paragraphs.[50] Additionally, she invokes a muse, alludes to a faraway setting, and adds epic similes throughout.[51] The poem begins with an invocation to a muse, Dante, which signals to the reader that the muse inspires the poet's voice to speak for the nation. Furthermore, she includes in the introduction an extended simile that compares medieval Europe to a peaceful and thriving garden:

---

[49] Lisa and the king both serve to represent the traditional values and practices of marriage. Lisa is the embodiment of female obedience, and the king is the embodiment of male mastery.

[50] Eliot inserts three interrupting alexandrines in which she highlights Lisa's desire to be thought of by the king (1:150), the king's reflection on Lisa's passionate expression of love (1:158), and the king's claim of one kiss by which to remember her (1:160). These insertions punctuate the romantic aspirations and effects of Lisa's love. The irregular meter highlights a passion that is at once irregular, improper, and efficacious.

[51] Epic similes are abundant. For example, Lisa compares herself to a pigeon or spot on the wall:

She watched all day that she might see him pass
With knights and ladies; but she said, "Alas!
Though he should see me, it were all as one
He saw a pigeon sitting on the stone
Of wall or balcony: some colored spot
His eye just sees, his mind regardeth not ..." (1:148)

Also, Lisa compares Minuccio to a trusted priest in another extended simile:
Finished the song, she prayed to be alone
With kind Minuccio; for her faith had grown
To trust him as if missioned like a priest
With some high grace, that, when his singing ceased,
Still made him wiser, more magnanimous,
Than common men who had no genius. (1:151)

> Six hundred years ago, in Dante's time,
> Before his cheek was furrowed by deep rhyme;
> When Europe, fed afresh from Eastern story,
> Was like a garden tangled with the glory
> Of flowers hand-planted and of flowers air-sown,
> Climbing and trailing, budding and full-blown,
> Where purple bells are tossed amid pink stars,
> And springing blades, green troops in innocent wars,
> Crowd every shady spot of teeming earth,
> Making invisible motion visible birth— (1:143)

The narrator invokes Dante for inspiration, and then offers thanks to another muse, Boccaccio, at the end of the story:

> Reader, this story pleased me long ago
> In the bright pages of Boccaccio,
> And where the author of a good we know,
> Let us not fail to pay the grateful thanks we owe. (1:163)

These bookend invocations serve to place Eliot in a tradition of great and timeless writers. By this means, and by suggesting that authors "of a good" merit gratitude, she implicitly asks her reader to thank her for her poem. This final joke serves as a reminder of the mocking purpose and playful tone of the poem.

The epic qualities of the introduction prepare the reader for a narrative about a great hero (Lisa) performing great deeds (loving greatly and marrying obediently) for the sake of ennobling the nation of Italy. Eliot also adds an epic element to the courtly love plot by magnifying the theme of love.[52] By elevating romantic love, a common theme of the poetess, Eliot gives the female hero the appearance of agency, thus preparing the reader to feel disappointed when she ends up in a loveless arranged marriage. The courtly love role reversal (a woman pining for a man) allows Lisa the appearance of control as the pursuer of love, and Eliot's heroine, unlike Boccaccio's, seeks the lofty goal of immortalizing herself with her great love.[53] In Eliot's version, she not only seeks the king's attention but also aims to make a permanent impression. Boccaccio offers no clue as to her intent for expressing her love to the king: "a thought came into [Lisa's] head, to make her love known to the king before her death" (500). But in Eliot's story:

---

[52]   Eliot's title, "How Lisa Loved the King," indicates at the outset that love will play a major role in the story.

[53]   Another poetess, Barrett Browning, employs such gender role reversal in her sonnet sequence, *Sonnets from the Portuguese*. In these sonnets, a woman declares her love for a man. Edith Simcox reports in her diary that Eliot discussed *Sonnets from the Portuguese* with her in 1878, but there is no direct evidence that Eliot had this series in mind when writing "How Lisa Loved the King" (*Letters* 9:236).

night and day, her unstilled thought
Wandering all o'er its little world, had sought
How she could reach, by some soft pleading touch,
King Pedro's soul, that she who loved so much
Dying, might have a place within his mind—
A little grave which he would sometimes find
And plant some flower on it—some thought, some
memory kind. (*CSP* 1:150)

Seeking immortality through love, Eliot's Lisa asks singer Minuccio to help express her love to the king:

She told him how that secret glorious harm
Of loftiest loving had befallen her;
That death, her only hope, most bitter were,
If when she died her love must perish too
As songs unsung and thoughts unspoken do,
Which else might live within another breast.
She said, "Minuccio, the grave were rest,
If I were sure, that lying cold and lone,
My love, my best of life, had safely flown
And nestled in the bosom of the king;
See, 'tis a small weak bird, with unfledged wing.
But you will carry it for me secretly,
And bear it to the king, then come to me
And tell me it is safe, and I shall go
Content, knowing that he I love my love doth know." (1:151–2)

Lisa's "loftiest" love, her "best of life," can afford peace in death if she can be assured that the knowledge of it resides in the king's breast. In contrast to Boccaccio's tale in which love comes to Lisa who languishes and prepares to die, in Eliot's poem, Lisa plays an active role in loving.[54] However, she needs Minuccio (a male singer) and Mico (a male poet) to express her love to the king. Men mediate Lisa's voice. As a woman, she can love, as a woman should, but she requires men to voice her love. Thus, Eliot sends the message that society elevates women for their natural and great ability to love and nurture while subjecting such love to male management.

Eliot also emphasizes Lisa's smallness to increase the epic value of her love. By contrasting Lisa's great and lofty love with her person, which the poem depicts as "small," "weak," "tiny," "miniature," "lowly," "frail" (1:146–9, 151, 154, 156, 161), Eliot creates in Lisa a love that takes on a life of its own and surpasses human capacity and understanding:

---

[54] Tuchman explains the significance of courtly love and the medieval concept of chivalry: "As formulated by chivalry, romance was pictured as extra-marital because love was considered irrelevant to marriage, was indeed discouraged in order not to get in the way of dynastic arrangements" (66). Lisa loves a married man, but this impropriety is never mentioned. Her class rank alone is what makes consummation inconceivable.

How Lisa's lowly love had highest reach
Of wingèd passion, whereto wingèd speech
Would be scorched remnants left by mounting flame.
Though, had she such lame message, were it blame
To tell what greatness dwelt in her, what rank
She held in loving? (1:147)

Minuccio sings to the king a song that voices Lisa's aspiring love:

I am a lowly maid,
No more than any little knot of thyme
That he with careless foot may often tread;
Yet lowest fragrance oft will mount sublime
And cleave to things most high and hallowèd,
As doth the fragrance of my life's springtime,
My lowly love, that soaring seeks to climb
Within his thought, and make a gentle bliss,
More blissful than if mine, in being his:
So shall I live in him and rest in Death. (1:154)

Eliot recreates the ordinary occurrence of falling in love into an extraordinary activity. Though born "of no noble line," Lisa loves like an epic hero and strives for immortality by loving superhumanly (1:144). Yet ironically, her epic ability to love does not result in her receiving love. Her love for one man results in marriage to another.

In addition to magnifying love to epic proportions, Eliot also elevates Lisa's marriage to an event with national importance. Marriage in Boccaccio's version does not take on great national importance. It is significant primarily for Lisa's family, who benefits from the king's marriage arrangement and dowry, and secondarily for the king, who secures his subjects' affection through his noble actions—marrying Lisa off and styling himself as her knight. However, these actions are among others that earn the king's favored status: "Such actions as these gain the hearts of the people, serve as an example for others to imitate, and secure in the end an everlasting fame" (504). Marriage in *The Decameron* provides a happy ending to a courtly love tale. Eliot imbues greater meaning to marriage in her version by changing the story so that the king represents the entire nation in his interaction with Lisa and makes it his great work, and one of national importance, to settle her marriage. Whereas Boccaccio's king addresses Lisa as a subject and speaks for himself alone, using the first person singular "I," "me," and "my" when addressing his subject Lisa, Eliot's king addresses Lisa as a collective entity, using the first person plural "we," "us," and "our." At times Eliot's king uses first person plural as an expression of the royal "we" to speak not as his own proper person but on behalf of the nation, as a divine representative of his people. For example, he uses the royal "we" when he addresses Lisa with his queen and courtiers in company: "Excellent maiden, that rich gift of love / Your heart hath made *us*, hath a worth above / All royal treasures" (*CSP* 1:160, emphasis added). At other times, however, he uses first person plural to describe himself and other people. For instance, he says: "'Twere dole to *all of us*, / The world should lose a maid so beauteous" (1:157, emphasis added).

In the many instances in which Eliot's king refers to himself in the first person plural in speaking to Lisa, whether or not he uses the royal "we," he speaks as representative of the people. Unlike Boccaccio's king who asks Lisa to get well for his sake—"Fair maid, how comes it that you are ill? You are young, and should be a delight to others; then why will you suffer this illness to prey upon you? For *my* sake be comforted and get well" (502, emphasis added)—Eliot's king charges Lisa to get well for the sake of himself, the queen, and the entire nation:

> Lady, what is this?
> You, whose sweet youth should others' solace be,
> Pierce *all our* hearts, languishing piteously.
> *We* pray you, for the love of *us*, be cheered,
> Nor be too reckless of that life, endeared
> To *us* who know your passing worthiness,
> And count your blooming life as part of *our* life's bliss. (*CSP* 1:157, emphasis added)

In Eliot's version, the king asks Lisa to get well and be cheerful for the betterment of society, suggesting that her youthfulness, beauty, and cheerful disposition contribute to the well-being of all the nation's people. He wants her to strive to be a delight to society rather than waste away unnaturally, for the "rich gift of love / Your heart hath made *us*, hath a worth above / All royal treasures" (1:160, emphasis added). The king interprets Lisa's love as a gift not only for him but for all the community.

The king also uses the royal "we" when he vows to be Lisa's cavalier and carry a token from her when he fights in battle or at festival tournament:

> *We* while *we* live your cavalier will be;
> Nor will *we* ever arm ourselves for fight,
> Whether for struggle dire, or brief delight
> Of warlike feigning, but *we* first will take
> The colors you ordain, and for your sake
> Charge the more bravely where your emblem is:
> Nor will *we* claim from you an added bliss
> To *our* sweet thoughts of you save one sole kiss.
> But there still rests the outward honor meet
> To mark your worthiness; and *we* entreat
> That you will turn your ear to proffered vows
> Of one who loves you, and would be your spouse. (1:160, emphasis added)

The king's offer to be Lisa's knight carries significance for the entire nation. He will garner courage to fight bravely from a visible reminder of her obedient love (her emblem). Both the king and Lisa, then, seek immortality: Lisa through loving the king, and the king through deeds in battle and increased territory. And they both succeed. The loyal subjects who benefit from the king's battle successes will always tell the story of how Lisa loved the king. The king uses "we" to urge Lisa to marry for the sake of the nation:

> *We* must not wrong yourself and Sicily
> By letting all your blooming years pass by
> Unmated: you will give the world its due
> From beauteous maiden and become a matron true. (1:161, emphasis added)

In other words, Lisa's remaining single while getting old would be a blight to all Sicily.

But her love does not result in a happy love relationship. She accepts as her duty the king's command to marry another man, Perdicone, saying:

> But, as you better know than I, the heart
> In choosing chooseth not its own desert,
> But that great merit which attracteth it;
> 'Tis law, I struggled, but I must submit,
> And having seen a worth all worth above,
> I loved you, love you, and shall always love.
> But that doth mean, my will is ever yours,
> Not only when your will my good insures
> But if it wrought me what the world calls harm. (1:161)

Lisa's love for the king translates to love of obedience: "she loving well / The lot that from obedience befell" (1:162). The king takes on a priestly role, uniting the two and proclaiming their union sacred and beneficial to all: "Now *we* claim *our* share / From your sweet love, a share which is not small: / For in the sacrament one crumb is all" (1:162, emphasis added). The community, too, participates in the divine sacrament of Lisa's marriage as if they partake in the sacrament of Christ's body. Lisa's marriage thus takes on sacred meaning for all of Sicily. The king, speaking in first person plural to represent the entire nation, vows to carry the married Lisa's emblem when he goes into battle and win territory in the name of feminine obedience. Lisa's obedient marriage ennobles the king and sanctifies the nation but offers little to Lisa herself. She will become the property of a husband she does not love. By exalting Lisa's arranged marriage to an event of national, sacred importance, Eliot points out the fact that society at once elevates women as the reproductive center of society while offering legal non-existence by virtue of their sex. Women carry on tradition by getting married and raising children who will continue to further male-dominant notions of marriage and gender status. By valuing women who perpetuate traditional gender ideals and marginalizing women who do not, men continue the cycle that gives them societal power.

Eliot further criticizes the male-controlled institution of marriage by presenting Lisa's marriage as a business exchange between men.[55] In *The Decameron*, the

---

[55] Compare Eve Sedgwick's model of marriage in which women serve as objects of exchange between homosocial men in *Between Men: English Literature and Male Homosocial Desire*.

king chooses Perdicone as Lisa's husband and, along with the queen, gives them "many jewels and other valuable presents" as well as two estates as a dowry (503). In Eliot's version, Bernardo, Lisa's father, seeks to elevate his social status by marrying Lisa to Perdicone, a man of higher birth and lesser fortune than himself. The narrator says of Bernardo:

> He loved his riches well,
> But loved them chiefly for his Lisa's sake,
> Whom with a father's care he sought to make
> The bride of some true honorable man,—
> Of Perdicone (so the rumor ran),
> Whose birth was higher than his fortunes were,
> For still your trader likes a mixture fair
> Of blood that hurries to some higher strain
> Than reckoning money's loss and money's gain.
> And of such mixture good may surely come:
> Lord's scions so may learn to cast a sum,
> A trader's grandson bear a well-set head,
> And have less conscious manners, better bred;
> Nor, when he tries to be polite, be rude instead. (*CSP* 1:144–5)

By adding this passage, Eliot addresses the problem of the commodification of women and the treatment of marriage as an exchange of property. Lisa's marriage results in her family's increased rank in society and Perdicone's increased financial status, but it is not based on love—the quality that the narrator has gone to great pains to explain most characterizes Lisa. Lisa seems to be greatly influential in matters of love but has no influence over her own love life. Once her father's property, Lisa becomes Perdicone's property after marriage, and marriage merely transfers her from one owner to another, no matter how much the king purports to honor her. The limited options for living independently forced many nineteenth-century women into marriages that were little more than financial contracts in which the husband, as owner of the wife, had the power to treat her as lovingly or as cruelly as he chose. By elevating the marriage of a common girl to an event of national significance, while adding an element of commodification, Eliot condemns the patriarchal practice of using women as vehicles for elevating status and restoring dwindling fortunes and implies a potential equation between Victorian and medieval arranged marriage.

Finally, Eliot expands upon the king's war exploits while elevating the theme of marriage to further her agenda. While Lisa performs romantic tasks worthy of a female hero, King Pedro performs manly heroic feats. Boccaccio relates that his tale takes place "at the time when the French were driven out of Sicily" and concerns King Pietro, who became "lord of the whole island" of Palermo (499).[56] Eliot elaborates the background information to amplify the elements of war and revenge:

---

[56]   In "Lisa," Eliot invoked a faraway time and place by choosing to recreate a story set in medieval Palermo. The poetess often reached to distant places and times to escape present-day cultural restrictions.

> Six hundred years ago, Palermo town
> Kept holiday. A deed of great renown,
> A high revenge, had freed it from the yoke
> Of hated Frenchmen, and from Calpe's rock
> To where the Bosporus caught the earlier sun,
> 'Twas told that Pedro, King of Aragon,
> Was welcomed master of all Sicily,
> A royal knight, supreme as kings should be
> In strength and gentleness that make high chivalry. (*CSP* 1:143)

The themes of marriage and war intersect at the end of Boccaccio's story, which concludes with the marriage of Lisa and Perdicone, the king's promise always to be Lisa's knight, and the king's fame for chivalry:

> So the marriage was solemnized, to the great joy of her husband, father, and mother; and many report that the king was very constant to his promise, for that, as long as he lived, he always styled himself her knight, and never carried any other token of favour upon his arms but what she sent him.—Such actions as these gain the hearts of the people, serve as an example for others to imitate, and secure in the end an everlasting fame. But there are few now-a-days that trouble their heads about that, the greater part of our princes being rather cruel tyrants. (504)

Boccaccio emphasizes the king's winning the favor of his people for his kind action and gentle chivalry, which contrasts with the usual tyrannical nature of kings. Eliot's conclusion at first resembles Boccaccio's in theme; she relates how the king pledges to "call himself fair Lisa's faithful knight; / And never wore in field or tournament / A scarf or emblem save by Lisa sent" (1:162). But then she adds a final note of war and revenge:

> Such deeds made subjects loyal in that land:
> They joyed that one so worthy to command,
> So chivalrous and gentle, had become
> The king of Sicily, and filled the room
> Of Frenchmen, who abused the Church's trust,
> Till, in a righteous vengeance on their lust,
> Messina rose, with God, and with the dagger's thrust. (1:162–3)

Eliot's bookend invocations to Dante and Boccaccio frame the story of King Pedro's vengeance against the hated, heretical Frenchmen. Accounts of the king's slaughterous revenge appear just after the first invocation and before the final one. These bloody reminders of the king's warlike exploits which led to territorial conquest likewise frame the story of Lisa's lofty love and the king's knightly behavior toward her. By juxtaposing masculine martial heroism and feminine heroic love, Eliot highlights the ironic intent of her epic additions. Lisa appears to have the power to influence a king and a nation, but in fact, she has no power at all. She performs the great deed of attracting the king's attention, but only with the help of two men, Minuccio and Mico. She appears to control history: the king will wear her emblem for the rest of his noble career to honor her great love, and subjects will remember her story when they see the king carry her emblem. Yet she has no control over her own marriage prospects. The concluding arranged marriage is deflating.

Though Lisa has no voice and no control, Eliot does. She exercises that control by immortalizing Lisa and her own message about marriage and women's lack of agency in matters of love in the poem. For Eliot, marriage represented a sacred union based on love between equals. Her relationship with Lewes was a true partnership, not a financial contract, and as such, in her view, more of a marriage than many that held legal status. Eliot suffered consequences for her choice to unite with Lewes. Her brother disowned her, and society branded her a fallen woman. A sensitive person by nature, she was deeply hurt by the rumors and societal alienation.[57] Telling Lisa's story allowed her to demonstrate the negative aspects of traditional marriage without directly announcing her own non-traditional views.

Conclusion

In "How Lisa Loved the King" and in "Brother and Sister," Eliot seemed to promote feminine obedience and traditional gender roles when she actually made subtle comments to the contrary. Her messages relating to gender matters in her poetry extended in purpose beyond fairness. She wanted a better society for women and for men, one that would allow women greater choices beyond marriage and domestic life and benefit all of society by bringing women's sensibility into the public sphere. Freeing women from rigid rules of decorum and allowing men and women greater access to communication with one another would promote greater understanding between the sexes. Likewise, she believed, equal education would create a more balanced society with the best minds of both sexes participating in civic life. By addressing issues of gender in her poetry, Eliot encouraged sympathetic relationships, greater respect for all, and thus a better society.

---

[57]   In a letter to her friend Charles Bray, she wrote emotionally:
   Of course many silly myths are already afloat about me, in addition to the truth, which of itself would be thought matter for scandal. I am quite unconcerned about them except as they may cause pain to my real friends. If you hear of anything that I have said, done, or written in relation to Mr. Lewes beyond the simple fact that I am attached to him and that I am living with him, do me the justice to believe that it is false. You and Mr. Chapman are the only persons to whom I have ever spoken of his private position and of my relation to him ... Pray pardon this long letter on a painful subject. I felt it a duty to write it ... I am quite prepared to accept the consequences of a step which I have deliberately taken and to accept them without irritation or bitterness. The most painful consequence will, I know, be loss of friends. If I do not write, therefore, understand that it is because I desire not to obtrude myself ... I am full of affection towards you all, and whatever you may think of me, shall always be ... Your true and grateful friend Marian Evans. (*Letters* 2:179)

Chapter 4
Mother to the Nation

Mothers ye, who help us all,
Quick at hand, if ill befall.
Holy Gabriel, lily-laden,
Bless the aged mother maiden
—George Eliot

George Eliot identified with a community of women poets who negotiated a sphere of domestic influence in Victorian England. As a young woman, Eliot cherished "our sweet Mrs. Hemans's language" (*Letters* 1:109) and found in her "a mothering voice and a sweetness of phrase and message which seemed to speak of the very nature of woman" (Leighton 16).[1] In 1857, she expressed deep admiration for the "feminine subtlety of perception," "feminine quickness of sensibility," and "feminine tenderness" of Elizabeth Barrett Browning's work ("Belles Lettres" 306). By addressing domestic themes and writing in a consciously feminine mode, Eliot identified with a larger community of women poets who had the power to comfort, console, and counsel; these poets relied on, and at times referred to, one another in their poetry. Though this community was highly influential in shaping Eliot's poetic persona and style, it was her interpersonal female community that informed the thoughts and values that her writing embodied. Throughout her life, female friends provided sympathy during times of loss and offered opportunities to exchange maternal affection in the absence of biological maternal relationships. This chapter examines how Eliot's experiences with female community and motherhood shaped her belief in sympathy's consoling power and edified her image as a spiritual mother to the nation. I will analyze *Armgart* and "Agatha" to show how she employed the themes of female community and motherhood to communicate the sacred value of sympathy in society.

George Eliot, Female Community, and Motherhood

Eliot's early relationships with women were emotionally intense and seemed to fulfill a need for maternal affection. Little is known about Eliot's mother as she is only mentioned twice in Eliot's surviving letters; however, most biographers agree that Christiana Evans was emotionally distant. Mrs. Evans's perpetual ill-

---

[1]   Eliot recommended and quoted Hemans's poetry to her friends Maria Lewis and Martha Jackson as a pious woman in her early twenties (*Letters* 1:72, 75, 109). Three decades later, she would draw on a feminine, spiritual sensibility like that of Hemans in her own poems.

health, household duties, and five children (three biological and two from Robert Evans's late first wife) prevented her from spending much time with her youngest daughter, who lived in boarding schools from ages five to seventeen.[2] In 1828, Mr. and Mrs. Evans sent Eliot to Mrs. Wallington's school in Nuneaton where she formed an intimate relationship based on religious affinity with Maria Lewis, the principal governess. Haight explains: "Miss Lewis gave the bright, eager little girl the sympathetic support and affection that she needed. Except from her father, she did not find it at home" (10). Eliot eagerly accepted the warmth of a caring mentor who provided the attention that she did not get from her mother. She quickly adopted Lewis's evangelical zeal and developed a pious and serious sensibility— one she would later have to reconcile with ambitious and creative instincts. Their relationship continued after Eliot left Nuneaton to attend the Franklins' school in Coventry (1832–1835) and throughout most of Eliot's years as her father's housekeeper after the death of her mother (1836–1842). In her many letters to Lewis, to whom she referred as Veronica (meaning "fidelity in friendship"),[3] Eliot shared feelings, frustrations, insecurities, and religious yearnings (*Letters* 1:68). Though Eliot developed close friendships with other women such as Martha Jackson, Lewis was the most important source of emotional support during the early years in which Eliot developed intellectually and creatively. The tone of Eliot's letters to Lewis changed over time to reflect an increasing awareness of her superior mind. Kathryn Hughes explains: "Her letters to Maria Lewis are didactic and pedagogic, anxious to display their superior knowledge. She lectures her former teacher on German pronunciation, recommends books, and generally acts like the older woman's spiritual and intellectual adviser" (32). Eliot's shifting into the role of spiritual advisor anticipated her shifting views on religion and ultimately her role as spiritual advisor to her readers. Her abandonment of Christianity in 1842 dissolved the religious bond that held together her ten-year relationship with Maria Lewis, and they eventually grew apart.[4]

---

[2]   Mrs. Evans sent all her young children to boarding school perhaps because she was too ill to manage household responsibilities. Kathryn Hughes attributes her mother's withdrawal of affection as the cause of Eliot's life-long depression and vulnerability to rejection (18–19).

[3]   Eliot used nicknames in her letters to her closest women friends to show affection. She called school friend Martha Jackson "Ivy" to signify constancy, and she referred to herself as "Clementis" (mental beauty) when writing to Lewis and Jackson. She later called Cara Bray "My own dear Heart's Ease" and frequently referred to Sara Hennell as "Lieber Gemahl" (My Dear Spouse) and "Beloved Achates" (faithful friend of Aeneas) (1:145, 161, 207).

[4]   Correspondence between Lewis and Eliot had ended by 1849, and when Eliot requested her letters back, Lewis complied with hurt feelings. In 1874, Eliot found her former friend's address and initiated contact with a gift of ten pounds. Lewis responded happily, and Eliot continued to send money with a letter once a year for the rest of her life. Lewis later told John Cross that she had known Eliot more intimately than any other (Harris, *Oxford Reader's Companion* 212).

After her move from Griff to Foleshill in 1841, Eliot developed friendships with Cara Bray and Sara Hennell, sisters and freethinkers who sympathized with her changing religious views and introduced her to others who also questioned the truth of Christianity. These friendships would provide strength to her during the difficult period of isolation from her family and friends following her apostasy. In 1852, she wrote to Sara to respond to a misunderstanding between them and to express deep gratitude for their relationship:

> I have as perfect a friendship for you as my imperfect nature can feel—a friendship in which deep respect and admiration are sweetened by a sort of flesh-and-blood sisterly feeling and the happy consciousness that I have your affection … It would be a sad day indeed for me in which I was "alienated" from you, for I should never replace you. It is impossible that I should ever love two women better than I love you and Cara—indeed it seems to me that I can never love any so well, and it is certain that I can never have any friend—not even a husband—who would supply the loss of those associations with the past which belong to you. (*Letters* 2:19)

Eliot expressed a sisterly affection for Cara and Sara, and her tenuous family ties made their friendship all the more cherished. However, two years later she would face the possibility of that "sad day" in which they too might alienate her. Her union with Lewes in 1854 amounted to withdrawal from Victorian society, and she understood the repercussions of her decision. She wrote to Charles Bray: "the most painful consequence will, I know, be the loss of friends" (2:179). Fear of their reaction hindered her from telling Sara and Cara of the elopement, and Sara especially was deeply hurt not by her actions but by her confiding in Charles, Cara's husband, and not them. Eliot responded to her disappointment with reassurance of her devotion:

> When you say that I do not care about Cara's or your opinion and friendship it seems much the same to me as if you said that I didn't care to eat when I was hungry … either I am a creature without affection … or, you, Cara and Mr. Bray are the most cherished friends I have in the world. (2:181)

In the same letter, she said: "Cara, you and my own sister are the three women who are tied to my heart by a cord which can never be broken and which really pulls me continually" (2:182). However, Eliot's own sister, Chrissey, would eventually break that cord which she thought could never be broken. Dependent on Isaac's financial support, Chrissey followed his orders to cease her relationship with Eliot, rendering complete the family's rejection. Cara and Sara showed their faithfulness and in time became part of the longed-for family that Eliot created in the absence of her own.

In addition to Cara Bray and Sara Hennell, Barbara Bodichon proved a faithful friend to Eliot. The two women met through Bessie Parkes and formed a close friendship based on mutual understanding. Bodichon was the first to discover that Eliot was the pseudonymous author of *Adam Bede*: "My darling Marian! … I saw the 1st review and read one long extract which … instantly made me internally exclaim that is written by Marian Evans, there is her great big head and heart and her wise wide views" (3:56). Eliot thanked Barbara for her "love and sympathy," explaining that she was "the first friend who has given any symptom of knowing me—the first heart that has recognized me in a book which has come from my heart of hearts" (3:63). Bodichon encouraged Eliot's writing and was one of the few women with whom Eliot discussed her work. As an illegitimate daughter of a radical politician, Bodichon could relate to living outside the bounds of societal propriety. She took trips with Eliot and Lewes, visited their home regularly, and gave advice on domestic matters. She was the first person to whom Eliot wrote after the death of Lewes and one of the few who knew of her impending marriage to John Cross (Nestor 150–1). In sum, Eliot's intimate friendships offered her sympathy throughout the painful experiences of her life. Through her female friends, she understood the necessity of community for the exercise of sympathy and recognized the power of community to restore those who suffer through tender interaction. These relationships would inspire her to encourage sympathy for others in her writing.

Eliot shared with her closest friends, Cara, Sara, and Barbara, the experience of not having children (Henry, *The Life* 230). However, Eliot's union with Lewes brought with it the duty of motherhood to his children, Charles, Thornton, and Herbert.[5] She corresponded with the boys regularly throughout their teenage and adult years, but she and Lewes made efforts to keep the boys from disrupting their home and literary lives. Rarely did the boys spend extended periods of time at their home. Eliot maintained a good relationship with Charles, who worked hard and secured a position as a clerk in the Post Office, but she and Lewes experienced frustration with the younger two boys who failed to live independently in Natal, South Africa. Eliot and Lewes dutifully supported the children financially into adulthood—and beyond in the cases of Thornie and Bertie, who often failed in their work and wrote to request money.[6] She grieved the loss of Thornie who died in her arms in 1869, and Lewes wrote that she "had lavished almost a mother's love on the dear boy, and suffered a mother's grief in the bereavement" (*Letters* 5:69). The experience of nursing Thornie through his illness provided one of the more powerful experiences of motherhood for Eliot but, as Bodenheimer explains, Eliot's stepsons "had never entered fully into her private emotional life, except during the brief periods when their strong needs overwhelmed her; the period of

---

[5]   Lewes also held legal responsibility for the four children Agnes had with Thornton Hunt but separated his own children by sending them to a boarding school in Switzerland. Lewes, with Eliot's help, financially supported all seven children who bore his name. For a detailed account of Eliot's role as a stepmother and the ways in which her experience played out in her novels, see Rosemarie Bodenheimer's chapter "George Eliot's Stepsons" in *The Real Life of Mary Ann Evans: George Eliot, Her Letters and Fiction*.

[6]   Eliot also assumed financial responsibility for Bertie's widow Eliza and her two children.

Thornie's dying was the most intense of these" (*The Real Life* 230). Eliot took her role as stepmother seriously, and she did her duty by helping to settle Lewes's children in life and by keeping good relationships, but her principle allegiance was to her writing. She and Lewes referred to her books as her children (*Letters* 3:117, 335). Bodenheimer notes that Eliot began using the metaphor of gestation and growth for the creative process at the time she became a stepmother suggesting "a wish to acknowledge that her primary womanly energies were reserved for the nurturing of her books" (*The Real Life* 202). She also notes Nancy Paxton's point that Eliot's definition of motherhood extended to women's creative insight and was not necessarily connected to procreation (231). Paxton explains that Eliot "chose to valorize the 'maternal' sensations and emotions that might be felt by all women rather than to idealize the bonds of biological motherhood" (24–5).

Eliot's connections with those she elected to bring into her inner circle of friendship were more emotionally satisfying than those with her stepsons. As she aged, she developed maternal feelings and formed attachments with younger men and women. In 1873, she wrote to Lucy Smith: "I have found quite a new interest in young people since I have been conscious that I am getting older" (*Letters* 5:381) and "it is one of the gains of advancing age that the good of young creatures becomes a more definite intense joy to us. With that renunciation of ourselves which age inevitably brings, we get more freedom of soul to enter into the life of others" (5:406). She explained her maternal inclinations to Oscar Browning: "I find the growth of a maternal feeling towards both men and women who are much younger than myself" (5:5), and to Emilia Pattison she wrote: "in proportion as I profoundly rejoice that I never brought a child into the world, I am conscious of having an unused stock of motherly tenderness, which sometimes overflows" (5:52). Her choices in life brought fame and emotional satisfaction with Lewes but resulted in broken family ties and no biological children of her own, and so Eliot came to rely on family ties of a spiritual nature with her friends and young devotees.

Young women worshiped Eliot as a mother-idol, and this devotion provided comfort in her later years. Eliot corresponded with Elma Stuart, a widow with a young son, from 1872 until her death, addressing letters with "my dear daughter" and signing "yours maternally," "your loving mother," and "Mutter" (the nickname used with her stepsons). The young woman lavished her spiritual mother with adoration in the form of gushing letters, photographs, and a flood of gifts, and Eliot did not refuse her worship, finding her "precious feelings and precious words ... sources of strength and comfort" (5:375). She warmly received Elma's many handcrafted gifts: "I half want to scold you for devoting too much of your time, strength and substance to creating pleasures for me. But I cannot find in my heart to say 'Do otherwise than your lovingness prompts you.' ... Bless you, dear, for all your tender thoughts and faithful affection" (6:403). Lewes named Elma "one of the *inner circle*" and in letters to her referred to Eliot as "Madonna," reinforcing the idolatrous nature of their mother-daughter relationship. In 1875, Eliot consented to Elma's request to write an article for a periodical that included an account of

Eliot's influence on her life: "You have a perfect right, my sweet daughter, to say what you think fit ... I don't of course mean that you will write any direct praise, but that your grateful ardour may easily seem to others more than George Eliot deserves" (6:167).[7] Eliot was willing to have private homage made public, but she urged her spiritual daughter not to overdo it. After the article's publication and reprinting, Eliot wrote to Elma: "As to the reprints, dear child, it was like your warm heart to get them done, but *they must be destroyed, please.* You could not hinder the suspicion that we had prompted the distribution—that would be the immediate conclusion of ordinary minds, and would by and by become their absolute statement" (6:230). Eliot invited public praise but was careful to avoid the appearance of self-promotion. Elma's wish to memorialize her relationship with Eliot extended even beyond death. She arranged to be buried next to Eliot in the Highgate Cemetery; the headstone, erected in 1903, read: "whom for 8 1/2 blessed years George Eliot called by the sweet name of 'Daughter.'"

Edith Simcox was another of Eliot's worshipful daughters, and she expressed her passion for Eliot in her journal, *Autobiography of a Shirtmaker*.[8] Her ardor exceeded even that of Stuart's. In her book she recorded her reverential devotion: "Day by day let me begin and end by looking to Her for guidance and rebuke, plan the future by what She would have thought best, and make a dread rule to myself out of the vow that every night what has been done ill or ill left undone shall be confessed on my knees to my Darling and my God" (Simcox 155). She described Eliot as "my goddess!" with a "net veil that could have grieved me but for the angelic way in which she took it off at my prayer" and wrote of kissing Eliot's feet with "passionate kisses that filled my eyes with tears" (26, 49). Eliot did not discourage Simcox's sexual and religious idolatry but did keep the one-sided love affair in check. At times Simcox's fawning was too much, and on one occasion Eliot asked her not to call her "Mother" as "her feeling for me was *not* at all a mother's" (110). On another occasion when Simcox, the "trembling lover," "kissed her again and again and murmured broken words of love," Eliot told her to save her love for "some imaginary he" and explained that she "had never all her life cared very much for women" but that she "cared for the womanly ideal, sympathized with women and liked for them to come to her in their troubles, but while feeling near to them in one way, she felt far off in another; the friendship and intimacy of men was more to her" (117–18). Eliot sought a motherly role, not a sexual one; she kept Simcox's advances at bay but did not discourage idolatry. With Simcox, Stuart, and other young women, she found an outlet for her "maternal

---

[7]   Four years earlier she had allowed Alexander Main to publish his book of worship, *Wise, Witty, and Tender Sayings in Prose and Verse, Selected from the Works of George Eliot.*

[8]   For a complete transcription of Simcox's journal, see *A Monument to the Memory of George Eliot: Edith J. Simcox's Autobiography of a Shirtmaker* (1998), edited by Constance Fulmer and Margaret Barfield.

feeling" as well as a gratifying source of homage. Nancy Henry explains Eliot's appeal to her young followers:

> People responded to her personally with an intensity greater than that generated by any of her contemporary authors, including Dickens. The Sundays at the Priory encouraged worshipful homage, but young men and women seemed to feel toward her a combination of moral reverence and sexual attraction. Young men confessed their loss of faith (Henry Sidgwick, F.W.H. Myers) and women confessed their domestic unhappiness (Georgiana Burne-Jones, Emilia Pattison). (*The Life* 237)

Pauline Nestor describes these relationships as limited: "Rather than close literary friendships, the most marked legacy of Eliot's celebrity was the host of admiring disciples ... who gathered around her in later life. They did not, however, offer Eliot any real opportunity for communality in the sense of the mutual exchange ... " (156). Elaine Showalter similarly states that Eliot had "an eager cult of female disciples who cast her in the role of 'spiritual mother' and adored her as someone superior, majestic, melancholy, and remote" ("Greening" 293). While it is true that Eliot's worshippers put her on a pedestal, it is not true that there was no mutual exchange. She welcomed the worship. She played the Madonna role to her beloved inner circle of women friends and found comfort in her maternal role.

   During these years of cultivating personal relationships as a spiritual mother, she also developed a motherly public image. Those outside her inner circle observed Eliot's maternal nature. Benjamin Jowett noted in 1879 her "sweet voice & soft sad humour" and "homely but motherly features" (Collins, *Interviews* 219). John Fiske also wrote of Eliot's maternal presence 1873 when he wrote:

> [She] looks simple, frank, cordial, and matronly ... I call her a good, honest, genuine, motherly woman with no nonsense about her ... There is nothing a bit masculine about her; she is thoroughly feminine and looks and acts as if she were made for nothing but to mother babies. But she has a power of stating an argument equal to any man ... Remember that ... George Eliot [is] just the age of my mother—a queer coincidence. (*Letters* 5:464–5)[9]

Eliot's maternal inclinations developed during her years of celebrity and poetry writing, and her personal relationships, public reputation, and poetry reflected her experience with and feelings about motherhood.

---

[9]   Eliot observed and appreciated the maternal in others as well. When in Rome with Lewes in 1860, she wrote to Mrs. Richard Congreve: "Oh, the beautiful men and women and children here! Such wonderful babies with wise eyes!—such grand-featured mothers nursing them! As one drives along the streets sometimes, one sees a Madonna and child at every third or fourth upper window" (*Letters* 3:288).

Motherhood in Eliot's Poetry

For Eliot and for the poetess in general, motherhood was a powerful symbol of self-resignation, duty, and spiritual nurturing. The poetess at once represented and promoted these attributes. By including maternal images in her poetry, Eliot reminded readers of her role as mother-poet while at the same time promoting motherly values such as sacrifice and sympathy. Kate Flint explains that the mother figure features prominently in Eliot's writing:

> ... partly because of the emotional resonance that it held for her, and partly because it provides an ideal site on which to examine the nexus of ideas concerning the social and the natural that lie at the heart of her treatment of gender. She invested the role of motherhood with sacredness, representing the highest form of duty of which most women were capable. (165)

Motherhood, for Eliot, represented sympathetic care for others. She wrote to Maria Lewis: "Maternal love [is] the only purely unselfish feeling that exists on this earth; the only affection which (as far as it appears) flows from the loving to the beloved object in one continual stream" (*Letters* 1:23). Flint notes that in this passage Eliot's notion of motherhood "appears as the purest form of George Eliot's often-commended virtue of sympathy" and explains that "Maternal feeling ... although it may encompass George Eliot's most cherished social values—sympathetic involvement, recognition of the demands of alterity, patient adherence to duty—is not a freestanding attribute, but must always be seen in its intersections with broader social relations and pressures" (167–8).[10] Eliot recognized the importance that society gave to motherhood, and she played upon this collective understanding of the sacred role of motherhood in her works to promote sympathetic understanding.

Abundant images of motherhood in her poetry reveal a writer who came to see herself as a mother to her readers, whom she guided in matters of morality. Although she did not believe women were morally superior to men, she took advantage of the perception of the English woman as spiritual guide and mother of the nation to impart moral lessons. Images of Mother Earth breast-feeding and child-rearing remind readers of the authority of the mother-poet. Most critics who discuss her portrayal of motherhood focus on her novels, investigating the figurative Madonnas or the fictional mothers who reject or abandon their children.[11] Few comment on the image of mother that appears throughout her poetry. Eliot did not present many portraits of actual mothers in her poetry, and mothers as characters

---

[10]   Flint qualifies this statement with an example from *Felix Holt, the Radical*, in which Eliot explored the idea of the unrequited love of a mother (Mrs. Transome) for her son (Harold) within a larger theme of women acquiescing to male power (168).

[11]   Critics often discuss Dinah, Dorothea, Mirah, and Romola as Madonna figures and Hetty, Molly Farren (Eppie's mother), and Contessa Alcharisi as unnatural mothers who in various ways abandon their children.

reside in the background of her poems as silent, passive figures.[12] More often, Eliot used motherhood metaphorically to convey the idea of mother as a strong, sacrificial leader who cares for and guides her children towards independence, productivity, and wisdom.

In several poems, Eliot relies on the image of Mother Earth to create such a picture. In "Agatha" Mother Earth is young, fertile, and nurturing. She "spreads soft and rounded breasts / To feed her children" (*Complete Shorter Poetry* 1:73).[13] Youthful Mother Earth enjoys the early stages of motherhood when her children are happy, dependent, and innocent. The poem "In the South" features earth as an older mother who has reared and sent off her children into the world: "O gentle brightness of late autumn morns! / The dear Earth like a patient matron left / By all she loved and reared, still smiles and loves" (2:103). Mother Earth is mature, patient, and loving. Her children have left her alone, but she finds contentment in her solitude, knowing that she has done her duty. The poem describes her as creator of all life around. She is productive and prophetic. "Scattered villages" are her children who have left her but still "sleep / In happy morning dreams" (2:103). Mother Earth smiles though she suffers the loss of her children who have moved on to independence. In "The Legend of Jubal," Eliot conveys a sense of loss by depicting a mother with a dead child. In a world in which "Death was now lord of Life" and suffering abounds, "a mother fair / Who folding to her breast a dying child / Beams with feigned joy that but makes sadness mild" (1:43). Eliot presents the grieving mother (a common poetess subject) to show that it is a mother's duty to bear pain and loss with strength and self-resignation. Linda Hughes points out the tendency of Victorian poets to filter loss through domestic imagery: "Victorians of all ages died at home and were usually prepared for burial there as well. The convergence of domestic ideals and the common domestic experience of death intensified society's focus on mourning and the need to articulate emotional response" (*Cambridge Introduction* 168). Motherhood could provide a powerful symbol of loss and mourning as well as nurture and new life. The reader encounters motherhood in poetry with a readiness to feel and express emotion.

---

[12]   Exceptions include brief mentions in *The Spanish Gypsy*, "Brother and Sister," and "The Legend of Jubal." In *The Spanish Gypsy*, mothers are mentioned but do not figure as characters (17, 29, 43, 101, 170, 238). The female narrator (sister) of "Brother and Sister" recollects her mother as doting on the brother and clinging while letting them go on their journey: "Our mother bade us keep the trodden ways, / Stroked down my tippet, set my brother's frill, / Then with the benediction of her gaze / Clung to us lessening, and pursued us still" (*CSP* 2:6). The narrator of "The Legend of Jubal" describes the "broad-bosomed mother of the strong"—presumably Cain's wife who sits next to her husband surrounded by her children looking "Like Demeter, placid o'er the throng" (1:53). She is mentioned just seven lines after Mother Earth, and both mothers (the figurative Mother Earth and the actual mother of Cain's children) are described as fertile, peaceful, and harmonious.

[13]   *The Spanish Gypsy*, completed only a few months before Eliot began "Agatha" (1868), offers a similar introduction in which Spain is described in motherly terms: "'Broad-breasted Spain, leaning with equal love / On the Mid sea ... / And on the untraveled Ocean's restless tides" (7). In both poems, Eliot equates motherhood with land and with a sense of home.

In "The Legend of Jubal," Mother Earth features prominently to represent community and harmony: "Earth and her children were at festival, / Glowing as with one heart and one consent— / Thought, love, trees, rocks, in sweet warm radiance blent" (1:52), and she fosters those traits as she guides Jubal throughout his journey. She provides sustenance, company, and counsel on his pilgrimage Eastward to "some far-off land" (1:55). When he arrives at the land of Seth's descendants, Jubal acknowledges Mother Earth's provision:

> Here have I found my thirsty soul's desire,
> Eastward the hills touch heaven, and evening's fire
> Flames through deep waters; I will take my rest,
> And feed anew from my great mother's breast,
> The sky-clasped Earth, whose voices nurture me
> As the flowers' sweetness doth the honey-bee. (1:56)

Mother Earth nurtures and provides rest for the wanderer and creates a home for him everywhere he goes. When after many years he returns to his origin of birth to complete his journey, he longs for his tribe to remember and "run to greet me, welcoming" (1:58), but his tribe does not recognize him. When he claims to be Jubal, creator of the music that binds the community, they mock him, accuse him of blasphemy, beat him with their flutes, and leave him for dead (1:62-3). Mother Earth alone, ever at his side, celebrates his return:

> Yea, the dear Earth, with mother's constancy,
> Met and embraced him, and said, "Thou art he!
> This was thy cradle, here my breast was thine,
> Where feeding, thou didst all thy life entwine
> With my sky-wedded life in heritage divine. (1:59)

Despite the rejection of his community, Jubal receives nurture and welcome from constant Mother Earth who helps him complete his spiritual journey and reminds him of his divine oneness with the earth.[14]

Throughout her poetry, Eliot creates a picture of Mother Earth who raises and sends off her children and who guides and provides for those under her watch. At times she nurtures and fosters community; at other times, she serves as a substitute for community. Sometimes she suffers, but she does not complain. She is constant, productive, and prophetic. She is home. Like the mother-poet herself, Mother Earth is a spiritual guide. Although Eliot did not subscribe to the idea of spiritual superiority by nature of gender alone, she did view mothers as spiritual, sacrificial

---

[14]   In the poem, the three sons of Cain are "heroes of their race," each seeking immortality through different means (1:45). Tubal-Cain creates industry, Jubal creates art and music, and Jabal is the mother figure who nurtures children, keeps family together, and spends time with the girls in the family (1:45–6). The three brothers represent three aspects of civilized society: home, industry, and art. Jabal appears to be a man but really is the embodiment of nineteenth-century standards of femininity. He is shepherd and spiritual leader of the nation.

leaders and demonstrators of sympathy. Eliot viewed her authorial role as that of a motherly guide in matters of sympathetic understanding and community bonding.

Sympathy and Female Community in *Armgart*

Eliot merged the themes of motherhood and community in *Armgart* (1870), a dramatic poem about the struggle of a woman artist who finds fulfillment in female friendship after suffering a great loss.[15] The poem strikingly recapitulates Eliot's feelings about her own role as a woman artist and as a mother figure.[16] *Armgart* critics examine in particular Armgart's lost voice (to discuss the silencing of women), her wasted female potential (to comment on women's limited choices in Victorian society), and her professional success (to remark on women's negotiation of the private and public spheres). Because these themes have been aptly discussed, I focus instead on the poem's expression of the redemptive power of sympathy and female community.[17]

---

[15] Eliot sold *Armgart* to *Macmillan's Magazine* and the *Atlantic Monthly* in 1871. In *Macmillan's*, it was titled "Armgart: A Tragic Poem." (*CSP* 1:91). The tragedy refers to Armgart's descent from fame to the ordinary women's lot in nineteenth-century society. It is interesting to consider Eliot's choice of the dramatic form given her earlier evangelical distaste for theater.

[16] On the whole, Eliot avoided autobiographical topics in her poetry. She did not address the issue of the fallen woman and dealt with marriage indirectly in "How Lisa Loved the King." "Brother and Sister," a poem inspired by her failed relationship with her brother, is perhaps her most autobiographical poem.

[17] Bonnie Lisle argues that Eliot associates art with death. For Eliot, to choose the artist's life is to choose death (271). The association of art and death relates to Eliot's assumption of the artist's role: the death of a former self (Marian Evans) and the birth of an artist (George Eliot) (271). Rosemarie Bodenheimer also reads *Armgart* as a representation of Eliot's artistic anxiety. She discusses Eliot's struggle with ambition, her fear of the "public woman" stigma, and her reservations about women on the stage ("Ambition and its Audiences" 8–9). Kathleen Blake proposes that the poem is about the incompatibility of love and art for women artists and says that though Eliot did not have to choose between love and art, the poem reflects her ambivalence about the conflict (75–6). Louise Hudd asserts that one of the aims of *Armgart* was to prompt discussion "about the way in which women approach sexual politics" and regards the poem as a "political critique of the idealistic feminism of Barrett Browning's *Aurora Leigh*, and in particular, the earlier text's problematic depiction of class politics and social reform" (62–3). Rebecca Pope addresses the role of opera and the significance of the diva's voice, explaining that the diva's voice in women's writing is "both a mode of and a metaphor for female empowerment in a culture that traditionally places women on the side of silence" (140). Susan Brown describes the form of *Armgart* as a closet drama and asserts that this form dramatized women's consciousness and agency ("Determined Heroines" 96). Grace Kehler argues that Eliot's use of the closet drama form allowed her to probe issues of agency and gender in *Armgart* and discusses form as it relates metaphorically to the poem's lament for the lost and suppressed voices (148). Rob Breton reads the poem in the context of the popular theatre and the Reform Act of 1867.

Armgart is a famous opera singer who must retire after losing her voice.[18] Eliot appropriately chose the verse drama form to portray the spiritual transformation of an opera singer, a performer whose own drama takes place off stage. The first scene opens with two pillars bearing the bronze busts of Gluck and Beethoven. Armgart performs in Christoph von Gluck's opera *Orpheus and Eurydice* (1762) at the beginning of the drama and loses the chance to perform in Ludwig van Beethoven's *Fidelio* (1805) at the end. Margaret Reynolds points out that Orpheus and Fidelio are cross-dressing roles; Orpheus is a male played by a woman and Fidelio is a woman dressing as a man (*Oxford Reader's Companion* 307).[19] The dramatic form of the poem, with reference to the cross-dressing performances, provides the backdrop for a story of spiritual transformation that entails masking and unmasking and multiple layers of drama. Armgart masquerades as a man for her part in the opera and perceives that she is a medium (a mask, in a sense), through which Gluck sings. She says that Gluck "sang, not listened: every linked note / Was his immortal pulse that stirred in mine" (*CSP* 1:96). After the performance, Armgart and Leo (her voice instructor) reenact the performance, and Graf (Armgart's suitor) refers to a "double drama"—the drama of her operatic performance and the drama of the audience's response to her performance. Armgart's theatrical disagreement with Leo over a trill provides another performance for an audience of two: Graf and Walpurga. Eliot's use of masking and dramatic layering at the poem's introduction prepares the reader for a story of unmasking and revelation.[20]

Initially, Armgart views herself worthy of the worship she receives as a celebrity. Graf claims to be her "votary," and Leo is "her priest" (1:104). She envisions her influence as extending far and wide:

> Shall I turn aside
> From splendours which flash out the glow I make,
> And live to make, in all the chosen breasts

---

[18]   For Eliot, music was the art that expressed emotional life. A number of her poems prominently feature the role of music: "O May I Join," "The Legend of Jubal," *Armgart*, "Arion," "Stradivarius," "Erinna," and *The Spanish Gypsy*.

[19]   Grace Kehler helpfully relates the historical significance of the role of Orpheus: Armgart, though she idealizes her feminine voice as superior to "tenor or baritone," literally assumes a role first performed by castrati, the role of Orpheus … According to legend, his most affecting songs follow the death of his wife, symbolically attaching song to trauma and loss. And of the many castrati and prima donnas who aspired to the more positive Orphic role in culture – that is, the role of the acknowledged, celebrated artist – but a handful garnered acclaim while the rest battled insignificance or deprecation during their lives. Armgart's history, too, remains a blank, not just because the drama ends so abruptly, but also because Armgart has not established herself as a full-fledged prima donna. She may be "the queen of song" in terms of her debut … but audiences are changeable and forgetful, notably when celebrity is short-lived. (160)

[20]   Patrick Brantlinger explains that Eliot uses dramatic form to underscore the power of the performing woman in *Armgart* while her novels feature women who are thwarted in their attempts to participate in the public sphere (213).

Of half a Continent? No, may it come,
That splendour! May the day be near when men
Think much to let my horses draw me home,
And new lands welcome me upon their beach,
Loving me for my fame. That is the truth
Of what I wish, nay, yearn for. Shall I lie?
Pretend to seek obscurity — to sing
In hope of disregard? A vile pretence!
And blasphemy besides. For what is fame
But the benignant strength of One, transformed
To joy of Many? Tributes, plaudits come
As necessary breathing of such joy;
And may they come to me! (1:103)

Armgart seeks worship from her audience and "new lands" and sings for accolades, not to uplift others. Obscurity, for her, is an intolerable, blasphemous thought. Armgart's grandiosity and egocentrism render her unable to care about others. Her audience, Graf, Leo, and Walpurga (her cousin and attendant) worship her, but in return she extends no sympathy to them. She cares only about how others can serve her. When Graf blasphemously asks Armgart to give up her ambition and concentrate her power "in home delights / Which penetrate and purify the world" (1:109), she replies indignantly:

What! leave the opera with my part ill-sung
While I was warbling in a drawing-room?
Sing in the chimney-corner to inspire
My husband reading news? Let the world hear
My music only in his morning speech
Less stammering than most honourable men's?
No! … The great masters write
For women's voices, and great Music wants me!
I need not crush myself within a mould
Of theory called Nature: I have room
To breathe and grow unstunted. (1:109)

Armgart prefers to play the role of a performer and receive worship rather than engage in intimate relationships as a wife, friend, or mother. She refuses the "renunciation" associated with domestic life and claims that her voice is her child (1:108), that she can "live unmated, but not live / Without the bliss of singing to the world, / And feeling all my world respond to me" (1:114). She prefers a life of self-interest rather than one involving sacrifice and giving: "No; I will live alone and pour my pain / With passion into music, where it turns / To what is best within my better self" (1:112).

However, when she loses her voice and livelihood, Armgart finds herself sharing the plight of the ordinary nineteenth-century unmarried woman. Grace Kehler explains that without an operatic career and without a family, Armgart has no secure position in society:

She had envisioned opera as an alternative to domestic feminine roles, as she indicates in her metaphoric placement of herself inside an operatic family: once the "bride" of art and "mother" of the child-voice ... Armgart as a prima donna acquired cultural merit that exempted her from the usual productive-reproductive gender binary, enabling her instead to nurture her talent. The metaphor of family, however, underscores the fragility of both nuclear and operatic structures of relationship, for like the domestic woman Armgart finds herself in a classic nineteenth-century dilemma: she has lost her only child (voice) and been deserted by her faithless husband (art/its audience), who has already found love elsewhere. (161)

Having cast away her chance to marry in favor of fame and worship, she becomes redundant—the "millionth woman in superfluous herds" without "a purpose, abject as the rest / To bear the yoke of life" (*CSP* 1:118, 120). She morosely embraces her new lot that she calls 'The Woman's Lot: a Tale of Everyday:' / A middling woman's, to impress the world / With high superfluousness" (1:125). This fall from fame to mediocrity forces Armgart to reflect on her self-devotion, and it is Walpurga who guides her to reflection by urging her toward a life of fellow-feeling. Throughout the first scenes, the audience has seen Walpurga arranging flowers, setting out an "offering" of food for Armgart, and providing emotional support (1:98). She is the domestic, feminine ideal, and when Armgart undergoes a crisis, Walpurga becomes her spiritual guide. She encourages Armgart to turn to a life of compassion by suggesting a reciprocation of sympathy. She says to Armgart: "you must see a future in your reach / With happiness enough to make a dower / For two of modest claims" (1:120), but Armgart rejects Walpurga as she rejected Graf: "Oh, you intone / That chant of consolation wherewith ease / Makes itself easier in the sight of pain" (1:120). Armgart associates intimacy (of marriage or friendship) with mediocrity and living as a wife, mother, and friend (rather than as an idol) as petty and meaningless. She perceives the average woman's life as miserable and requiring a pretense of happiness: "All the world now is but a rack of threads / To twist and dwarf me into pettiness / And basely feigned content, the placid mask / Of woman's misery (1:127). Walpurga points out that Armgart's perception of the average woman wearing a "placid mask" to conceal misery shows her inability to understand the feelings of other women:

Ay, such a mask
As the few born like you to easy joy,
Cradled in privilege, take for natural
On all the lowly faces that must look
Upward to you! What revelation now
Shows you the mask or gives presentiment
Of sadness hidden? (1:127)

Armgart has not looked beyond the placid masks of ordinary women to recognize the suffering of individuals, but now that she has become ordinary herself, she is forced to sympathize. Patrick Brantlinger states that Walpurga points out that "everyday performances of unexceptional women, including herself, went unnoticed by Armgart until she lost her talent" and that Walpurga "prefers her own concealed misery to Armgart's inability to see beyond masks and sympathize with the thousands of individuals who were her audience" (214).[21] Walpurga complains that Armgart has never noticed her suffering though she has been attending to her daily:

> You who every day
> These five years saw me limp to wait on you,
> And thought the order perfect which gave *me*,
> The girl without pretention to be aught (*CSP* 1:127)

Consumed with her own life of fame and then with her miserable lot as an unmarried woman, Armgart has never noticed Walpurga's worse lot as an unmarried woman who is also lame. She has never recognized that Walpurga has been serving, sympathizing with, and adoring her for many years without receiving any support or understanding in return. Walpurga speaks against the nature of one "who can live / In mere mock knowledge of their fellows' woe" (1:128) and disabuses Armgart of the notion that she and her audience were in sympathy with one another. She scolds Armgart for her lack of fellow-feeling for others and for assuming a "rebel's right" not to join the lot of humanity (1:128):

> Are you no longer chartered, privileged,
> But sunk to simple woman's penury,
> To ruthless Nature's chary average—
> Where is the rebel's right for you alone?
> Noble rebellion lifts a common load;
> But what is he who flings his own load off
> And leaves his fellows toiling? Rebel's right?
> Say rather, the deserter's. Oh, you smiled
> From your clear height on all the million lots
> Which yet you brand as abject. (1:128–9)

Walpurga tells Armgart "a lame girl's truth," that Armgart does not "bear a human heart" and cannot sympathize with humanity because she thinks herself superior to others.

> For what is it to you that women, men,
> Plod, faint, are weary, and espouse despair
> Of aught but fellowship? Save that you spurn
> To be among them? Now, then, you are lame—
> Maimed, as you said, and leveled with the crowd:
> Call it new birth—birth from that monstrous Self
> Which, smiling down upon a race oppressed,
> Say, 'All is good, for I am throned at ease.' (1:130)

---

[21] Brantlinger also connects Armgart to the Alcharisi in *Daniel Deronda*. Like Armgart, the Alcharisi is isolated, alone, and unable to understand her audience (214).

Armgart's "lameness"—which unmasks her by taking her from the position of a distanced, idolized performer to the level of the rest of society—allows the chance for a "new birth." She accepts Walpurga's rebuke and for the first time understands her own lack of sympathy: "Yet you speak truth; / I wearied you, it seems; took all your help / As cushioned nobles use a weary serf, / Not looking at his face" (1:128). Armgart, once "blind / With too much happiness" was not able to see the suffering of others, but sorrow brings her "true vision"—an understanding of the value of sympathy:

> Were there one
> This moment near me, suffering what I feel,
> And needing me for comfort in her pang —
> Then it were worth the while to live; not else. (1:129)

Armgart's enlightenment prompts her to try to understand the feelings of others. Practicing fellow-feeling for the first time, she asks Leo how old he is and remarks: "Strange! since I have known you / Till now I never wondered how you lived" (1:131). Armgart shows concern for Leo and learns that his heart is "half broken" because of his failure as a composer. Her recognition of and identification with his sorrow is a sign of redemption.

With Walpurga as her spiritual guide, she drops the mask of the distanced performer and joins humanity as "a broken thing" who is better able to feel the suffering of others. Mathilde Blind explains that Eliot creates in Armgart a woman with high artistic aims and ambition and then implies that what is valuable about her is "the part of her nature which she shares with ordinary humanity" (230). For Eliot, Blind argues, the multitude "claims the deepest sympathy and tenderest compassion; so that all greatness, in her eyes, is not a privilege, but a debt, which entails on its possessor a more strenuous effort, a completer devotion to the service of average humanity" (231). Armgart says to Leo: "We must bury our dead joys / And live above them with a living world" (*CSP* 1:134). She decides to make a humble living as a music teacher, to care for herself and her cousin, and to use her gift to uplift others rather than herself:

> I would take humble work and do it well —
> Teach music, singing — what I can — not here,
> But in some smaller town where I may bring
> The method you [Leo] have taught me, pass your gift
> To others who can use it for delight.
> You think I can do that? (1:133)

Rob Breton asserts that the poem reveals Eliot's discomfort with the idea of the female spectacle: "That Armgart chooses teaching over acting suggests that Eliot subscribed to the conventionally Victorian idea that acting is morally questionable, generating a kind of reckless voyeurism. Singing is less objectionable because it is not simply a performance but rather an utterance of genuine emotion" (120). Breton may have a point here, but I think Armgart's choice of teaching as a profession also speaks to a desire to exercise her gift in an altruistic manner, rather than a selfish one. Furthermore, Armgart's choice to live in Freiburg, Walpurga's small hometown, is a sacrificial gift to repay Walpurga's loyalty. Armgart buries her "dead joy" as a mother buries her dead child: "Mothers do so, bereaved" (*CSP* 1:134). Armgart, having lost her own child (her voice) will adopt "another's living child" (1:134). The adopted child may refer to the voice students she plans to instruct or the community in general that she plans to serve. She admits that "it is hard / To take the little corpse, and lay it low, / And say, 'None misses it but me'" (1:134), but she renounces her fame and her operatic role, saying: "Paulina sings Fidelio, / And they will welcome her to-night" (1:135). Armgart has learned fellow-feeling through suffering and finds solace in sympathetic female community. She will embrace the role of sacrificial mother who will serve and sympathize with others.[22]

Eliot conveys a message about the importance of female community in *Armgart* to promote the value of sympathy. Brantlinger explains that "Eliot's elision of the literary character with which Armgart identifies and the author who writes about that character underscores how the performing woman serves as a figure for the female writer" (213).[23] Unlike Armgart, Eliot did not have to sacrifice the worship of acolytes to perform the role of spiritual mother. As a poetess, she guided readers to spiritual truth through a dramatic rendering of a story involving loss and gain, spiritual death and rebirth.

---

[22]   For an insightful reading of *Armgart* as an expression of same-sex love, see Wendy Bashant's "Singing in Greek Drag: Gluck, Berlioz, George Eliot." Bashant argues that Eliot chose opera and poetry, rather than the familiar novel, to "transgress against her society's notions of women loving other women" (225). I agree with Bashant's reading of the poem as a celebration of the power of female relationships and allow for the possibility of Eliot's condoning lesbian love. However, I believe female community in the poem serves more forcefully as a depiction of the power of female sympathy in a society that did not offer many life options for women beyond the confinements of idealized womanhood.

[23]   Bodenheimer discusses *Armgart* in terms of Eliot's anxiety about authorship; however, she remarks that Eliot refused to make a direct association between her life and her career. John Cross, she explains, quotes Eliot's reply to his suggestion to write an autobiography: "The only thing I should care much to dwell on would be the absolute despair I suffered from of ever being able to achieve anything. No one could ever have felt a greater despair, and a knowledge of this might be a help to some other struggler ... but, on the other hand, it might only lead to an increase of bad writing" (Cross 1:29). Bodenheimer asserts that Eliot's response reveals elements of ambition and self-aggrandizement. She states: "The justification of her writing as an art that fulfilled a need in others comes into play for a moment, raised only to be quenched by the old prohibitive fear, turned against the fledgling ambitions of others. George Eliot was ready to teach others to suffer, but not to aspire" ("Ambition and its Audiences" 31). It is true that suffering and resignation play a role in this poem, but I believe the poem offers a redemptive reading as well. Eliot reveals the limitations that women, especially unmarried women, faced in nineteenth-century society. However, the conclusion is not entirely negative. Armgart finds refuge in female society, she becomes more human by learning the value of sympathy, and she will redirect her ambition and talent to help others.

Sympathy and Motherhood in "Agatha"

"Agatha," written one year before *Armgart* in 1869, also involves the theme of female community. Both poems present the main characters' names as titles, both are located in a foreign land (Germany), and both feature women who, while not biological mothers, are mothers to a community.[24] Both women create a home with other supportive females for whom they care, and both garner strength within those female communities to serve the larger community. Eliot uses the dramatic verse form for both *Armgart* and "Agatha"; however, the action in *Armgart* is immediate, and the reader assumes, at the end of the poem, the development of a female community not yet complete. The action in "Agatha," on the other hand, occurs in the past: the story of female community has already taken place. In the poem, the narrator speaks of women who are dead but still remembered. *Armgart* concerns an egocentric person who learns through hardship to practice sympathy, and the poem concludes with her enlightenment: a new life will begin as the poem ends. Conversely, Agatha's story, from the beginning, is an example of a life sympathetically lived. A discussion on the setting and character of "Agatha" will show how Eliot appealed to poetess themes of home, female community, and motherhood to relay a sympathetic message to her readers.

An understanding of Eliot's treatment of home in "Agatha" rests on familiarity with the traditional usage of setting in women's poetry. Armstrong explains that contemporary critics associated women's poetry with an "impassioned land" or emotional space that lay beyond the boundaries of the poet's nationality and culture. She states: "movement across and between cultural boundaries ... could be seen as a search for the exotic, an escape from restrictions into the 'other' of bourgeois society" (*Victorian Poetry* 325). West-Burnham argues that the concept of traveling is important for women's poetry because it implies personal and spiritual transformation as well as an understanding of a wider social context ("Travelling" 91). Women writers, she explains, change their landscapes from the domestic, stereotypically feminine sphere to unfamiliar territory (a different

---

[24] Critics who discuss motherhood in Eliot's poetry focus primarily on Fedalma as Madonna figure in *The Spanish Gypsy*. I examine "Agatha" instead since it is a critically underrepresented poem. Both heroines are equated with motherhood despite being childless, and both are the sole spiritual leaders of their communities. Eliot, also childless, presents herself as spiritual mother to the nation in the creation of these poems and in her role as a poetess.

country and cultural context).[25] The motif of the traveler allowed women to challenge perceived versions of self, life, and women's writing (92).[26]

Despite her interest in travel and knowledge of foreign cultures, Eliot set most of her novels in the provinces of England.[27] But her poems were often set in foreign places and times.[28] Just as Eliot was able to escape societal alienation early in her career through travel, so she provided a space in which her characters could navigate their lives outside of traditional English codes of conduct. Armgart, Agatha, and Fedalma (*The Spanish Gypsy*), for example, reject marriage, decline

---

[25] Eliot's *The Spanish Gypsy*, for example, moves to fifteenth-century Spain, allowing Eliot to ask questions about gender, race, religion, and class in a "safer" space while still maintaining propriety (West-Burnham, "Travelling Towards Selfhood" 91–2). West-Burnham states:

> In the abandonment of the personal life, George Eliot depicts a heroine who foregoes a life of personal happiness and love in favour of "mothering" her tribe and working for the greater good of others. Eliot thus begins to ascribe to many of the social and political challenges taking place in the nineteenth century, using religion as one of the key areas of growth, development and "home" for women's self-identification. Indeed, Eliot is using religion as a discursive framework: its legitimate status is primary, but she is also subversively deploying it in relation to women's autonomy and their public role. (92)

[26] Eliot's personal experience with travel no doubt influenced her decision to set her poetry in foreign lands. Foreign countries were often home for Eliot, and she found living abroad rejuvenating. She traveled all over Europe to study foreign languages and cultures and to escape social alienation—she found solace in Germany after her elopement with Lewes. In her biography of Eliot, Barbara Hardy adds: "Her need for foreignness was political as well as personal. Before Geneva she had thought feelingly about nationalism and criticized English culture. She was not just tolerant of foreignness but, at times, sounds positively xenophiliac" (47). In *George Eliot and Europe*, John Rignall explains that Europe, for Eliot, "was no monolithic 'other' but a naturally accepted part of her heritage as an educated Englishwoman" (xi). Her knowledge of the world, he notes, was in part due to her interaction with other nations and races (xi). Nancy Henry discusses Eliot's investigations of people who lived "beyond the bounds of her personal lot" (*George Eliot* 13). Eliot, she argues, studied Jewish history, culture, and religion to better understand the "other" within England (13).

[27] *Romola*, set in fifteenth-century Florence, is the exception. Rignall notes: "With the exception of *Romola* ... George Eliot's extensive foreign travels left no novels as their direct product. Only the Roman scenes of *Middlemarch* and a few brief and scattered episodes elsewhere, most notably in *Daniel Deronda*, bear immediate testimony to her European journeys" ("The Idea of Travel" 139). He points out that the idea of travel only plays a central role in one novel, *Daniel Deronda*. Eliot's poetry, however, features prominently the motifs of travel and journeying.

[28] "Agatha" and *Armgart* are located in nineteenth-century Germany, and "How Lisa Loved the King" and *The Spanish Gypsy* are set in medieval Spain. The action of "The Legend of Jubal" and "The Death of Moses" takes place in biblical times, and the main character of "The Legend of Jubal" journeys from the Middle East to India. "Erinna" takes place in seventh-century BCE Greece.

to have children, and form atypical families. However, as they are foreigners and travelers, audiences did not expect them to conform to British nineteenth-century societal standards of femininity. By setting her stories abroad, Eliot was free to portray her own idea of society, in which female members clung to one another out of necessity and took on atypical maternal roles in their communities. Leighton discusses how Hemans relocated her poems of motherhood to her own mother's Italian-German lands; in their "woman-to-woman atmosphere," Hemans's poems "not only look at history from the angle of forgotten mothers, daughters, widows and wives, but also build up a powerful mythology of motherhood as a socially self-sufficient state and a metaphorically longed-for ideal" (17). Along the same lines, Eliot set her poems of motherhood (*The Spanish Gypsy*, *Armgart*, and "Agatha") in foreign places and allowed her main characters to travel as they sought spiritual transformation and fulfillment through self-sacrifice.

In "Agatha," Eliot relocated home to a rural town in the Black Forest to portray her own idea of domesticity, which elevated female community, and to make universal the moral value of womanhood. Her poem was inspired by a trip in 1868 to Germany where she and Lewes, along with acquaintances Gräfin von Baudissin and her daughter, paid a visit to the cottage of an old peasant woman in Sankt Märgen (Haight 404, *CSP* 1:67–9).[29] In order to emphasize the centrality of home in the story, she provides a detailed description of the setting that repeatedly reinforces a connection between motherhood, sacredness, and home. First, she describes an area of the Black Forest, an idyllic natural area in which fertile Mother Earth welcomes all:

---

[29]   In the poem, the old peasant woman figures as Agatha and von Baudissin figures as an angel named Countess Linda (*CSP* 1:69). Eliot described Sankt Märgen to John Blackwood during her visit in 1868:

> We got your letter yesterday here among the peaceful mountain tops ... The monks as usual found out the friendly solitude, and this place of St. Märgen was originally nothing but an Augustinian monastery. About three miles off is another place of like origin, called St. Peter's, formerly a Benedictine monastery, and still used as a place of preparation for the Catholic priesthood. The Monks have all vanished, but the people are devout Catholics. At every half mile by the roadside is a carefully kept crucifix, and last night as we were having our supper in the common room of the inn we suddenly heard sounds that seemed to me like those of an accordion. "Is that a zittern?" said Mr. Lewes to the German lady by his side. "No, it is prayer." The servants, by themselves—the host and hostess were in the same room with us—were saying their evening prayers, men's and women's voices blending in unusually correct harmony. The same loud prayer is heard at morning noon and evening from the shepherds and workers in the fields. We suppose that the believers in Mr. Home and in Madame Rachel would pronounce these people "grossly superstitious." The land is cultivated by rich peasant proprietors, and the people here as in Petersthal look healthy and contented. This really adds to one's pleasure in seeing natural beauties. (*Letters* 4:457)

> Come with me to the mountain, not where rocks
> Soar harsh above the troops of hurrying pines,
> But where the earth spreads soft and rounded breasts
> To feed her children; where the generous hills
> Lift a green isle betwixt the sky and plain
> To keep some Old World things aloof from change.
> Here too 'tis hill and hollow: new-born streams
> With sweet enforcement, joyously compelled
> Like laughing children, hurry down the steeps,
> And make a dimpled chase athwart the stones ... (1:73)

Heavenly terminology describes the nurturing paradise ("A little world whose round horizon cuts / This isle of hills with heaven for a sea"), and oxymoronic phrases using feminine language ("sweet enforcement" and "joyously compelled")[30] draw the reader's attention to the connection of theme and place (1:73). The pastoral setting is isolated and protected from the outside world "save in clear moments when southwestward gleams / France by the Rhine" (1:73).

Next, the description of setting homes in on a religious town, named after Saint Mary, a place formerly inhabited by Augustinian monks:

> The monks of old chose here their still retreat,
> And called it by the Blessed Virgin's name,
> Sancta Maria, which the peasant's tongue,
> Speaking from out the parent's heart that turns
> All loved things into little things, has made
> Sanct Märgen,— Holy little Mary, dear
> As all the sweet home things she smiles upon. (1:73)

Feminine, diminutive language ("loved things," "little things," "Holy little Mary, dear") connects the domestic Holy Mary and the "sweet home things" upon which she smiles. With this passage, the narrator seems to smile upon the reader with the same sweetness with which the Virgin Mary smiles on domestic life in the town. Mary blesses "the children and the cows, the apple-trees, / The cart, the plough," sanctifying the agricultural town (1:73). She sets a feminine example of humility and domestic service to others despite her divine origins:

---

[30] Eliot employs oxymora and paradox in other poems that contain feminine and religious themes as well. In "Ex Oriente Lux," Eliot presents a double birthing image (the birth of the earth and of Thought) along with oxymoronic and paradoxical expressions ("sweet imprisonment," "Dividing towards sublime union," and "Clove sense and image subtilly in twain") to emphasize the complexity of religious and philosophical matters and to promote sympathy and appreciation for Eastern culture and religion (*CSP* 2:99). In "O May I Join the Choir Invisible," oxymoronic phrases such as "immortal dead" and "divinely human" challenge readers to consider the notion that human sympathy constitutes divine action (2:85–6). In "Erinna," Eliot refers to the "darling dragon Hate," "rage divine," and "terrible beauty" to describe the suffering of an innocent girl and elicit the pity of the reader (2:115).

> What though a Queen? She puts her crown away
> And with her little Boy wears common clothes,
> Caring for common wants, remembering
> That day when good Saint Joseph left his work
> To marry her with humble trust sublime. (1:74)

The town reveres Mary as the community mother and caregiver. The Matriarch, despite her divine connections, assumes a humble stature: she resides with, not above, the community and serves as divine intercessor for all:

> Grandames and mothers and the flute-voiced girls,—
> Fall on their knees and send forth prayerful cries
> To the kind Mother with the little Boy,
> Who pleads for helpless men against the storm,
> Lightning and plagues and all terrific shapes
> Of power supreme. (1:74)

The townspeople venerate domesticity and femininity in their adoration of the Holy Mother. The holy monks (representing a patriarchal divine order) that founded the Augustinian monastery of Sankt Märgen in the twelfth century are gone and forgotten: "monks are gone, their shadows fall no more." Now, domestic men replace holy men ("their silent corridors / Are turned to homes of bare-armed, aproned men" / Who toil for wife and children") in the sacred place where church bells "pealing on high from two quaint convent towers" summon "To grave remembrance of the larger life / That bears our own, like perishable fruit / Upon its heaven-wide branches" (1:74). The image of men wearing aprons recalls the image of Joseph leaving his work to marry the Holy Mother. The feminine men in this once patriarchal town bear witness to the Holy Mother's salutary influence. Though the monks are gone, the bells from the monastery still "ring the Catholic signals," marking the continuity of religion and community (1:74). Saints living and dead share the same sacred location and participate in a community life that continues to thrive under the blessing of the Holy Mother.

After describing the broad landscape and then the town, the narrator focuses in on the setting even more closely on the "prettiest hollow of these hills" where Agatha's cottage and a small chapel are located. Again, the narrator goes into elaborate description of the scene to draw attention to the hallowed importance of the home. Near the cottage "on the farthest height" stands a chapel "with a little tower" decorated with "heaven-planted, incense-mingling flowers" with an altar to the Virgin Mary:

> Within, the altar where the Mother sits
> 'Mid votive tablets hung from far-off years
> By peasants succoured in the peril of fire,
> Fever, or flood, who thought that Mary's love,
> Willing but not omnipotent, had stood
> Between their lives and that dread power which slew
> Their neighbor at their side. (1:75)

The chapel[31] is a pilgrimage site where worshippers come to pray to the Virgin Mary, who acts as intercessor to the community. The descriptions of Sankt Märgen, the monastery, and the chapel preface that of Agatha's home, which like the chapel is "one room" in which "everything within the four low walls [is] / An honoured relic" (1:75). Agatha's home is a holy place, containing Catholic books, pictures of immortalized women saints ("little pictures hung a-row, / Telling the stories of Saint Ursula, / And Saint Elizabeth, the lowly queen"), and pictures over her bed, including one of the Virgin's death and one of her "flowering tomb" above which she "smiling bends and lets her girdle down / For ladder to the souls that cannot trust / In life which outlasts burial" (1:76–7). The picture of a smiling Mary acting as divine intercessor by means of her feminine garment serves as daily inspiration to Agatha who also serves others by means of her feminine goodness. Agatha keeps the company of "kings and queens / And mitred saints who sat below the feet / Of Francis with the ragged frock and wounds" in pictures on her walls (1:77). Like Saint Francis who chose to live in poverty, Agatha finds nice clothes "not worth while" and instead finds her worth in "Duty ... / ... done worthily" and "humblest service" (1:82, 77). Inside this consecrated home, Agatha performs the sacred task ("the higher gift") of caring for her cousins Kate and Nell, who "Are housed by her in Love and Duty's name, / They being feeble, with small withered wits, / And she believing that the higher gift / Was given to be shared" (1:75). She also keeps a quiet home where "all things round / Seemed filled with noiseless yet responsive life, / As of a child at breast that gently clings," and she is an immaculate housekeeper: "all the household goods ... polished fair / By hands that cherished them for service done" (1:76). The poem's lengthy descriptions of setting establish the religious significance of home and caring for others.[32] The

---

[31] Judas-Thaddäus Chapel on the Ohmen, twelfth century.

[32] "A London Drawingroom," in contrast to "Agatha," relies on setting to provide a picture of a life without sympathy:

> The sky is cloudy, yellowed by the smoke.
> For view there are the houses opposite
> Cutting the sky with one long line of wall
> Like solid fog: far as the eye can stretch
> Monotony of surface & of form
> Without a break to hang a guess upon.
> No bird can make a shadow as it flies,
> For all is shadow, as in ways o'erhung
> By thickest canvass, where the golden rays
> Are clothed in hemp. No figure lingering
> Pauses to feed the hunger of the eye
> Or rest a little on the lap of life.
> All hurry on and look upon the ground,
> Or glance unmarking at the passers by
> The wheels are hurrying too, cabs, carriages
> All closed, in multiplied identity.

narrator uses second person ("just as you enter ... you will find") to take the reader from a broad landscape (mother Earth) to a closer view of the area (Sankt Märgen and the Augustinian monastery), to a chapel within the valley, and then to Agatha's cottage which—like the other sites described—is a holy living shrine (1:73–7). The reader finally enters this holy of holies after a three-page descriptive journey to learn the significance of a life sympathetically—and therefore sacredly—lived.

Eliot elevates the domestic realm and the role of motherhood by presenting Agatha as a divine representation of the feminine ideal. Through interaction with the angelic Countess Linda and through association with the Virgin Mary, Agatha attains an otherworldly status as domestic perfection itself. The "old knitter" lives in a sacred home and receives visits from angels like the Holy Mother Mary: "For in the slanting sunbeams angels come / And visit Agatha who dwells within" (1:75). One such angel is Linda, who appears to be a beautiful noblewoman. It is unclear whether Linda is alive or appearing in spirit form, as when she enters, the action shifts from the present tense (for the description of setting) to the past tense (for the relation of the story). Linda was either a member of the community who was young at the time of the narrator's story or one who died while young—either way, "her years were few" (1:76). As Eliot describes her, Linda was the picture of feminine perfection:

> Taught in all seemliness that fits a court,
> All lore that shapes the mind to delicate use,
> Yet quiet, lowly, as a meek white dove
> That with its presence teaches gentleness. (1:76)

It is not known whether this "angel in the house"[33] was married or had children of her own, but she was known by the town's orphans as "Mamma Linda" and devoted her life to caring for the helpless. Agatha, too, has devoted her life to caring for others. She cared for "an old afflicted pair, / Who wore out slowly" thirty years ago and left her their cottage after they died, and then she cared

---

> The world seems one huge prison-house and court
> Where men are punished at the slightest cost,
> With lowest rate of colour, warmth and joy. (2:91)

The narrator in the London drawing-room looks out the window to a scene in which people rush through the smoggy, dark, and lonely city without eye contact or care for one another. Apathy replaces sympathy in this prison-like dystopia. "Agatha," by contrast, portrays a peaceful, idyllic heaven on earth characterized by a community that loves and sympathizes.

[33] Referring to Countess Linda as an angel and presenting Agatha as spiritual perfection might be a nod to the "angel in the house" ideal. Coventry Patmore coined the phrase in the title of his poem, "The Angel in the House," which portrayed the perfect Victorian woman (his wife) as devoted and submissive to her husband. Eliot's letters do not make clear whether or not she read this poem, but the popularization of the concept by the 1860s makes it likely that she was familiar with the expression. Eliot's angels in "Agatha," however, are either dead or unmarried, and they are not beholden to one husband and one household, but to other women and to the entire community.

for Kate and Nell, her feeble-minded cousins, in her cottage. Linda and Agatha comprise a composite of the feminine ideal. With no mention of biological children, the narrator nevertheless describes them as mothers to the community. They are both likened to the Holy Mother Mary who, having the status of a Queen, "puts her crown away" and cares for "common wants" (1:74, 77). Linda represents Mary, the Queen; whereas, Agatha—the poor, old woman whose "grey hair is a crown"—represents the common Mary (1:82). Both care for the "common wants" of the community as symbolic mothers to all.

The purpose of the dialogue between Linda and Agatha is to reveal the character of Agatha and present a picture of sympathetic female community. Through Linda's questions, the reader learns that Agatha, like Mary, is the community's divine intercessor:

> … I pray, I pray
> For poor young Hans. I take it much to heart
> That other people are worse off than I,—
> I ease my soul with praying for them all.
> ………………………………………..
> … the Virgin's heart
> Is kinder far than mine; and then I stop
> And feel I can do nought towards helping men,
> Till out it comes, like tears that will not hold,
> And I must pray again for all the world. (1:79)

Agatha takes pilgrimages to purge her life of sin in order to be a perfect intercessor for the community: "I try / All ways I know of to be cleansed and pure. / I would not sink where evil spirits are. / There's perfect goodness somewhere: so I strive" (1:80). She has taken one pilgrimage to the Einsiedeln Abbey in Switzerland, and plans to go again despite her old age. Like Jubal, she undertakes the pilgrimage for the sake of the community and finds the travel experience regenerating and purifying (1:56, 79-80). Also like Jubal, she alone takes on the atoning responsibility for all the community. Agatha explains:

> … people are busy here
> The beasts want tendance. One who is not missed
> Can go and pray for others who must work.
> I owe it to all neighbours, young and old;
> For they are good past thinking,—lads and girls
> Given to mischief, merry naughtiness,
> Quiet, as the hedgehogs smooth their spines,
> For fear of hurting poor old Agatha.
> 'Tis pretty: why, the cherubs in the sky
> Look young and merry and the angels play
> On citherns, lutes, and all sweet instruments.
> I would have young things merry. See the Lord!
> A little baby playing with the birds;
> And how the Blessed Mother smiles at him. (1:81)

Agatha prays for the young people who are given to mischief and merriment, and she sees in them a vision of heaven in which angels similarly appear young and merry as they play their "sweet instruments." Though they quiet their "merry naughtiness" in Agatha's presence, she does not judge them but "would have young things merry" (1:81). As the Blessed Mother smiles on baby Jesus and angels in the sky, Blessed Agatha smiles on the youth in her community; she sees in them the continuity of life. She is the "old stalk to be plucked away: / The garden must be cleared for young spring plants" and will "go / Right willingly" to a new "home beyond the grave" where "most are there / All those we pray to" (1:81). She will join the saintly choir in heaven, and the new generation will be connected to her through prayer and memory. Like the Virgin Mary and other saints depicted in the monastery, the chapel, and her home, Agatha will live on after death in the minds and hearts of those she touched through her sacrificial devotion to others; the Catholic bells in the town will summon "To grave remembrance of the larger life / That bears our own" (1:74).[34]

At the end of the dialogue between Linda and Agatha, the narrator shifts to first person and explains that though once an outsider, she decided to remain in Sankt Märgen and become part of the community—"I stayed among those hills" (1:83). During her stay, she "oft heard more / Of Agatha" and "liked to hear her name, / As that of one half granddame and half saint" (1:83). By reminding the reader of her presence, the narrator—having begun the story by entreating the reader to "Come with me to the mountain …"—concludes the poetic pilgrimage by enshrining Agatha's legacy for future generations of readers. Just as the Catholic Church canonized the saints on Agatha's wall, the poet canonizes the life of Saint Agatha by recording the community's account of her life and influence.

The Sankt Märgen community recognizes Agatha as the community's patron mother-saint by giving her diminutive nicknames as a sign of affection and by remembering how she served the community as a loving intercessor:

> … The lads
> And younger men all called her mother, aunt,
> Or granny, with their pet diminutives,
> And bade their lasses and their brides behave
> Right well to one who surely made a link
> 'Twixt faulty folk and God by loving both:
> Not one but counted service done by her. (1:83)

---

[34] In death, Agatha will join the ranks of the female saints on her cottage walls— Saints Ann, Elizabeth, Ursula, and Mary—to represent chastity (like Saint Ursula) and motherhood (like Saints Ann, Elizabeth, and Mary). Saint Ann was the mother of Mary; Saint Elizabeth was the mother of John the Baptist. Both were barren and became mothers as a result of divine intervention. Ursula was a virgin martyr and never had the chance to marry or have children, and the Virgin Mary conceived immaculately. All embody in various ways an idealized femininity that evokes motherhood and virginity.

The community also remembers her as a sweet grandmother who enjoyed the friendly tricks of groups of merry revelers "for the love it showed" (1:83). The poet Hans—possibly the same Hans that Agatha prayed for when he went off to war, now safely returned—"wrote [for] them songs / That grew from out [of] their life," one of which the narrator relates that "They oft sang, wending homeward from a feast" (1:83). Hans's ten-stanza folk song is a prayer that celebrates the community and invokes the aid of Agatha and other saints. Drunken merrymakers form choirs that sing "In quaintly mingled mirth and piety" together as they return home from celebrations: "Midnight by the chapel bell! / Homeward, homeward all, farewell! / I with you, and you with me, / Miles are short with company" and petition the "Holy Babe" to "Bind us fast to one another!" (1:83–4). They remember those who have passed on, like Toni whose "ghost is wandering now, / Shaped just like a snow-white cow," and superstitiously they give his ghost "good cheer" (1:84).[35] They sing "good words" for Agatha, Kate and Nell as they pass the cottage and wish the "Little maidens old, sweet dreams! / Sleep one sleep till morning beams" (1:85). They praise them for helping as mothers to the community: "Mothers ye, who help us all, Quick at hand, if ill befall," and they ask "Holy Gabriel" to "Bless the aged mother-maiden!" (1:85). Each six-line stanza ends with a two-line refrain asking "Heart of Mary" (six times), "Holy Babe, our God and Brother," "Good Saint Joseph," "Meek Saint Anna," and "Holy Gabriel" for protection, comfort, unity, faithfulness, joy, blessings for the elderly, uprightness, and a place with the saints (1:83–5). This prayer-song and the poem itself celebrate the life of the community, including members and events past and present, and summon "To grave remembrance of the larger life / That bears our own" (1:74).

The narrator has taken the reader on a journey to a foreign place where saintliness resides in community living, and idealized femininity involves spiritual (rather than biological) motherhood. Religion consists of Catholicism that has been redefined to include feminized men and maternal leaders. Women are valued for their ability to foster community and care for others, not for their ability to marry well and give birth to children. Superstition, drinking, and merry-making are all acceptable elements of the community that thrives in its togetherness. The saintly women in the story are all dead but remain a vibrant part of the community and provide a sacrosanct model for future generations. By depicting motherhood metaphorically rather than literally, by connecting femininity and sainthood, and by presenting the home as a sacred environment, Eliot takes advantage of nineteenth-

---

[35] McCormack remarks on the disparity of the superstitious element at the end and the celebration of Agatha's Catholicism: "The conclusion of the poem thus presents an unanticipated, rawly superstitious, male-dominated scene that contrasts with the female saintliness gone before in Agatha's cottage" (*George Eliot in Society* 51). Her point is well-taken, especially given the young men's bidding girlfriends and brides to behave well to Agatha. One could read these details as a sign of the community's patriarchal regression; however, since this male action is mediated by the abiding influence of Agatha's maternal example, I see the overall message as one that upholds the values, and potentially transformative power, of motherhood and community.

century domestic values to communicate a message that appears to reflect those values but in fact offers a different model of spirituality. By taking the reader outside of England, where rigid laws of decorum reflect traditional values, to a foreign home that appears to be a true sanctuary in its lack of religious and societal stricture, Eliot conveys the idea that sympathy for others creates a vibrant, blessed community. Eliot, like Agatha, was not a biological mother, but she was a spiritual mother to the community who presented herself as a non-traditional feminine ideal—a poetess with divine authority to act as intercessor for her readership.

Conclusion

Eliot relied on the poetess themes of female community and motherhood, which were associated with a stance of sympathy. She celebrated motherhood in her poems by displacing biological motherhood and direct care for children with non-traditional female families. Agatha, mother to her community, represents the sympathetic ideal that Armgart acquires. Agatha lives on in the singing voices of the young people in the community that she touched, and Armgart will live on in singing voices of the young women she will teach.

Likewise, Eliot will live on through the female voices she brought to life in her poems. Like her characters, she too identified with motherhood, and neither her status as a fallen woman nor her rejection of traditional Christianity hindered her from assuming a position as spiritual leader to the nation later in life. She guided others toward a better way of life—that of caring for others—by writing poetry within a tradition that associated itself with feminine piety and spiritual authority. For Eliot, exercising sympathy for others was the highest achievement for humanity, and she wrote to teach the value of such an achievement. Readers who take into account Eliot's poetess treatment of community and motherhood come to view her not only as a writer of fiction, an intellectual, and a social commentator but also as a woman who longed to nurture, participate in, and foster human relationships.

Chapter 5
The Future of George Eliot Studies

George Eliot struggled with depression, anxiety, and relentless self-doubt throughout her life. She was painfully conscious of her plain looks, the cause of rejection by John Chapman and Herbert Spencer, and she feared becoming a spinster. When she boldly commenced a liaison with Lewes, she suffered the rejection of her family and society. Writing, too, provided an endless source of anxiety. Eliot took on a male pseudonym to protect herself from detractors who would denigrate her work based on her reputation as a fallen woman. Hiding her identity suited her because she had a deeply ingrained fear of failure. Extremely self-conscious and often in need of reassurance, she worried about not writing well and about the criticism of her work. Benjamin Jowett wrote that her "extraordinarily sensitive, pathetic, & sympathetic emotions" were the "secret of her not writing until she was 40 years of age" and that she was "deeply affected by what is said of her" (Collins, *Interviews* 157). He also said that she "seemed to fear too much that her writing would not be appreciated" (205). Novelist Mary Ward wrote of Eliot's need for sympathy from others:

> I am conscious of something very human and womanly, which seems still to lay an appealing hand upon one, as though it asked above all for sympathy—and to be understood. She was abnormally, pitifully dependent upon sympathy; it explains the false step of her life. But it also explains the infinitely receptive and plastic temper which was the source of her best art. She who craved for sympathy had first given it in good measure—poured down and running over—to the human life about her. (143)

Eliot's emphasis on sympathy arose from her own experience as an outsider in society who longed to be understood and to be a part of the community. She valued human relationships and was hurt by societal alienation. She chose a lifestyle that many deemed immoral, yet she championed morality by upholding the notion that sympathy itself embodied that which was best in religion and suggested that those who treated others with understanding and compassion best understood the concept of God. Her personal choices meant that she would not be a legal wife or biological mother. Yet, she assumed these roles and accomplished a domestic and spiritual ideal in her life and writing. Writing as a poetess, she transformed her pains and troubles into an impulse to convey the redemptive value of sympathy in poetry.

Eliot experienced the ministering potential of poetry. She absorbed herself in poetry after the deaths of her father, her step-son, and Lewes, "finding it absolutely

necessary to get into an emotionally different sphere" (Collins, *Interviews* 205).[1]
She, too, wanted to provide a poetic source of solace and inspiration for others, and
to that end she spent a great deal of her artistic energy writing and publishing poetry.
She interrupted *Middlemarch* to write poetry and set aside *Daniel Deronda* to
collect her poems in a volume (*The Legend of Jubal, and Other Poems*) even though
many of them had already been published in magazines. Nancy Henry explains
that Eliot turned to poetry, "the highest and most serious form of writing," out of
a "sense of what a great author should do for mankind" (*Cambridge Introduction*
83). She explains that "perhaps Eliot simply could not feel herself the equal of
contemporaries such as Tennyson, much less past greats such as Wordsworth,
Scott, Goethe, Milton or Shakespeare, until she had tried her hand at both epic
and lyric poetry" (83–4). She aspired to be ranked alongside past and present great
poets, and others viewed her as achieving such renown (calling her the "Female
Shakespeare"), but whether or not she saw herself as a success in this regard is not
clear. What is clear is that she viewed her purpose as an artist to awaken sympathy
in others; and she assumed a prophetic voice as a poetess "to propagate as far as
[she could]" the ideas for which she cared so strongly (*Letters* 6:26).

Eliot adopted the feminine poetess persona only after her early public writing
career as an anonymous reviewer and after the pseudonymous (supposedly male)
authorship of her first five novels. Her readers ultimately associated her famous
male name with the feminine poetess. Readers of her novels would have seen her
poetry as works of moral instruction rather than as works of entertainment, and
they would have understood Eliot's role as that of a public novelist taking on a
poetess stance to voice a guiding message for her readership. As LaPorte states,
she "embraces stereotypically feminine poetic models as an influence that should
change the cultural landscape, and even have a guiding influence akin to that of
the Bible ("Poetess as Prophet" 159). She was famous, influential, and prominent
in changing the thought in nineteenth-century England via her novels and German
translations. As a poetess, she used her influence to write with a moral imperative
to make a better society. Modern readers as a whole, however, remain unfamiliar
with this important genre of Eliot's oeuvre because the poems had not been easily
accessible and because modern criticism, until very recently, had largely classified
her verse as inferior and unworthy of study. But to understand more fully George
Eliot and her place in the canon of Victorian literature, one must include study of her
poetry. An accurate picture of Eliot and her work includes an understanding of the
novelist who presented herself as a man *and* the poetess who used her femininity.

This book has demonstrated one way to view Eliot's work as a poet: through
her stance as a poetess who propagated the feminine value of sympathy through a
voice of moral and spiritual authority. I have argued that Eliot assumed the stance
of a poetess to encourage sympathetic relations between the sexes and among those

---

[1]   She wrote "As Tu Vu la Lune se Lever" after her father's death and "The Legend of
Jubal" after Thornie died (*CSP* 1:27, Haight 465). After Lewes's death, she stayed alone in
her room reading and copying sections of *In Memoriam* (Haight 516–17).

with different religious views and lifestyles. For Eliot, sympathy led to a moral society, and the role of a poet was to heighten the readers' awareness of the salvific power of sympathy and guide them toward a better way of living. Eliot took on the converging roles of poetess, sage, moral leader, and mother to the nation and aspired to the highest of cultural influence while appropriating the most modest and feminine means to further this end. In much of her poetry, she appeared to uphold traditional, domestic values while sometimes inserting controversial views in order to promote compassion, fairness, and fellow-feeling. Poetry was not a departure from her artistic aim but rather an extension of it. She could comment on social issues more assertively in her poetry than in fiction because poetry allowed for a measure of disguise behind feminine expression and within the confined quarters of verse form. Scholars may wish to further examine how Eliot fits into the poetess tradition by discussing poems not discussed here and by interpreting her poems alongside those of other poetesses who inspired her and whom she inspired. Such analyses would make more complete the understanding of nineteenth-century women poets. Eliot's conspicuous presence as one of the century's great authors renders her near omission from critical discussions of poetry quite surprising.

Poetic Themes

Examining Eliot's poetry through her feminine stance as a poetess is but one way to view her poetic oeuvre. Her poetry invites further exploration from other perspectives as well. Many of her unanalyzed (or under-analyzed) poems shed light on her social views, and thematic studies of these poems will bring about a better understanding of Eliot's thought and expression thereof. For example, Eliot criticism still wants a thorough examination of religion in her poetry. LaPorte provides excellent examples of such studies in "George Eliot: The Poetess as Prophet" and in *Victorian Poets and the Changing Bible*, in which he shows how Eliot uses domestic, sentimental tropes and relies on biblical subjects in her poems to demonstrate the vatic power "that derived from sympathy, from a sentiment that in Eliot's culture had become the province of women" (*Victorian Poets* 226). Eliot's interest in Judaism, prophecy, and biblical myths invites fuller examinations into her poems that deal with religious themes.

An in-depth discussion of the role of music in Eliot's poetry is also still needed. "O May I Join the Choir Invisible," "The Legend of Jubal," *Armgart*, "Arion," and "Stradivarius" all present music as a central theme. Music in these poems provides the means to immortality, and the musician (and by extension, the poet) comments on the immortalizing power of music.[2] For example, in "Stradivarius" and "The

---

[2]   Beryl Gray's *George Eliot and Music* discusses the importance of music in the life and works of Eliot, and Phyllis Weliver's *The Figure of Music in Nineteenth-Century British Poetry* includes some of Eliot's poems in its analysis of music in the nineteenth-century. However, the prevalence of music in her poems calls for a more focused analysis of its role.

Legend of Jubal," central characters create an instrument that brings sacred music to the community. Both characters struggle with the egoistic ambition that comes from their power as creators and lose sight of the real purpose for their gift—to serve God by uniting the community through the saving power of music. Stradivarius views his master skill in making violins as a gift that helps God rather than as a gift from God. He "should rob God" if he did not make violins because "not God Himself can make man's best / Without best men to help him" (*Complete Shorter Poetry* 2:18). Eliot punishes such creative hubris in "The Legend of Jubal." Jubal's "burning need / To claim his fuller self" by declaring himself the creator of the lyre to gain fame leads to rejection and ultimately death; his community, in disbelief, beats him for blasphemy and leaves him for dead (1:61–3). An examination of these two poems would add to an understanding of the religious function of music in Eliot's work and shed light on her personal struggle with artistic ambition.

The concept of memory also pervades Eliot's poetry. She grapples with memory, time, and change in "As Tu Vu la Lune se Lever," "O May I Join the Choir Invisible," "How Lisa Loved the King," "Brother and Sister," "The Legend of Jubal," "Two Lovers," "Self and Life," "Sweet Evenings Come and Go, Love," "Agatha," "I Grant You Ample Leave," and *The Spanish Gypsy* to comment on how invocations of memory recall the natural process of the development of the individual and the community. In "Brother and Sister," the narrator "cannot choose but think upon" formative years of life with her brother, including "dire years whose awful name is Change" (2:5, 11). Memory forces her to analyze how life's painful transitions molded her into the person she ultimately becomes. In "The Legend of Jubal," memory shapes not just the individual but also the community as a whole: "Memory [discloses] her face divine" to remind people of death and change and urge them to seek immortality through artistic creation which will live on in others' memories (1:44). Memory in "The Legend of Jubal" concerns herself not with the individual but with collective identity. Jubal seeks the familiarity of "those first eager years," and longs for the recognition of his tribe but instead encounters "Dread Change, with dubious face and cold / That never kept a welcome for the old" (1:59). Dreadful change creates a new world that worships artistic inventions, such as music, and appropriates human innovation to develop collectively without regard for the wishes of the development's originator. Jubal's seeking fame shows that he lost sight of the communal purpose of creating. The poem thus urges the artist to create and then relinquish personal claims to the art with the understanding that the art exists to serve an ever-changing society. These brief examples show how Eliot's treatment of memory calls for further investigation in her poems.

My discussion of female community in Chapter 4 only brushes the surface of the overarching theme of community in Eliot's poetry. Eliot addresses the themes of community and isolation in "Farewell," "Sonnet," "In a London Drawingroom," "Two Lovers," "O May I Join the Choir Invisible," "Agatha," "How Lisa Loved the King," *Armgart*, "Brother and Sister," "Erinna," "The Legend of Jubal," and *The Spanish Gypsy*. She approaches these themes from various angles. For example,

"Sonnet" and "In a London Drawingroom" create a mood of disillusionment by depicting an isolating setting. Both these poems create a mood of imprisonment and alienation. In "As Tu Vu la Lune se Lever" and "Two Lovers," on the other hand, Eliot creates a mood inspired by romantic love. The narrator of "As Tu Vu" compares the beautiful sight of stars reflected in dew drops and the scent of a flower in one's coat pocket to the beauty of a noble soul (1:29). The narrator urges his/her lover (and readers) to hold on to such sweet memories that unite one to another. "Two Lovers" binds together lovers not through memories triggered by moments in time but through the collective memories of a life spent together. Both poems celebrate the joy of togetherness. These poems present vivid portraits of community and isolation, and a number of other poems contrast these ideas to promote Eliot's cherished belief in the value of living in cooperation and with mutual understanding.[3] Examining Eliot's use of religion, music, memory, and community in her poetry would add new dimensions to current readings of her works.

Overlapping Themes in Poetry and Novels

Many themes in Eliot's poetry also find life in her fiction, and thematic comparisons can expand the meaning of the fiction, particularly (but not exclusively) in the cases in which she wrote poetry at or around the same time as novels. Margaret Reynolds states that Eliot's poetry "functions as a parallel text to the novels; many of the same concerns and themes are taken up there, and quite often a poetic text, composed at about the same time as a novel, will reflect and enlarge upon the prose" (*Oxford Readers Companion* 304).[4] Reynolds is right. Eliot interrupted writing *Middlemarch* (1869–1872) to compose "How Lisa Loved the King" (1869), "Brother and Sister" (1869), and *Armgart* (1870), and one can find parallel themes in all of these works. For example, as I discussed in Chapter 3, Eliot makes

---

[3]   Other thematic avenues for exploration in Eliot's poems, all of which overlap with the theme of religion, include suffering (see "How Lisa Loved the King," "Question and Answer," *Armgart*, "Erinna," "Self and Life," "The Legend of Jubal," "Arion," and *The Spanish Gypsy*), death (see "Farewell," "O May I Join," "How Lisa Loved the King," "Sweet Evenings," "Death of Moses," "The Legend of Jubal," *Armgart*, "Arion," "Self and Life," and *The Spanish Gypsy*), the concept of the soul (see "Mid the Rich Store," "O May I Join," "Agatha," "How Lisa Loved the King," "As Tu Vu," "Brother and Sister," "Erinna," "Death of Moses," *The Spanish Gypsy*), and renunciation (see "How Lisa Loved the King," "The Legend of Jubal," *Armgart*, "Arion ," "Death of Moses," and *The Spanish Gypsy*).

[4]   Nancy Henry also points out the fact that Eliot's novels and poetry contain parallel themes, explaining that "in the poems she intentionally distills ideas which in the novels are diffused in the larger artistic project of creating a realistic, multi-faceted fictional world" (*Cambridge Introduction* 83). Henry observes that Eliot's poems "single out for emphasis ideas and emotions that are present in the novels" while at the same time, they "provide insight into what she thought poetry ought to be and do and in turn what she thought fiction should be and do" (84).

subversive comments on marriage in "How Lisa Loved the King"; however, her simultaneous treatment of marriage in *Middlemarch* is less controversial. Dorothea does not need to marry, but she does. She renounces her wealth and philanthropic aspirations to take on the traditional role of wife and mother. In the finale, the narrator comments: "Many who knew her, thought it a pity that so substantive and rare a creature should have been absorbed into the life of another, and be only known in a certain circle as a wife and mother. But no one stated exactly what else that was in her power she ought rather to have done" (836). Such is the view of many readers and critics today. Dorothea's marriage seems like capitulation to society's gender normative expectations, but as the narrator states, what else was she to do? She did what was expected. Eliot offered a less risky view of marriage in her widely read novel, and in doing so avoided censure.[5] Both the poem and the novel leave the reader somewhat dissatisfied with the marriage of the protagonists; however, Eliot made a much bolder statement condemning nineteenth-century marriage practices in her poem.

The most obvious case in which Eliot's poetry functions as a parallel text includes "Brother and Sister" and *The Mill on the Floss*, although they were not written at the same time. Like "Brother and Sister," *The Mill on the Floss* details the lives of two siblings who grow up in a rural setting. Both the novel and the poem depict the tension between the siblings due to the sister's non-conformity to gender rules and the brother's disapproval. The novel concludes with the death of the reunited siblings, and the poem concludes with a divorce and a liberated sister-poet. Eliot frees the non-conforming sister in "Brother and Sister" and drowns her in *The Mill on the Floss*. The sister in the poem suffers the loss of her brother but thrives personally through the power of imagination and her ability to express herself through the art of writing. The sister in the novel regains her brother's affection but dies in the end. Both sisters suffer because they are female, but the sister-narrator has the power to recreate her life through verse and live on in the minds of her readers. Eliot was able to speak out on gender matters more freely in her poetry because her poetry presented the material in a less overt manner. Aware of the fact that readers scrutinized novels more thoroughly than poetry, Eliot developed these themes more discreetly through verse.

---

[5]   Some marriages are emotionally fulfilling (such as the unions of Fred and Mary in *Middlemarch* and Adam and Dinah in *Adam Bede*), and some result in disillusionment and unhappiness. Women in Eliot's novels, though not the sole sufferers, more often suffer in bad marriages because of their greater need to marry. Without many options for work and with no legal entitlement to property, women had to rely on marriage for survival and were expected to be dutiful, loyal, and submissive to their husbands. Most of Eliot's wives submit to their husbands. Rosamond Lydgate in *Middlemarch* is an obvious exception. Her strong will and self-centeredness clash with her husband's expectations for submissiveness, and consequently the relationship is a disaster.

Poetic Epigraphs

Another avenue for future Eliot studies includes examination of her poetic epigraphs. Eliot's epigraphs served as chapter headings in some of her novels to offer thematic parallels and metaphoric evaluations of characters.[6] J.R. Tye explains that Eliot used these epigraphs (or "mottoes" as she called them) in the tradition of Scott, Dickens, and Thackeray, and he examines Eliot's painstaking process of writing and incorporating epigraphs in her later novels (*Felix Holt, the Radical*; *Middlemarch*; and *Daniel Deronda*), the reasons she used them, and the function they served (235). He focuses on her own prose and poetic epigraphs as opposed to ones she borrowed from other authors. David Higdon helpfully notes that of the 225 epigraphs in her works, 96 are original and 129 are borrowed from 56 identified authors and eight anonymous authors to point out the fact that though she drew from a variety of sources, she often relied on her own creativity to craft introductory statements (128–9). Higdon shows that she consciously designed the epigraphs to form a central part of the structure of her novels, and he refers to her comments in "Notes on Form in Art" about the wholeness of a work evolving from a union of smaller parts. Eliot's concern with the relationship between the parts and the whole of a work, explains Higdon, implies that "she was highly selective in admitting into her novels only that which was consistent with the overall design" (133–4). He analyzes various epigraphs to show how they served a structuring function in the novels. Reynolds also explores the function of Eliot's epigraphs:

> The epigraphs serve both as a clue to what will follow in each chapter, and as an alternative, often ironic, commentary on what has gone before—depending on whether you read them before, or after, or even refer to them during, the reading of a chapter. The mixture of "real" quotations borrowed from Shakespeare, Wordsworth, and the Bible, as well as many other sources, put alongside the "made up" quotations which are George Eliot's own means that Eliot makes herself into one of the sages whose word is a form of law, a yardstick for moral reading and thinking. (*Oxford Reader's Companion* 304)

Few critics have found interest in the overall structural function of Eliot's epigraphs. Further analysis of the epigraphs as parallel texts to Eliot's novels could provide rich insight into her participation in a tradition of novelists relying on poetry and her use of her own poetry to provide a guiding, moral voice in her novels. Eliot incorporated more epigraphs in her later novels than in early ones; she wrote these final novels at a time when she was establishing herself as a poetess. She thus used her poetess persona in her novels not only to provide parallel themes but

---

[6]   For more on Eliot's use of epigraphs, see van den Broek's discussion in *Complete Shorter Poetry* (2:129–30) and his entry on epigraphs in the *Oxford Reader's Companion* (100). Also, to read Eliot's own thoughts on incorporating epigraphs, see her letters to her publisher John Blackwood in 1876 (*Letters* 6:241) and 1873 (5:458–9).

also to remind her readers that she wrote fiction as an entertainer and as a moral guide. She therefore encouraged readers to enter into the lives of the characters with a sense of moral obligation to feel and relate to the characters' struggles and sorrows. In this way, she was able to encourage sympathy in her fiction with the authority of a poetess.

Sympathy in Poetry and Novels

Scholars might also consider a comparative study of Eliot's approach to sympathy in her poetry and novels.[7] Though she encourages sympathy in most of her works, she approaches sympathy differently in her poetry. Readers of her novels enter into the lives of characters by empathizing with the hardships of some characters, condemning the selfish motives of other characters, and identifying with the noble and ignoble alike through Eliot's careful creation of flawed, realistic personages. In her poetry, on the other hand, she relies less on characterization and realistic portrayals to invoke sympathy. Instead, she draws on the power of verse form and poetic techniques, her own relationship to the reader as moral guide, and, at times, religious themes and language to convey a message of sympathy. For example, in her lyric poem, "O May I Join the Choir Invisible," Eliot assures the reward of immortality for those who strive for "generosity," "deeds of daring rectitude," and "thoughts sublime." Her use of religious language and themes and the musical iambic pentameter uplifts the reader, making her feel a part of a chanting choir aspiring to otherworldly greatness. Readers identify not with a struggling, realistic character but rather with a nameless narrator who, like any reader, feels moved by the beauty of the poem's language and spiritual message and who feels connected by a desire to join the choir invisible. In "Brother and Sister," Eliot employs meter, sonnet form, and contrasting images of confinement and freedom to create a mood in which the reader identifies with the female narrator, seeking to escape unfair gender boundaries and to live a life of freedom, truth-seeking, love, and creative expression. In both poems, Eliot invites the reader to identify with the narrator by entering into the life of the poem via meter, form, and musical expression.[8]

In her dramatic and narrative poetry (*Armgart*, "Agatha," "A Minor Prophet," The Death of Moses," "The Legend of Jubal," "How Lisa Loved the King," and *The Spanish Gypsy*), Eliot extols the virtue of sympathy through stories

---

[7]   In her article, "On Suffering and Sympathy: *Jude the Obscure*, Evolution, and Ethics," Caroline Sumpter illustrates one possibility for future Eliot studies focusing on sympathy. She argues that Thomas Hardy's fascination with the "natural history" of sympathy prompted him to participate in a conversation about the evolutionary significance of sympathy in *Jude the Obscure*. Eliot scholars might also find it fruitful to examine her poetry and fiction as they reveal her views on social evolution, sympathy, and morality.

[8]   Henry states that Eliot freed herself from her self-imposed restrictions of realism and conformed to the metrical restrictions of poetry in order to express purely a set of beliefs (*Cambridge Introduction* 84).

of characters who embark on spiritual journeys.[9] In these poems, Eliot creates characters, but she does not develop them through psychological realism as she does in her novels. Thus, the readers encounter poetic characters not as people but as representations of ideas. For example, readers identify with Armgart and Jubal, both of whom represent artistic creation, through quests in which they learn to overcome ego and discover the greater values of community and selflessness. Similarly, Fedalma in *The Spanish Gypsy* faces a dilemma in which she must choose between personal and community good. Unlike Armgart and Jubal, Fedalma is not egocentric; rather, she faces two paths, and both are arguably virtuous, though one is more admirable than the other. She chooses the higher calling and overcomes her desire for personal happiness for the greater good of the community. Fedalma weds the curse of her outcast Zincali people instead of her lover, Don Silva, and sacrifices her chance to have children in order to take on the higher calling of being a mother to a nation. Critics debate Eliot's meaning in offering such choices to her main character; such a debate reveals the poem's ability to draw readers into the story. By having Fedalma choose to sympathize with an outcast tribe and renounce personal desire, Eliot challenges readers to question what they would do in the character's position. Eliot successfully engenders reader sympathy not by developing Fedalma as an identifiable character through means of realism, but rather by upholding her as an ideal representation of duty and compassion. In these and many of her poems, Eliot elicits sympathy through various means, including meter, form, and representation of ideals. Adding Eliot's treatment of sympathy in poetry to similar discussions of her novels would further illuminate Eliot's views on this encompassing ideology.

Poetry Within Poetry

Another avenue for future study involves Eliot's drawing attention to the art of poetry in her poems. Eliot comments on the role of the poet and the craft of writing poetry through the narrator's self-referential "lines" in "Brother and Sister" and in the self-creating "words" and "definitions" in "I Grant You Ample Leave." She extends this technique in two other poems ("How Lisa Loved the King" and *The Spanish Gypsy*) by including whole lyric poems within the title poems and by having the narrator and characters comment on the power of the poetry. In "How Lisa Loved the King," a young girl enlists the help of a musician (Minuccio) who enlists further the help of a poet (Mico) to compose a song about Lisa's great love

---

[9]   For a discussion of Eliot's cult of duty, her view of poetry as a higher art form than prose, and the motivation behind her epic ambitions, see Charles LaPorte's discussion of *The Spanish Gypsy* and "The Legend of Jubal" in *Victorian Poets*. LaPorte treats Eliot's connecting poetry and religious sentiment "through an affective, implicitly feminine poetics compatible with secularization and materialism but plainly growing out of English Christian tradition" (197–8).

for King Pedro.[10] Minuccio asks Mico to write lyrics for the love song, and Mico explains the poetry-writing process: "that thought is poesy, / I need but listen as it sings to me" (*CSP* 1:152). After three days, "When linkèd notes had perfected the lay," Minuccio sings the song to the court to powerful effect:

> The strain was new. It seemed a pleading cry,
> And yet a rounded, perfect melody,
> Making grief beauteous as the tear-filled eyes
> Of little child at little miseries.
> Trembling at first, then swelling as it rose,
> Like rising light that broad and broader grows,
> It filled the hall, and so possessed the air,
> That not one living, breathing soul was there,
> Though dullest, slowest, but was quivering
> In Music's grasp, and forced to hear her sing.
> But most such sweet compulsion took the mood
> Of Pedro (tired of doing what he would).
> Whether the words which that strange meaning bore
> Were but the poet's feigning, or aught more,
> ....
> For, though they came behind all former rhymes,
> The verses were not bad for these poor times.
> "Monsignor, they are only three days old. . . ." (1:154–5)

By commenting on the careful crafting of lyrics and by presenting the collaborative efforts of poet and musician, the narrator emphasizes the relationship between artist and audience. The artist painstakingly creates a work of art that takes on a life of its own with the power to elicit the strong emotions of an audience. Likewise, the poetess carefully chooses her words and meter to write a song that will move the reader to a heightened state of feeling and understanding.

Eliot pronouncedly employs this metapoetic technique as she punctuates the dramatic *The Spanish Gypsy* throughout with lyric poems. Early in the poem,

---

[10] To prepare the reader for the effect of the love poem, the narrator first reports the rejuvenating effect of Minuccio's music on Lisa who is dying from love for the king:

> . . . he preluded
> With magic hand, that summoned from the strings
> Aerial spirits, rare yet vibrant wings
> That fanned the pulses of his listener,
> And waked each sleeping sense with blissful stir
> ....
> . . . her faith had grown
> To trust him as if missioned like a priest
> With some high grace, that when his singing ceased
> Still made him wiser, more magnanimous
> Than common men who had no genius. (1:151)

Minuccio's music soothes Lisa and wakes her from the throes of death. The musician-priest prays for her through song, and the prayer has a salutary effect.

musician (Pablo) and poet (Juan) sing odes to spring to mourn the transience of beauty and express hope for renewal (46–7, 50–1). The narrator describes the moving effect of Pablo's music in the plaça:

> Pablo awakes the viol and the bow—
> The masculine bow that draws the woman's heart
> From out the strings and makes them cry, yearn, plead,
> Tremble, exult, with mystic union
> Of joy acute and tender suffering.
> To play the viol and discreetly mix
> Alternate with the bow's keen biting tones
> The throb responsive to the finger's touch,
> Was rarest skill that Pablo half had caught
> ……………………………………………………
> The wingéd sounds exalt the thick-pressed crowd
> With a new pulse in common, blending all
> The gazing life into one larger soul
> With dimly widened consciousness: as waves
> In heightened movement tell of waves far off. (45–6)

The narrator describes the crowd gathering in a physical, emotional, and spiritual union that widens consciousness and raises community awareness. The music inspires Fedalma to move "as, in dance religious, Miriam, / When on the Red Sea shore she raised her voice / And led the chorus of her people's joy" and as the "spirit in her gravely glowing face / With sweet community informs her limbs" (48–9). The gathered crowd responds with collective amazement: "They hold their breath, and live by seeing her" (49). The narrator describes Fedalma's dance as a song; she dances with the "grand chord / Of her harmoniously bodied soul" (49). Eliot the poet presents Pablo the musician who sings a song that unifies the audience and inspires Fedalma's rapturous dance, all of which highlights the beauty of artistic expression and its power to inspire communal awe. Eliot also has characters directly comment on their experience with poetry/music. After Juan sings of his love for the virtuous Fedalma, Blasco remarks, "Faith, a good song, sung to a stirring tune / I like the words returning in a round; / It gives a sort of sense. Another such!" (34). Eliot creates a poem that points to its own power and invites the readers to follow the characters' lead and express strong emotions and act for the common good. *The Spanish Gypsy* is thus a poem that regularly reminds readers to feel the music of the poem, adopt a greater sensibility to the issues presented, and express emotions through acting out the message of the poem. The poem within a poem also reminds readers of the performing role of the poetess. As poets and musicians perform their music in the poetic scenes, the poetess performs her music and demonstrates the emotional expression she hopes to elicit. There are many more examples of Eliot's inclusion of lyric poems within *The Spanish Gypsy*, and a full-length study of these poems and their effects could provide valuable new insight into one of her most discussed poems.

These are but a few possible avenues for future Eliot studies that focus on her poetry. Such studies will offer greater insight into the imagination and sensibility of one of the nineteenth-century's greatest writers. Additionally, exploration of her poems in coordination with the work of other Victorian poets will shed light on the poetess tradition and Victorian poetry as a whole. By excavating Eliot's poems from their unvisited tombs, readers and scholars will restore life to art that has the power to stir pulses to generosity, "urge man's search to vaster issues," and "breathe beauteous order" into the growing life of all humanity (*CSP* 2:85).

Bibliography

Ablow, Rachel. *The Marriage of Minds: Reading Sympathy in the Victorian Marriage Plot*. Stanford, CA: Stanford UP, 2007. Print.

Anger, Suzy. *Victorian Interpretation*. Ithaca, NY: Cornell UP, 2005. Print.

Armstrong, Isobel. "The Gush of the Feminine: How Can we Read Women's Poetry of the Romantic Period?" *Romantic Women Writers: Voices and Countervoices*. Ed. Paula R. Feldman and Theresa M. Kelley. Hanover, NH: UP of New England, 1995. 13–32. Print.

———. "Msrepresentation: Codes of Affect and Politics in Nineteenth-Century Women's Poetry." *Women's Poetry, Late Romantic to Late Victorian: Gender and Genre, 1830-1900*. Ed. Isobel Armstrong, Virginia Blain, and Cora Kaplan. Basingstoke, UK: Macmillan, 1999. 3–32. Print.

———. "Preface." *The Cultural Place of George Eliot's Poetry*. Ed. Kyriaki Hadjiafxendi. *George Eliot-George Henry Lewes Studies* 60–61 (2011): 3–7. Print.

———. *Victorian Poetry: Poetry, Poetics and Politics*. London, UK: Routledge, 2003. Print.

Arnold, Matthew. *Culture and Anarchy*. London: Smith, Elder, and Co., 1869. Print.

Ashton, Rosemary. "Evans, Marian [George Eliot] (1819–1880)." *Oxford Dictionary of National Biography*. May, 2008. Web. <http://www.oxforddnb.com.ezproxy.tcu.edu/view/article/679>.

———. *George Eliot: A Life*. London, UK: Penguin Books, 1997. Print.

Bashant, Wendy. "Singing in Greek Drag: Gluck, Berlioz, George Eliot." *En Travesti: Women, Gender, Subversion, Opera*. New York, NY: Columbia UP, 1995. Print.

Beer, Gillian. *George Eliot*. Bloomington, IN: Indiana UP, 1986. Print.

Beshero-Bondar, Elisa. *Women, Epic, and Transition in British Romanticism*. Newark: U of Delaware P, 2011. Print.

Billone, Amy Christine. *Little Songs: Women, Silence, and the Nineteenth-Century Sonnet*. Columbus, OH: Ohio State UP, 2007. Print.

Blain, Virginia. "Letitia Elizabeth Landon, Eliza Mary Hamilton, and the Genealogy of the Victorian Poetess." *Victorian Poetry* 33.1 (1995): 31–51. Print.

Blair, Kirstie. *Form and Faith in Victorian Poetry and Religion*. Oxford: Oxford UP, 2012. Print.

Blake, Kathleen. "'Armgart'—George Eliot on the Woman Artist." *Victorian Poetry* 18.1 (1980): 75–80. Print.

Blind, Mathilde. *George Eliot*. Boston, MA: Roberts Brothers, 1883. Print.

Boccaccio, Giovanni. *The Decameron, Or Ten Day's Entertainment of Boccaccio.* Trans. Walter Keating. London, UK: Henry G. Bohn, 1855. Print.

Bodenheimer, Rosemarie. "Ambition and its Audiences: George Eliot's Performing Figures." *Victorian Studies* 34.1 (1990): 7–33. Print.

———. *The Real Life of Mary Ann Evans: George Eliot, Her Letters and Fiction.* London: Cornell UP, 1994. Print.

———. "A Woman of Many Names." *The Cambridge Companion to George Eliot.* Ed. George Levine. Cambridge, UK: Cambridge UP, 2001. 159–80. Print.

Boos, Florence. "Morris' Radical Revisions of the 'Laxdaela Saga.'" *Victorian Poetry* 21.4 (1983): 415–20. Print.

Brantlinger, Patrick, William B. Thesing, eds. *A Companion to the Victorian Novel.* Malden, MA: Blackwell, 2002. Print.

Bray, Charles. *The Philosophy of Necessity: Or, the Law of Consequences; as Applicable to Mental, Moral, and Social Science.* London, UK: Longman, 1841. Print.

Breton, Rob. "The Thrill of the Trill: Political and Aesthetic Discourse in George Eliot's *Armgart*." *Victorian Review* 35.1 (March 2009): 116–31. Print.

Brown, Susan. "Determined Heroines: George Eliot, Augusta Webster, and Closet Drama by Victorian Women." *Victorian Poetry* 33.1 (1995): 89–109. Print.

———. "The Victorian Poetess." *Victorian Poetry.* Ed. Joseph Bristow. Cambridge, UK: Cambridge UP, 2000. 180–202. Print.

Browning, Elizabeth Barrett. *The Poems of Elizabeth Barrett Browning.* 2 Vols. London, UK: Edward Moxon, 1844. Print.

Carlyle, Thomas. *Sartor Resartus: The Life and Opinions of Herr Teufelsdröckh.* London, UK: Chapman and Hall, 1831. Print.

Carroll, Alicia. *Dark Smiles: Race and Desire in George Eliot.* Athens, OH: Ohio UP, 2003. Print.

Chapman, Alison. "Poetry, Network, Nation: Elizabeth Barrett Browning and Expatriate Women's Poetry." *Victorian Studies* 55.2 (2013): 275–85. Print.

Chase, Karen. "The Woman Question." *Oxford Reader's Companion to George Eliot.* Ed. John Rignall. Oxford, UK: Oxford UP, 2000. 443–8. Print.

Cicero, Marcus Tullius. *Letters to Atticus.* Trans. Eric Winstedt. Vol 3. London, UK: William Heinemann, 1918. Print.

Collins, K.K. *Interviews and Recollections.* Houndmills, UK: Palgrave Macmillan, 2010. Print.

Collins, Rowland L. "George Eliot." *Victorian Poets After 1850.* Dictionary of Literary Biography Vol. 35. Ed. William E. Fredeman and Ira Bruce Nadel. Detroit, MI: Gale Research, 1985. *Literature Resource Center.* Web. 13 May 2014.

Cottom, Daniel. *Social Figures: George Eliot, Social History, and Literary Representation.* Minneapolis, MN: U of Minnesota P, 1987. Print.

Creeger, George R., ed. *George Eliot: A Collection of Critical Essays.* Englewood Cliffs, NJ: Prentice-Hall, 1970. Print.

Creel, George W. *The Poetry of George Eliot*. Diss. U of California, Berkeley, 1948. Print.

Darwin, Charles. *The Origin of Species*. Ed. Gillian Beer. Oxford, UK: Oxford UP, 1996. Print.

David, Deirdre. *Intellectual Women and Victorian Patriarchy: Harriet Martineau, Elizabeth Barrett Browning, George Eliot*. Ithaca, NY: Cornell UP, 1987. Print.

Davidoff, Leonore. "Gender and the 'Great Divide': Public and Private in British Gender History." *Journal of Women's History* 15.1 (2003): 11–27. Print.

Dentith, Simon. *Epic and Empire in Nineteenth-Century Britain.* Cambridge, UK: Cambridge UP, 2006. Print.

Dolin, Tim. *George Eliot*. Oxford, UK: Oxford UP, 2005. Print.

Dowling, Andrew. "'The Other Side of Silence': Matrimonial Conflict and the Divorce Court in George Eliot's Fiction." *Nineteenth-Century Literature* 50.3 (1995): 322–36. Print

Easley, Alexis. "Poet as Headliner: George Eliot and Macmillan's Magazine." *The Cultural Place of George Eliot's Poetry*. Ed. Kyriaki Hadjiafxendi. *George Eliot-George Henry Lewes Studies* 60–61 (2011): 107–25. Print.

Eliot, George. *Adam Bede*. Ed. Carol A. Martin. New York, NY: Oxford UP, 2001. Print.

———. "Belles Lettres." *Westminster Review* (January 1857): 306–10. Print.

———. *The Complete Shorter Poetry of George Eliot*. Ed. Antonie Gerard van den Broek. 2 Vols. London, UK: Pickering and Chatto, 2005. Print.

———. *Daniel Deronda*. London, UK: Penguin, 2003. Print.

———. *Essays of George Eliot*. Ed. Thomas Pinney. New York, NY: Columbia UP, 1963. Print.

———. *George Eliot: Collected Poems*. Ed. Lucien Jenkins. London, UK: Skoob, 1989. Print.

———. *The George Eliot Letters*. Ed. Gordon Sherman Haight. 9 Vols. New Haven, CT: Yale UP, 1954. Print.

———. *George Eliot's Life as Related in Her Letters and Journals*. Ed. John Walter Cross. 3 Vols. New York, NY: Harper & Brothers, 1885. Print.

———. *Middlemarch*. London, UK: Penguin, 2003. Print.

———. *The Mill on the Floss*. London: Norton, 1994. Print.

———. *Scenes of Clerical Life*. Ed. David Lodge. New York, NY: Penguin, 1973. Print.

Ermarth, Elizabeth Deeds. "George Eliot's Conception of Sympathy." *Nineteenth-Century Fiction* 40.1 (1985): 23. Print.

———. "Woman in France: Madame De Sable." *Oxford Reader's Companion to George Eliot.* Ed. John Rignall. Oxford, UK: Oxford UP, 2000. 442–3. Print.

Essays and Reviews. Farnborough, UK: Gregg, 1860. Print.

Ferreira-Buckley, Linda and Winifred Bryan Horner. "Writing Instruction in Great Britain: The Eighteenth and Nineteenth Centuries." *A Short History of Writing Instruction: From Ancient Greece to Modern America*. Ed. James Jerome Murphy. 2nd ed. Mahwah, NJ: Hermagoras Press, 2001. 173–212. Print.

Feuerbach, Ludwig. *The Essence of Christianity*. Trans. Marian Evans. London, UK: John Chapman, 1857. Print.

Fleishman, Avrom. *George Eliot's Intellectual Life*. Cambridge, UK: Cambridge UP, 2010. Print.

Flint, Kate. "George Eliot and Gender." *The Cambridge Companion to George Eliot*. Ed. George Levine. Cambridge, UK: Cambridge UP, 2001. 159–80. Print.

Fulmer, Constance M. and Margaret E. Barfield, eds. *A Monument to the Memory of George Eliot: Edith J. Simcox's Autobiography of a Shirtmaker*. New York, NY: Taylor and Francis, 1998. Print.

Graver, Suzanne. *George Eliot and Community: A Study in Social Theory and Fictional Form*. Berkeley, CA: U of California P, 1984. Print.

Gray, Beryl. *George Eliot and Music*. New York, NY: St. Martin's, 1989. Print.

Hadjiafxendi, Kyriaki. "Introduction: George Eliot and the Poetics of Disbelief." *The Cultural Place of George Eliot's Poetry*. Ed. Kyriaki Hadjiafxendi. *George Eliot-George Henry Lewes Studies* 60–61 (2011): 7–16. Print.

———. "Voicing the Past: Aural Sensibility, the Weaver-Poet, and George Eliot's 'Erinna.'" *Studies in the Literary Imagination* 43.1 (2010): 95–118.

Haight, Gordon Sherman. *George Eliot: A Biography*. New York, NY: Oxford UP, 1968. Print.

Hardy, Barbara Nathan. *George Eliot: A Critic's Biography*. London, UK: Continuum, 2006. Print.

Harris, Ruth. "Lewis, Maria." *Oxford Reader's Companion to George Eliot*. Ed. John Rignall. Oxford, UK: Oxford UP, 2000. 211–12. Print.

Haskin, Dayton. "George Eliot as a 'Miltonist': Marriage and Milton in *Middlemarch*." *Milton and Gender*. Ed. Catherine Gimelli Martin. Cambridge, UK: Cambridge UP, 2004. 207–22. Print.

Hennell, Charles. *An Inquiry Concerning the Origin of Christianity*. London, UK: Smallfield, 1838. Print.

Henry, Nancy. *The Cambridge Introduction to George Eliot*. Cambridge, UK: Cambridge UP, 2008. Print.

———. *George Eliot and the British Empire*. Cambridge, UK: Cambridge UP, 2002. Print.

———. *The Life of George Eliot: A Critical Biography*. Chichester, UK: Wiley-Blackwell, 2012

Higdon, David Leon. "George Eliot and the Art of the Epigraph." *Nineteenth-Century Fiction* 25.2 (1970): 127–51. Print.

Hodgson, Peter Crafts. *The Mystery Beneath the Real: Theology in the Fiction of George Eliot*. Minneapolis, MN: Fortress Press, 2000. Print.

Holmes, John. *Dante Gabriel Rossetti and the Late Victorian Sonnet Sequence: Sexuality, Belief and the Self*. Aldershot, UK: Ashgate, 2005. Print.

The Holy Bible, King James Version. New York, NY: American Bible Society, 1999. Print.

Houston, Natalie. "Valuable by Design: Material Features and Cultural Value in Nineteenth-Century Sonnet Anthologies." *Victorian Poetry* 37 (1999): 243–72. Print.

Hudd, Louise. "The Politics of a Feminist Poetics: 'Armgart' and George Eliot's Critical Response to *Aurora Leigh*." *Essays and Studies* 49 (1996): 62–83. Print.

Hughes, Kathryn. *George Eliot: The Last Victorian*. New York, NY: Farrar Straus Giroux, 1999. Print.

Hughes, Linda K. *The Cambridge Introduction to Victorian Poetry*. Cambridge, UK: Cambridge UP, 2010. Print.

Jaffe, Audrey. *Scenes of Sympathy: Identity and Representation in Victorian Fiction*. Ithaca, NY: Cornell UP, 2000. Print.

Julian, Linda. "Laxdaela Saga and 'The Lovers of Gudrun': Morris' Poetic Vision." *Victorian Poetry* 34.3 (1996): 355–71. Print.

Keble, John. *Keble's Lectures on Poetry, 1832–1841*. Trans. Edward Kershaw Francis. 2 Vols. Oxford, UK: Clarendon Press, 1912. Print.

Kehler, Grace. "Armgart's Voice Problems." *Victorian Literature and Culture* 34.1 (2006): 147–66. Print.

Knight, Mark, and Emma Mason. *Nineteenth-Century Religion and Literature: An Introduction*. Oxford, UK: Oxford UP, 2006. Print.

Krueger, Christine L. *The Reader's Repentance: Women Preachers, Women Writers, and Nineteenth-Century Social Discourse*. Chicago, IL: University of Chicago Press, 1992. Print.

LaPorte, Charles. "Atheist Prophecy: Mathilde Blind, Constance Naden, and the Victorian Poetess." *Victorian Literature and Culture* 34.2 (2006): 427–41. Print.

———. "George Eliot, the Poetess as Prophet." *Victorian Literature and Culture* 31.1, Victorian Religion (2003): 159–79. Print.

———. "Postscript." *The Cultural Place of George Eliot's Poetry*. Ed. Kyriaki Hadjiafxendi. *George Eliot-George Henry Lewes Studies* 60–61 (2011): 142–6. Print.

———. *Victorian Poets and the Changing Bible*. Charlottesville, VA: U of Virginia P, 2011. Print.

Leighton, Angela. *Victorian Women Poets: Writing Against the Heart*. Charlottesville, VA: U of Virginia P, 1992. Print.

Lisle, Bonnie J. "Art and Egoism in George Eliot's Poetry." *Victorian Poetry* 22.3 (1984): 263–78. Print.

Main, Alexander. *Wise, Witty, and Tender Sayings in Prose and Verse, Selected from the Works of George Eliot*. Edinburgh: William Blackwood and Sons, 1871. Print.

———. *The George Eliot Birthday Book*. Edinburgh: William Blackwood and Sons, 1878. Print.

Mandell, Laura. "Introduction: the Poetess Tradition." *Romanticism on the Net.* Feb–May 2003. Web. <http://www.erudit.org/revue/ron/2003/v/n29-30/007712ar.html#no40>.

Mattingly, Carol. *Appropriate[ing] Dress: Women's Rhetorical Style in Nineteenth-Century America.* Carbondale, IL: Southern Illinois UP, 2002. Print.

McCormack, Kathleen. *George Eliot in Society: Travels Abroad and Sundays at the Priory.* Columbus, Ohio: Ohio State UP, 2013. Print.

———. "*The Spanish Gypsy:* Geography, Photography, and Ethnography in Spain." *The Cultural Place of George Eliot's Poetry.* Ed. Kyriaki Hadjiafxendi. *George Eliot-George Henry Lewes Studies* 60–61 (2011): 47–61. Print.

McGann, Jerome J. *The Poetics of Sensibility: A Revolution in Literary Style.* Oxford, UK: Oxford UP, 1996. Print.

Mellor, Anne K. "The Female Poet and the Poetess, Two Traditions of British Women's Poetry, 1780-1830." *Women's Poetry in the Enlightenment, the Making of a Canon, 1730–1820.* Ed. Isobel Armstrong and Virginia Blain. New York, NY: St. Martin's Press. 1999. 81–98. Print.

Melnyk, Julie. *Victorian Religion: Faith and Life in Britain.* Westport, CT: Praeger, 2008. Print.

———. *Women's Theology in Nineteenth-Century Britain: Transfiguring the Faith of their Fathers.* New York, NY: Garland, 1998. Print.

Mermin, Dorothy. "The Damsel, the Knight, and the Victorian Woman Poet." *Critical Inquiry* 13.1 (1986): 64–80. Print.

Müller, Karl Ottfried. *History of the Literature of Ancient Greece.* London: Baldwin and Cradock, 1840. Print.

Nestor, Pauline. *Female Friendships and Communities: Charlotte Brontë, George Eliot, Elizabeth Gaskell.* Oxford, UK: Oxford UP, 1985. Print.

Neufeldt, Victor. "The Madonna and the Gypsy." *Studies in the Novel* 15.1 (1983): 44–54. Print.

Newey, Katherine. "The 'British Matron' and the Poetic Drama: The Case of Augusta Webster." *The Cultural Place of George Eliot's Poetry.* Ed. Kyriaki Hadjiafxendi. *George Eliot-George Henry Lewes Studies* 60–61 (2011): 126–41. Print.

Nord, Deborah Epstein. *Gypsies & the British Imagination, 1807–1930.* New York, NY: Columbia UP, 2006. Print.

OED Online. Oxford University Press, March 2014. Web. 22 May 2014.

Paley, William. *Natural Theology: or, Evidences of the Existence and Attributes of the Deity, Collected from the Appearances of Nature.* Oxford, UK: Oxford UP, 1802. Print.

Paris, Bernard J. "George Eliot's Unpublished Poetry." *Studies in Philology* 56.3 (1959): 539–58. Print.

———. "George Eliot's Religion of Humanity." *George Eliot: A Collection of Critical Essays.* Ed. George R. Creeger. Englewood Cliffs, NJ: Prentice-Hall, 1970. 11. Print.

Patmore, Coventry Kersey Dighton. *The Angel in the House.* London, UK: J.W. Parker and Son, 1854. Print.

Paxton, Nancy. *George Eliot and Herbert Spencer: Feminism, Evolutionism, and the Reconstruction of Gender.* Princeton: Princeton UP, 1991. Print.

Peterson, Linda H. "Rewriting *A History of the Lyre*: Letitia Landon, Elizabeth Barrett Browning and the (Re)Construction of the Nineteenth-Century Woman Poet." *Women's Poetry, Late Romantic to Late Victorian: Gender and Genre, 1830–1900.* Ed. Isobel Armstrong, Virginia Blain, and Cora Kaplan. Houndmills, UK: Macmillan, 1999. 115–32. Print.

———. *"The Spanish Gypsy* as George Eliot's Poetic Debut." *The Cultural Place of George Eliot's Poetry.* Ed. Kyriaki Hadjiafxendi. *George Eliot-George Henry Lewes Studies* 60–61 (2011): 31–46. Print.

Phelan, J.P. *The Nineteenth-Century Sonnet.* Houndmills, UK: Palgrave Macmillan, 2005. Print.

Pinch, Adela. *Strange Fits of Passion: Epistemologies of Emotion, Hume to Austen.* Stanford, CA: Stanford UP, 1996. Print.

———. *Thinking about Other People in Nineteenth-Century British Writing.* Cambridge, UK: Cambridge UP, 2010. Print.

Plant, I.M., ed. *Women Writers of Ancient Greece and Rome: An Anthology.* Oklahoma: U of Oklahoma P, 2004. Print.

Pope, Rebecca A. "The Diva Doesn't Die: George Eliot's *Armgart.*" *Embodied Voices: Representing Female Vocality in Western Culture.* Ed. Leslie C. Dunn and Nancy A. Jones. Cambridge, UK: Cambridge UP, 1994. 139–51. Print.

Pratt-Smith, Stella. "Inside-Out: Texture and Belief in George Eliot's 'Bubble-World.'" *The Cultural Place of George Eliot's Poetry.* Ed. Kyriaki Hadjiafxendi. *George Eliot-George Henry Lewes Studies* 60–61 (2011): 62–76. Print.

Prins, Yopie. "Personifying the Poetess: Caroline Norton, 'the Picture of Sappho'." *Women's Poetry, Late Romantic to Late Victorian: Gender and Genre, 1830–1900.* Ed. Isobel Armstrong, Virginia Blain, and Cora Kaplan. Houndmills, UK: Macmillan, 1999. 50–67. Print.

Pyle, Forest. *The Ideology of Imagination: Subject and Society in the Discourse of Romanticism.* Stanford, CA: Stanford UP, 1995. Print.

Qualls, Barry. "George Eliot and Religion." *The Cambridge Companion to George Eliot.* Ed. George Levine. Cambridge, UK: Cambridge UP, 2001. 119–37. Print.

Reynolds, Margaret. "Poetry of George Eliot." *Oxford Reader's Companion to George Eliot.* Ed. John Rignall. Oxford, UK: Oxford UP, 2000. 304–8. Print.

Reynolds, Margaret, and Angela Leighton, eds. *Victorian Women Poets: An Anthology.* Oxford, UK: Blackwell, 1995. Print.

Richards, Bernard Arthur. *English Poetry of the Victorian Period, 1830–1890.* 2nd ed. London, UK: Longman, 2001. Print.

Rignall, John. "George Eliot and the Idea of Travel." *The Yearbook of English Studies* 36.2 (2006): 139–52. Print.

———. *George Eliot and Europe.* Aldershot, UK: Scholar Press, 1997. Print.

———, ed. *Oxford Reader's Companion to George Eliot.* Oxford, UK: Oxford UP, 2000. Print.

Ryken, Leland, ed. *Dictionary of Biblical Imagery*. Downers Grove, IL: InterVarsity Press, 1998. Print.

Sanders, Valerie. "'My father shook my soul awake:' Salvaging Family Relationships in Eliot's Poetry." *The Cultural Place of George Eliot's Poetry*. Ed. Kyriaki Hadjiafxendi. *George Eliot-George Henry Lewes Studies* 60–61 (2011): 77–90. Print.

Scheinberg, Cynthia. *Women's Poetry and Religion in Victorian England: Jewish Identity and Christian Culture*. Cambridge, UK: Cambridge UP, 2002. Print.

Secor, Cynthia Ann. "The Poems of George Eliot." Diss. Cornell University, 1969. Print.

Sedgwick, Eve Kosofsky. *Between Men: English Literature and Male Homosocial Desire*. New York, NY: Columbia UP, 1985. Print.

Shaw, W.D. "Poetry and Religion." *A Companion to Victorian Poetry*. Ed. Richard Cronin, et al. Malden, MA: Blackwell, 2002. 457–74. Print.

Showalter, Elaine. *A Literature of their Own: British Women Novelists from Brontë to Lessing*. Princeton, NJ: Princeton UP, 1998. Print.

———. "The Greening of Sister George." *Nineteenth-Century Fiction* 35.3 (1980): 292–311. Print.

Smith, William. *Dictionary of Greek and Roman Biography and Mythology*. 3 Vols. London, UK: C. Little, and J. Brown, 1870. Print.

Staves, Susan. "Church of England Clergy and Women Writers." *Huntington Library Quarterly* 65.1 (2002): 81–103. Print.

Stern, Kimberly. "The Poetics of Criticism: Dialogue and Discourse in George Eliot's Poetry." *The Cultural Place of George Eliot's Poetry*. Ed. Kyriaki Hadjiafxendi. *George Eliot-George Henry Lewes Studies* 60–61 (2011): 91–106. Print.

Strauss, David Friedrich, and George Eliot. *The Life of Jesus, Critically Examined*. 6th ed. London, UK: G. Allen, 1913. Print.

Sumpter, Caroline. "On Suffering and Sympathy: Jude the Obscure, Evolution, and Ethics." *Victorian Studies* 53.4 (2011): 665–88. Print.

Tasker, Meg. "Aurora Leigh, Barrett Browning's Novel Approach". *Tradition and the Poetics of Self in Nineteenth-Century Women's Poetry*. Ed. Barbara Garlick. New York, NY: Rodopi, 2002. 23–41. Print.

Tate, Gregory. *The Poet's Mind: The Psychology of Victorian Poetry 1830–1870*. Oxford: Oxford UP, 2012. Print.

Tennyson, Alfred. *Tennyson's The Princess*. Ed. Albert Cook. London, UK: The Athenaeum Press, 1897. Print.

Tennyson, G.B. *Victorian Devotional Poetry: The Tractarian Mode*. Cambridge, MA: Harvard UP, 1981. Print.

Thain, Marion. "What Kind of a Critical Category is 'Women's Poetry'?" *Victorian Poetry* 41.4 (2003): 575–84. Print.

Thompson, Andrew. *George Eliot and Italy: Literary, Cultural, and Political Influences from Dante to the Risorgimento*. Houndmills, UK: Macmillan, 1998. Print.

Tuchman, Barbara Wertheim. *A Distant Mirror: The Calamitous 14th Century.* New York, NY: Knopf, 1978. Print.

Tucker, Herbert F. *Epic: Britain's Heroic Muse, 1790–1910.* Oxford, UK: Oxford UP, 2008. Print.

———. "Quantity and Quality: The Strange Case of George Eliot, Minor Poet." *The Cultural Place of George Eliot's Poetry.* Ed. Kyriaki Hadjiafxendi. *George Eliot-George Henry Lewes Studies* 60-61 (2011): 17–30. Print.

———. "Poetry: The Unappreciated Eliot," *A Companion to George Eliot.* Hoboken, NJ: John Wiley & Sons Inc. 2013. Print

Tye, J.R. "George Eliot's Unascribed Mottoes." *Nineteenth-Century Fiction* 22.3 (1967): 235–49. Print.

Uglow, Jennifer S. *George Eliot.* New York, NY: Pantheon Books, 1987. Print.

Van den Broek, Antonie Gerard. "Epigraphs." *Oxford Reader's Companion to George Eliot.* Ed. John Rignall. Oxford, UK: Oxford UP, 2000. 100–101. Print.

Vogeler, Martha. "The Choir Invisible: The Poetics of Humanist Piety." *George Eliot: A Centenary Tribute.* Ed. Gordon Height and Rosemary Van Arsdel. Totowa, NJ: Barnes and Noble, 1982. 64–83. Print.

Weliver, Phyllis. *The Figure of Music in Nineteenth-Century British Poetry.* Aldershot, UK: Ashgate, 2005. Print.

West-Burnham, Joss. "Fedalma—'The Angel of a Homeless Tribe': Issues of Religion, Race and Gender in George Eliot's Poetic Drama, *The Spanish Gypsy.*" *Women of Faith in Victorian Culture: Reassessing the Angel in the House.* Ed. Anne Hogan and Andrew Bradstock. Houndmills, UK: Macmillan, 1998. 78–90. Print.

———. "Travelling Towards Selfhood: Victorian Religion and the Process of Female Identity." *Women's Lives into Print: The Theory, Practice and Writing of Feminist Auto/Biography.* Ed. Pauline Polkey. Houndmills, UK: Macmillan, 1999. 80–95. Print.

Worrall, B.G. *The Making of the Modern Church: Christianity in England since 1800.* London, UK: SPCK Publishing, 2004. Print.

Index